PORKOPOLIS

PORK

American Animality, Standardized Life,
& the Factory Farm ALEX BLANCHETTE

OPOLIS

Duke University Press *Durham and London* 2020

Designed by Aimee C. Harrison
Typeset in Minion Pro and Trade Gothic
by Westchester Publishing Services

Library of Congress Cataloging-in-Publication Data
Names: Blanchette, Alex, author.
Title: Porkopolis : American animality, standardized life, and the
factory farm / Alex Blanchette.
Description: Durham : Duke University Press, 2020. | Includes
bibliographical references and index.
Identifiers: LCCN 2019043393 (print) | LCCN 2019043394 (ebook)
ISBN 9781478007890 (hardcover)
ISBN 9781478008408 (paperback)
ISBN 9781478012047 (ebook)
Subjects: LCSH: Swine industry—United States. | Swine breeders—
United States. | Factory farms—United States. | Agriculture—
Economic aspects—United States.
Classification: LCC HD9435.U62 B53 2020 (print) | LCC HD9435.U62
(ebook) | DDC 338.1/76400973—dc23
LC record available at https://lccn.loc.gov/2019043393
LC ebook record available at https://lccn.loc.gov/2019043394

Cover art: Sean Sprague, *Locker*, 2013–2015. Courtesy of the
photographer.

CONTENTS

Part IV. Carcass

Part V. Viscera

ILLUSTRATIONS

All images courtesy of Sean Sprague, unless noted otherwise.

ACKNOWLEDGMENTS

I AM THANKFUL THAT academic books place their acknowledgments at the beginning. I am not sure how far into this book friends and acquaintances from Dixon will read. For better and for worse, it is a fair bit more "academic" than a lot of others on this kind of subject matter. This might ring hollow to some of these friends—but the detail and density of these pages is the result of many years of work, and it is a reflection of my respect for you. I think that your home is complicated, I think that it matters, I do not believe it can be reduced to a simple take-away message, and (though this might be my own failing) I do not know how else to depict your unique lives than in thick sentences and twisting paths of thought. This book is critical. Everyone that I met in Dixon will disagree with at least some parts, and I realize that some will object to all of it. But it tries to always be critical of the broader world in which we find ourselves. It is not a critique of people, their decisions, or their beliefs. I do not purport to know how to live your lives or do your jobs differently. This book admittedly does not do a good enough job of communicating how much I enjoyed living in Dixon, and how residents made it feel like home. But I appreciate every moment—the insights, the debates, the patience, the critique of me, the skepticism, and the support. I cannot name names here, but there are many people to thank. Unfortunately, some who taught me the most—not just what to think about, but how to think—are not explicitly in these pages. But they should know that they were with me across every sentence, including those that I chose not to write.

ACKNOWLEDGMENTS

Sean Sprague's photographic talents have greatly improved this book, as did his keen eye and observations during the three months we lived together in Dixon. I also owe thanks to the village that helped raise me. The only thing that makes Bayfield, Ontario, remarkable is the people who live there. Caitlin Ferguson asked me, when I said that I might like to study anthropology for a living, whether I was going to write something that mattered to Bayfield. I do not know whether I did. But her nudge is what sent me down this path.

I was gifted with a brilliant and faithful dissertation committee in the Department of Anthropology at the University of Chicago. All of the (good) pages of this book are tied to the unique privilege of having Joe Masco as a mentor. His combination of creativity, far-reaching thought, deep critical acumen, and dedication to his students is singular. Jessica Cattelino is a model of everything I want to be as a scholar and a person, and I still cling to every piece of insight that she shares. Judy Farquhar instills in her students the desire, capacity, and confidence to try to craft something new. Brad Weiss helped me see why my arguments matter and gave me the faith to pursue particular lines of inquiry when I was not sure where they might lead. Susan Gal is an ideal of rigorous scholarly engagement, and I would not have been able to arrive at this approach to factory farms without her coursework. Although they were not on my dissertation committee, Michael Silverstein and Kaushik Sunder Rajan were invaluable intellectual supports at pivotal times during graduate school. Anne Ch'ien is the bedrock of the University of Chicago's Department of Anthropology. Finally, I owe a special debt to my first real academic teacher and mentor, Bonnie McElhinny. In just twelve brief months of engagement during my senior year of college at the University of Toronto, her pedagogy, brilliance, and towering example transformed me from a lackadaisical student with fleeting interests into someone who was ready to pursue study for life.

The Tufts University Department of Anthropology is an open-minded and inspiring place to write and teach. Cohorts of students have pushed my ideas, and I am grateful to Diane Adamson and Cass Madden for serving as exemplary research assistants on elements of this project. My colleagues are a model of support and generous critique. Thank you especially to Amahl Bishara, Tatiana Chudakova, Coco Gomez, Jamie Gorman, David Guss, Kareem Khubchandani, Lisa Lowe, Sarah Luna, Zarin Machanda, Kris Manjapra, Colin Orians, Sarah Pinto, Nick Seaver, Rosalind Shaw, Cathy Stanton, and Lynn Wiles.

I am grateful for Ken Wissoker's longstanding interest in this project, his careful editorial interventions, and his unending patience throughout the process. Thanks to Elizabeth Ault, Susan Albury, Aimee Harrison, Chad Royal,

Joshua Tranen, and Toni Willis at Duke University Press, and the two incisive peer reviewers, for their diligent work in sharpening this book.

I completed my doctoral dissertation in 2013 while living as a Weatherhead Fellow at the School for Advanced Research (SAR) in Santa Fe, New Mexico. I will forever be thankful that I was able to spend time at such a studious, intellectually nourishing, and beautiful place. A large part of that experience is owed to the staff, scholars, and artists that give SAR its special alchemy. Thank you to James Brooks, Linda Cordell, Doug Dearden, Elise Edwards, Dean Falk, Melissa Henry, Laura Holt, John Kantner, Nancy Owen Lewis, Jonathan Loretto, Fibian Kavulani Lukalo, Danika Medak-Saltzman, Margaret Wickens Pearce, Elysia Poon, Leslie Shipman, Karla Slocum, Ageeth Sluis, Nicole Taylor, and Carla Tozcano. I had the privilege to return to SAR for an advanced seminar on changing relations between nature and labor that shaped some of this book's ideas. In addition to that seminar's participants, whose insights still help me think more clearly, I thank Michael Brown, Paul Ryer, and Maria Spray.

The first draft of this book was completed while I was an S. V. Ciriacy-Wantrup Visiting Fellow in the Department of Geography at the University of California, Berkeley. Berkeley Geography is a dedicated and politically engaged place, the kind of department that expands your ambition simply by being in its orbit. Thanks especially to Jake Kosek, Nathan Sayre, and Michael Watts for their ideas and support. I also benefited enormously from studying with the members of the 2016 Alterlife seminar.

The research and photography for this book was made possible by grant support from the Social Science and Humanities Council of Canada, the Wenner-Gren Foundation for Anthropological Research, the National Science Foundation, and the Toronto Arts Council.

Portions of this book have appeared as journal articles and book chapters. I thank the editors of those venues, and the work of anonymous peer reviewers in helping to shape them. A modified version of chapter 1 appeared as a section of the longer article, "Living Waste and the Labor of Toxic Health on American Factory Farms," *Medical Anthropology Quarterly* 33, no. 1 (2019): 80–100. An earlier version of chapter 2 was published as "Herding Species: Biosecurity, Posthuman Labor, and the American Industrial Pig," *Cultural Anthropology* 30, no. 4 (2015): 640–69. Parts of chapter 5 appeared as sections of a longer chapter, "Making Monotony: Bedsores and Other Signs of an Overworked Hog," *How Nature Works: Rethinking Labor on a Troubled Planet,* edited by Sarah Besky and Alex Blanchette, 59–76. Albuquerque, NM: University of New Mexico/SAR Press, 2019. Two earlier sections of chapter 6

ACKNOWLEDGMENTS

ACKNOWLEDGMENTS

appeared in "Infinite Proliferation, or the Making of the Modern Runt," in *Life by Algorithms: How Roboprocesses Are Remaking Our World*, edited by Catherine Besteman and Hugh Gusterson, 91–106 (Chicago: University of Chicago Press), 2018.

Every page of this book was critically nurtured over many steadfast years by the insights of the Hive writing group. There is just no way to thank Tatiana Chudakova, Kate Goldfarb, Elayne Oliphant, and Carly Schuster enough. Some of this book's chapters have also been strengthened through participation in varied writing collectives with Susanne Freidberg, Bridget Guarasci, Julie Guthman, Lisa Haushofer, Alison-Marie Loconto, Whythe Marschall, Nick Shapiro, Sarah Vaughn, and Jerry Zee. Sarah Besky has been an inspiring collaborator on writing projects and has pushed my thinking in many new directions. Eli Thorkelson has simply taught me a lot of things, about both academia and the good life.

An enormous number of people have provided encouragement, ideas, and sharp critiques when various versions of this book needed them the most. Their varied commentary on talks and drafts have all made it into this manuscript in some manner. Some engagements were sustained over many years, and others were off-the-cuff comments during presentations that stuck with me for a long time. Thank you to Thomas Andrews, Hannah Appel, Debbora Battaglia, Lindsay Bell, Lucas Bessire, David Bond, Rob Blunt, Summerson Carr, Lily Chumley, Jane Collins, Molly Cunningham, Naisargi Dave, Kathryn Marie Dudley, Joe Dumit, Jan Dutkiewicz, Cassie Fennell, María Elena García, Stefanie Graeter, Phillip Drake, Akhil Gupta, Joe Hankins, John Hartigan, Karen Hébert, Deborah Heath, Kregg Hetherington, Karen Ho, Richard Horwitz, Elizabeth Johnson, Eleana Kim, Yongjin Kim, Mazen Labban, Marcel LaFlamme, Hannah Landecker, Marianne Lien, Kristina Lyons, Paul Manning, Andrew Mathews, Kate McHarry, Amelia Moore, Jason Moore, Amy Moran-Thomas, Michelle Murphy, Alex Nading, Timothy Pachirat, Jan Padios, Anand Pandian, Juno Parreñas, Heather Paxson, Josh Reno, Justin Richland, Gabriel Rosenberg, Shiho Satsuka, Kristen Simmons, Bhrigupati Singh, Harris Solomon, Heather Swanson, LaShandra Sullivan, Christien Tompkins, Gabe Tusinski, Wim Van Deale, Jason Weideman, Kaya Williams, Andrew Yale, Emily Yates-Doerr, and Noah Zatz.

My parents, Janet and Gaetan Blanchette, are an unending well of love and support. They taught me most of what I know. Tatiana, Mira, and Motya make things worthwhile.

PREFACE **WATCHING HOGS WATCH WORKERS**

ON A COLD FALL EVENING IN 2010, I met a man in his late forties named Juan at a house party. A former businessman in his native Mexico, Juan had reluctantly moved with his family to the American Great Plains in the mid-2000s, trying to escape the escalating borderland drug violence in Ciudad Juárez. He was curious about my research, asking me what I had been learning in this remote agribusiness company town. A couple years back, Juan explained, he had worked in a 2,500-head sow breeding barn that was similar to the one where I was currently employed. He wanted to communicate a haunting impression of hogs locked in tiny gestation crates that was seared into his memory. "They have almost 360 degrees vision," he said. He slowly moved his pointing index fingers from his eyes to the back of his head, keeping his digits trained onto my face. "They are always watching you," he continued. "Sometimes they look like they are not looking at you . . . , but if you look at their eyes, you will see that they are always following you." His body gave off an involuntary shiver—and it was not due to recalling the damp barn heat from thousands of bodies or the smell of feces, memories that can still make my skin tingle years later. He seemed to visibly shake at the feeling of thousands of confined animals scanning his every movement.

They are always watching you. In retrospect, Juan was not the only person I met who had tried to become attuned to the thick sentience of animal agribusiness. Someone who taught me how to artificially inseminate sows, for instance, sternly told me to never look a hog in the eyes. If the animals think you are looking at them, they will freeze. If this happens when sows are being escorted from the gestation to the delivery barns, he explained, it can cause injuries as advancing lines of animals pile up and crawl over each other. We would walk sideways with our faces to the walls to avoid making eye contact whenever we saw hogs moving through the hallways. Another person instructed me to never touch a gestating pregnant sow. She said this seemingly casual act of individual attention can alarm the animal, make it bellow, and lead to an entire row of overexcited neighboring hogs. As hogs have been gradually bred to bear larger litters, to the very limits of what their bodies can sustain, the simple gesture of touching a sow could potentially lead to waves of miscarriages throughout the barn. Otherwise mundane human actions, such as a sideways glance or a stroke of fur, had apparently become imbued with powers to physically affect animals and the broader project of cheap American meat. These people were being taught that their every random behavior was freighted with the potential to manifest in pigs' bodies and flesh.

In pork industry periodicals, animal agribusiness is presented as a site of biosecure, engineered, and controlled confinement. It is often articulated in popular media as the outcome of technoscientifically precise automation, a matter of well-ordered (if cruel) anthropocentric domination over animal lives in mechanized buildings. But following the sharpening stare of industrial hogs allows us to glimpse something else: how new intensities and forms of intimacy are emerging between hogs and the few human beings with whom they still remain in physical contact in these hyperindustrialized spaces. Within these cramped barns underpinned by extreme productivity, where the efforts of as few as five people now help conceive and birth fifty-five thousand animals per year, the very meaning and efficacy of human life and labor is subtly shifting alongside hogs' bodily conditions.

This book is about the politics of industrialism in an ostensibly postindustrial United States, articulated through the changing forms of being human that underlie porcine life and death. It further reinterprets the shifting logics of agribusiness through ethnographic analyses of overworked animals' immune systems, pheromones, instincts, hormones, ovulation, muscle fibers, tendon distribution, fatty acids, and sentience. I begin with an image of highly observant animals, then, because it suggests that even *how pigs look at human beings* is a historical product with evolving consequences as farm industrialization intensifies. The modern porcine gaze, along with how it can biophysically affect hogs, is itself inseparable from the many waves and epochs of industrialization that have been compounded into this animal over the past two hundred years. Compulsively staring hogs can be read as an embodied metaphor for the factory farm as a whole. They are a lively symbol of how much human work has been absorbed by the porcine species—how many economic demands are now built into this creature's genetics and carcass—along with, in turn, how biophysically attuned industrial hogs have become to human labor. As I suggest in the pages to come, this might also be seen as a potent image to trouble the tenuous yet tenacious—even totalizing—state of industrial capitalism, labor, and livelihood in select pockets of rural America today.

A NOTE ON PHOTOGRAPHY

THE PHOTOGRAPHS IN THIS BOOK are the result of two periods of collaboration with Sean Sprague, a Canadian photographer. The first series, rapidly shot over ten days in late 2010, is featured in brief photographic chapters that initiate each of the main parts of the book. The short opening chapters, acting as interludes, preview each part's main arguments and transition between worksites on the route from pigs to pork. This first series of photographs features very few human workers, effectively depicting one kind of managerial ideal of total automation without the messy contingencies of human engagement (see chapter 2). Put differently, the focus of this series on the serene environments and aesthetics of pork production should be viewed itself as a kind of capitalist dream image of the factory farm.

Selections from the second series, a set of images compiled over three months in 2013, are featured mainly at the opening of each part. Each of these images is composed from more than one thousand separate photographs, and then, through a laborious process, digitally stitched together to give the appearance of a single large-scale shot (see, for examples, figures 3.1, 5.1, 7.1, or 7.2). In a sense, the scenes in these images never happened: each one is a composite of action unfolding in place over hours. From another perspective, however, they are more realistic and detailed as a representation of these scenes of labor than one can achieve by taking a single image at a moment in time (see Butet-Roch 2015).

Although I allow these images to evoke their own impressions of modern meat making—accompanying and even standing in tension with the text—

they should not be viewed as documentary in nature. They are conditioned by the sites that managers allowed Sprague to depict, how (or whether) those managers prepared sites prior to our arrival, the poses and tasks that some workers felt worthy of depiction over the course of hours, and the process itself generated reflections that result from self-consciously slowing down tasks. The presence of the fraught camera in these kinds of hidden spaces, where meat lobbies' efforts to combat undercover exposés have made it illegal in some states to visually depict agribusiness without an owner's permission (see Pachirat 2011), also sometimes unveiled new ways of sensing work. To this end, my brief and sporadic comments on images focus on what their execution opened up and made apparent during the photographic process.

It was what happened after these images were completed, however, that really taught me something new about how the factory farm is imagined in the public sphere. Although Sprague was solicited by junior editors to submit his images to a major photography outlet, a senior editor balked at being the first to feature them. Perhaps they just did not like the photographs. But it was their explanation that surprised me. Recounting how the news media was once engulfed in scandal after digital photographers had secretly doctored their documentary images, this editor was concerned—even if Sprague was forthright that these images are not "real"—that the subject matter was too sensitive for this kind of art. Viewers expected that a depiction of agribusiness would be purely documentary in nature. I empathize with where the editor is coming from, especially given how the camera has been pivotal to activist projects seeking to unveil the truth of factory farms. But I also take this as a minor reflection of the broader kinds of cultural work people put in to insist that things like modern slaughterhouses (and the people who occupy them) are distinctive sites that come with special rules of representation. Animal agribusiness is deemed scandalous in popular culture, a special domain, an exceptional deviation from some people's imagined norms of American capitalism and society. Rightly or wrongly, I hear in these concerns a sense that this site is unique, and all of these unspoken rules of depiction seem to insist that *this is not us*. What if, instead, we took these operations as not exceptional at all—as normal, and even prescient, reflections of American industrial worlds to come in the near future?

INTRODUCTION
The "Factory" Farm

THE RED MEAT CAPITAL OF THE WORLD

"If it wasn't for the hogs, there'd be nothing here. This would be a ghost town." An elderly man first said these words to me in a coffee shop in the town that I call Dixon, the central hub of some fifteen thousand residents in a recently formed one hundred-mile-radius region that cuts across the Great Plains and Midwest of the United States. He would not be the last. A hairdresser. An art gallery director. A breeding farm manager. A young man who had spent much of his adult life scraping muck from animal intestines in a slaughterhouse. After learning that I had moved to the region to live among those who labor within some of the world's largest pork corporations, the first thing some of these people wanted to know was whether I was "pro- or anti-hog." I would shrug, not yet sure what it meant to firmly ensconce myself in either of these camps. "Neither," I'd say. A few of them nodded that this was a sensible position. They then repeated a version of the ambivalent motto: without the millions of hogs to sustain our livelihoods, everything would disappear. Some of these people had likely read prior writers' dystopian portraits of their home. They seemed to be suggesting, for this new visitor's benefit, that they know the air can get thick with hydrogen sulfide and the soil is oversaturated with fecal nutrients. But what are they supposed to say? Without all the hog excrement, they would not be here. They would not have enjoyed the unique lives they have lived. Dixon would be an empty shell of a ghost town rather than, to invoke another local slogan, one of "the red meat capital[s] of the world."[1]

By 1863, Chicago was officially named the global "Porkopolis," surpassing Cincinnati as the city that killed more animals than any other. Also known as "the hog butcher to the world," Chicago's many slaughterhouses in combination knifed, bled, and eviscerated 970,000 hogs in that year's killing season (Wade 2003, 33). The city's trials to kill pigs quickly and distribute their perishable body parts across continents helped generate the organizational forms that underlie industrial capitalism as many still think of it today: the (dis)assembly line, global transportation networks, and commodities trading (Dutkiewicz 2018; Freidberg 2009; Shukin 2009). Chicago's seas of animal bodies—driven on foot through the city from the countryside, and on display in the Union Stock Yards—were, back then, a popular tourist attraction (Pacyga 2015). This may be hard to imagine today, when animal death offends some sensibilities and is hidden from public visibility (Pachirat 2011; Vialles 1994). But in those times, Chicago's kill floors were fabled places that travelers visited to physically see myths of American progress. As animals were dismembered with the regularity of clockwork, some believed they were witnessing the roots of an incipient future where nature was harnessed for human prosperity.[2] Chicago's scale and sensory overload amazed onlookers, imbuing nineteenth-century mass-slaughter with the quality of what Susan Buck-Morss (2000, xi) elsewhere calls a dream world, or an expression of "social arrangements that transcend existing forms." These were scenes of exploitation, for hogs and workers alike, but they were seen by some as heralding human mastery: "the optimistic vision of a mass society beyond material scarcity, and the collective, social goal, through massive industrial construction, of transforming the natural world" (Buck-Morss 1995, 3).[3]

Industrialism no longer enthralls in this manner. Factories and workshops still generate most of the world's material goods. But they rarely spawn dreams of being on the cusp of history, of summoning a new world (Grandin 2009; Nye 1996). For many communities, large-scale manufacturing has not led to the remaking of nature in service to human flourishing but, instead, left behind unruly polluted and toxic environs.[4] The culture of industry lingers as an idealized object of American nostalgia for a mid-twentieth-century period of stable jobs and social relations that politicians pledge to revitalize after each new and euphoric face of capitalism—from neoliberal globalization to digital entrepreneurialism—fails to realize its social promises. But while industrialism may not be hegemonic as it was in Chicago of the 1890s, Dixon and places like it suggest that it did not cease evolving. Disenchanted industrial technics for extracting value from hogs and the people who kill them have only been intensifying across the twentieth and twenty-first centuries. Waves upon waves of industrialization have been compounded into the porcine body over that long stretch of time, and there is nothing familiar or stable about the emerging result.

In 2013, 150 years after Chicago was crowned the global Porkopolis, the agribusiness corporation that I call Dover Foods would kill some 5.6 million hogs in a single slaughterhouse.[5] At a butcher rate of roughly nineteen thousand hogs dismembered across an eighteen-hour working day—that is, a new pig killed every three seconds—there are more animal carcasses inside Dixon at any given moment than there are living human beings. Each day leads to approximately 2,815,800 pounds of edible muscle being shipped to more than two dozen countries. A portion of the daily harvest of 793,300 pounds of bones is eventually processed into gelatin, bone glue, or soup stock for Japanese ramen. Some 736,440 pounds of varied organs will travel to pet food plants and to pharmaceutical companies for biomedical drugs; 287,000 pounds of blood drip from the kill floor and flow to rendering, where the blood is recycled into plasma for feeding baby piglets. Another derivative of the rendering process is 281,500 pounds of lard for use as biodiesel feedstock or as glycerin in cosmetics. Even the roughly 8,700 pounds of fecal material from hogs held at slaughter, kept in misted pens for an hour-long destressing period after travel from barns, is processed into methane biogas to heat water sanitation systems.[6] Beyond Dover Foods, three other companies that I call Berkamp Meats, Trenton Produce, and Cardinal Packing bring the number of piglets born across this one hundred-mile-radius region each year to well over seven million. This small place was responsible for the conception of more than 6 percent of the 112 million American hogs slaughtered in 2013.

Dixon is something of a nineteenth-century Porkopolis reborn, an ardent experiment in industrialization unfolding in the middle of an otherwise postindustrial United States. It is thus a paradoxical place that is both timely and untimely: it is an unusual attempt to resuscitate select values and aesthetics from the prior ledger of twentieth-century capitalism, yet it is also a project that feels fitting and even iconic of a rural United States that is more broadly being reshaped through corporate biotechnology and racialized inequality. But I do not call this small outpost a new Porkopolis simply because it has become one of a small handful of global centers for the mass-production of animal flesh; I do not label it as such based on its sublime numerical quantity of hogs alone. Instead, what distinguishes this company town as a postmodern Porkopolis are the ways that everyday human life and labor have become qualitatively infused with, and organized through, dimensions of capitalist swine. Dixon has been built up, and is now being continuously remade, to unlock new forms of value within the hog's body, mind, and behavior. This town marks a zone where corporations' efforts to manifest a highly uniform version of the porcine species, at a massive scale, have transformed the industrial hog into an omnipresent, world-defining creature.

This book is an ethnography of that industrial pig. Developed through the distinct views of people whose planning and labor underpin this creature's prolific and fragile existence, its chapters arch across every stage of the American hog's life and death. They are about what it means to live, work, and be human in industrial porcine worlds—places built through (and for) the exploitation of capitalist animals.[7] The chapters to come trace an array of topics: attempts to rekindle industrial capitalism in a culturally postindustrial United States; the possibilities of (more-than-human) labor struggle in dilapidated environments; the politics of animal intimacy and care in spaces marked by violence; the shifting place of the human body within cheap meat; and the corporate monopolization of an entire species. At root, however, this book boils down to a simple argument. My claim is that agribusiness is not a project of human mastery over hogs. It is not a simple site of anthropocentric domination over another species. That is too faithful to our inherited fantasies and hopes from nineteenth-century Porkopolises. Instead, the "factory" farm is a matter of reorganizing human communities through the life-and-death cycles of the porcine species. Modern meat, as the model is unfolding in the United States, revolves around remaking the lives and labor of human beings to make them amenable to capitalist animality. This shift in the object of agribusiness engineering, I further argue, is a reflection of the ways industrialism is reaching some tensions—some two centuries after companies first started engineering animality in 1800s Cincinnati—as it grapples with a biological being that has little obvious room left for capitalist expansion.

....

At a time when many insist that we should call the United States postindustrial because fewer people in cities are employed in manufacturing jobs, this book immerses itself in a pocket of that country where things just keep becoming unendingly more industrialized. The process we have labeled "deindustrialization" in the global North since the 1970s, it is worth underlining, has not resulted in a situation in which the material world—from the objects that compose our everyday lived environments to the planet's climate patterns—is less conditioned by industrial processes (Fortun 2012; Moore 2015). It has meant fewer jobs. In practice, deindustrialization marks the social abandonment and ostracizing of manual laborers—the devaluation of their existence—amid factory closures (Walley 2013; Finkelstein 2019), along with intensified exploitation of the few remaining manual laborers employed in factories in the United States and elsewhere. Depending on the location from which you write, deindustrialization can just as easily be renamed a time of hyperindustrialization: fewer people, places, and species now bear the unacknowledged weight of making the world's material artifacts; it means select people live through unprecedented intensities of work. A key premise of this book is that we err when we think that industrialism is a fixed and prior epoch receding in the rearview mirror, outmoded by new forms and strategies of capitalist accumulation. It is, instead, a process that continues to unfold in novel ways. In turn, the chapters that follow are built around queries that aim to put the very nature of animal agribusiness to question: What is the "factory" in the factory farm? What is the "industrial" in the industrial pig? And each does so to glimpse what it might mean to more radically deindustrialize work, the environment, and the imagination.

Concretely, *Porkopolis* is divided into five parts. Each of these parts offers an interpretation of this experiment in cultivating industrial animality as a whole—yet they illuminate that broader project from the very specific vantage point of one discrete phase of porcine life or death. They include portraits of how diverse people live and labor with industrial boars, sows, meat hogs, carcasses, and viscera. The material textures at each of these sites that compose modern meat are different, and there are many such sites: feed mills, genetics facilities, hog growing barns, slaughterhouses, pet food factories, fat-*cum*-biodiesel plants, bone rendering operations, distribution centers, trailer parks, hospitals, and churches. This path moves from semen extraction to biodiesel transesterification, from a biosecure boar stud to the gelatins that compose your house. Such an effort will not lead to a single conclusion. We will see there are many factories within the factory farm. But what does suture these chapters is an attempt to defamiliarize the contemporary state of industrial capitalism in rural America—and even to deindustrialize the assumptions that we bring to the anthropological study of labor and productivity—by illuminating how agribusiness is not just, or even primarily, an economic matter of making pork and profit. It is also an eminently political project of channeling human energy and imagination toward preserving the social categories, values, and aesthetics of inherited industrialisms.

The remainder of this introduction, however, stays outside the hog muck and blood to develop some propositions about the nature of the "factory" farm. For now, please think back to that slogan: "If it wasn't for the hogs, Dixon would be a ghost town." Let me be clear, first of all, that this is not a neutral statement to make in this region. Many locals who are unconnected to the pork industry would strenuously dispute its implications. And nor is it a neutral ground from which to develop an anthropological analysis. There are many stories that can be told about such a cosmopolitan outpost, and the diverse ambitions that ripple through this place cannot be reduced to an outgrowth of "the hogs." Yet, hearing people constantly invoke that phrase informed how I experienced this region over the course of years, the kinds of things that captured my attention; it has even come to underlie some of the political and ethical commitments of this book. It raises the question *What is the industrial pig in the first place?*, for the motto can be read as a statement about *totality*: one capitalist species supports all forms of human livelihood in this town. It requires asking how the porcine species has been reenvisioned and carnally remade to carry such a burden. Such a statement is also about more than pigs alone. It is about the state of American human life today. It reflects the necessity of wage labor in that country; it indicates how most of us can only live where there are things that put us to work (Weeks 2011). It suggests that this Porkopolis is one where thousands of people are made to toil within a model of animal life.

A TOWN OF GHOSTS

Readers familiar with the rural Great Plains may recognize ghost towns as a frequent figure in conversation—and perhaps for good reason. Trips to cities take residents past boarded-up Main Streets and dilapidated homes that suggest grinding poverty and loneliness for the few who must remain once everything else leaves. Mentions of ghost towns recall the region's recurrent histories of settlement, slow bouts of depopulation, and abandonment in the face of an arid geography that can be hostile to many of agricultural capitalism's key life forms (LaFlamme 2018; Worster 1979). I know no better way to encapsulate this rural predicament than to tell the story, or at least the one I was told, of how pork corporations first entered Dixon and its vicinity. Facing the loss of small-scale manufacturing facilities and jobs, much as the rest of the United States did in the 1980s, the town council hired a rural business developer. Despite diligently searching for well-paying factories and dairies that could stem the flow of residents moving to cities for work, he came back with only three options. Representatives of just a few industries would consider relocating to this sparsely populated and remote area: private prisons; a nuclear waste facility; or an industrial pork installation. Opting to pursue the more familiar agricultural option, the town's residents voted to make what a friend called "a Faustian bargain" and allowed their home to become host to what is now amongst the planet's densest concentrations of nonhuman mammal life.

After the closing of most of its manufacturing facilities in the late 1980s, the town of Dixon shrank from ten thousand people to an aging population of 7,500. By 2010, however, the town was bustling, with a population estimated at between twelve thousand and sixteen thousand people. The wide discrepancy in population numbers that were recounted to me is due to Dover Foods' 60–100 percent annual turnover rate across its operations, the growth of surrounding enclaves and hamlets, and the unreliability of census figures in a boom-town setting where migrant workers clandestinely pack into trailer homes because of a shortage of affordable housing (see also Stull and Broadway 2013; Shapiro 2015; Stuesse 2016). When running at full capacity, Dover employs approximately two thousand people on the "plant side" (slaughterhouse), two thousand on the "live side" (farms), and five hundred more in an array of "support functions" that can range from grounds maintenance to trucking routes. This is in addition to some 1,500 other people employed at internationally significant pork firms and subsidiaries for processing hog parts. Some would argue that these paychecks support much of everything else, from retail to government. But even they are the tip of the iceberg—or so I learned— in terms of how industrial hogs have been remade to absorb human activities.

When I moved to the town of Dixon, I initially heard that stock phrase about ghost towns as a statement of corporate dependency, one riddled with weariness about living in a company town. Everything that surrounds us is tied to hog production, it suggests, and everything could disappear with shifts in the price of oil and grain. Public life ignored divisions between work and home. Dover Foods was the sponsor of every event. Radio DJs lauded the company's reliable jobs, pay, and medical benefits. People shopping at Wal-Mart wore the Dover Foods insignia on their T-shirts and the puffy winter jackets they used to keep warm in the cold meatpacking plant. I came to recognize the managers because they wore these crests as badges of identity on their crisp green oxford shirts, signaling that they are freshly starched embodiments of the corporation's values, whether they are cooking pork burgers at charity football games, attending church, or socializing with friends at a bar. Workers' company-sponsored clothing was often more disheveled, reflecting the pressure of long work hours matched with the parental demands on the young-bodied people who disproportionally endure meatpacking disassembly's "grueling monotony."[8]

Worries about corporate desertion would flash up at unexpected times. Friendly conversations at bars would be punctured by semi-joking threats, such as when a burly middle-aged white biker cut me off and said, "My wife works as a secretary at Dover Foods. If you write anything bad about them, I'll drag you outside and beat your ass." I was surprised, during an interview, when a Dover transportation manager initially ignored my questions about the technical challenges of shipping hogs. He insisted that much of his time was spent managing company appearances. When he was hired, he tried to reduce operating costs in his department. His strategy was to prioritize maintenance on the functional innards of company-branded trucks over their shiny exteriors. Within weeks, his office was getting angry calls from people who had spotted a dent, or a recycled pink replacement bumper, as those trucks drove through town. These residents thought Dover had ceased investing in its infrastructure and all the hogs were soon moving elsewhere.

When I started what would become twenty-seven months of ethnographic research, between 2009 and 2013, such flashes of sympathy and interdependence with the state of "the hogs" took me by surprise. I had expected to find the simmering rubble of what Richard Horwitz (1998) dubbed the national Hog Wars in reference to the ferocity of resistance that marked small farmers' confrontation with pork corporations. In the 1990s, newspaper articles and scholarly reports from rural places across the country were filled with notes recounting strife among neighbors, fecal stench, water pollution, the rediscovery of agrarian values, and—in an otherwise important debate's low moment—white nativist fretting about workers of color arriving from around the world (see also DeLind 1995; Halverson 2000). Out-of-the-way places such as Dixon, along with a handful of other pockets of industrial animality stretching from North Carolina to California, came to occupy an outsize role in how a food-conscious urban public imagines the current state of rural life and the ethics of eating. The quantity of books that depict scenes of epochal confrontation between "family" and "factory" farmers is stunning, such that Carolyn Johnsen's (2003) dust-jacket claim captures the spirit of that time when it states that corporate pork constitutes a definitive "struggle for the heart and soul of rural America."

My intention is not to belittle such convictions, even if I am skeptical of the exclusionary premises behind the idea that white farmers are the indispensable backbone of rural life or that there is a fixed and currently existing "heart and soul" to rural America. I even admit that similar kinds of sentiments are what first drew me to look for places like Dixon. This book was motivated by wanting to make some kind of contribution to the tight-knit agrarian community in Canada where I grew up. In the early 2000s, that region was taking on larger quantities of confined animals, and its bases of life and livelihood seemed to be changing. I attended graduate school in anthropology in part to search after places that—however naïvely, in retrospect—may forecast what my childhood home could one day become and learn from those who have refused to acquiesce. So when I arrived in Dixon, my first move was to call the older generation of antiagribusiness activists—people who I also figured would gladly speak with an outside researcher not from these parts.

These countryside residents, who had lived here their entire lives, waged a battle over the materially and symbolically overwhelming stench of hog manure. A generation of grandparents, they wrote op-eds that developed vocabularies for enunciating the horror of breathing vaporized hog shit. They posed for photographs wearing gas masks on their lawns, portraying the outdoors as an uninhabitable zone. They organized community forums and lobbied the politicians who gave tax breaks to pork corporations and relaxed environmental standards for manure pits. They brokered alliances between ranchers and environmentalists while educating distant communities about how industrial hogs remake sociality and ecology. I had a dozen names that I had gathered from old newspaper clippings at the local library. Some had died of old age. One was now a recluse, holed up on his ranch. Another told me that she was about to take a vacation every time I called over the course of two months, gradually making clear, in the politest of ways, that she did not want to meet with me. One person finally picked up, and, to my relief, invited me over for sweet tea the following afternoon.

When I left my motel the next day, I drove along the bustling old-timey Americana main street. Thinking of that motto about ghost towns—and the eye-opening yet reductive way it makes you look for "the hogs" everywhere—it is strange to recall that everything I saw through my windshield can be traced back, if you try really hard, to the meeting of human muscles and pig metabolisms. There were the Guatemalan-owned clothing stores and Burmese fruit markets that tend to open from 4 p.m. to 10 p.m., only after first-shift workers were released from slaughterhouses and breeding barns. This route passes near an elementary school where children speak a total of twenty-six different languages, and side streets where South Sudanese refugees organize Dinka street dances and festivals on select weekends. The path crosses a barnlike banquet hall that is a key destination on major Mexican *cumbia* bands' touring schedules. Along the highway, I drove past fuel stations strangely adorned with signs that read "100% Gas," which I would later learn advertised that the vendors refused to blend corn-based ethanol into pumps, as this increases the cost of animal feed. As I continued into the countryside, past mile-long sprawling trailer parks, squat silver confinement barns appeared on the horizon next to gravel side roads buried in cornfields. But with the exception of a pink snout sticking out of a truck, on its way to slaughter, I never did see a single intact, living pig outside. Traces of industrial hogs were everywhere and nowhere. They undergird a thriving rural locale that is at once cosmopolitan—a place bursting at the seams with diverse lives and ambitions, portending radically other senses of what rural America could yet become—and a palpable expression of global dispossession and injustice, reflecting how people from other countries are disproportionately displaced for the mere privilege of earning a living (Miraftab 2016).

I pulled into the lane of a modest country home. Tall fields of grain ready for harvest engulfed the surrounding property. The blinds were drawn on the glass front door. A blue plastic bag was hanging on the doorknob; a $5 bill and a yellow note was stapled to its front. The note apologized for wasting my time. The money was for my gas. The note's author claimed the corporation had become too powerful over the years and could refuse to buy their crops.[9] This former activist had decided they did not want to further risk their family's livelihood by becoming part of new media scandals. Inside the blue plastic bag were some weathered anti-factory farm booklets distributed by the Sierra Club in the 1990s. The note explained that these booklets had once been helpful as this person tried to learn what their home was becoming. Their pages' dog-eared corners indexed decades-old struggles that now felt buried, subdued to waning memories and hushed voices in diners among close friends.

The terms of my research would change shortly after that nonencounter. In the years to follow, I would shadow Dover Foods' managers during their routine workdays across most stages of pork production while participating over eight months in post–World War II manufacturing theory classes with corporate executives developing new epistemologies for mass-producing pigs.[10] I worked as an entry-level laborer in the artificial insemination and birthing departments for another company, Berkamp Meats, and assisted an ESL (English as a second language) class for Karen-speaking Burmese refugees working the midnight sanitation shift at the slaughterhouse. I lived and volunteered for a summer in a homeless shelter that housed people from a dozen countries who were newly employed in the slaughterhouse and were awaiting their first paycheck, and I was selected for a yearly Chamber of Commerce program that taught a dozen future community leaders about the rural economy. This was in addition to more fleeting senses of place garnered from residents during conversations at town social clubs, churches, bars, and public events. But I still think that short note suggested more about what it means to live amid industrial animality than I would subsequently glean from in-depth conversations over the course of nearly one hundred interviews.

The former activist and their fellow generation of farm families had waged an agrarian campaign in the name of their property rights—symbolic of their land, their place, their home—against disruption from the invading stench of industrial hogs on neighboring land that was quietly purchased by corporations from banks and estate trusts.[11] Their story is similar to that of others fighting through the courts using nuisance suits against all-encompassing odors. Many have lost because of the invisibility of scent and the use of "right-to-farm" laws that were originally supposed to protect small farmers from the complaints of encroaching suburbs (DeLind 1995).[12] I do not recall smelling excrement lingering in the wind at that exact afternoon moment (but see chapter 1). But "the hogs" were there. They were tied up with this person's livelihood—helping motivate crop choice and growth in their farm fields—such that the working, embodied actions of even prior generations of activists had been yoked to become interdependent with hog diets and metabolisms. This former activist's everyday actions, the farming practices their family had done for generations, had been converted to fulfill one dimension of industrial porcine nature. As the note described the corporation, it was a force that had become too powerful, its control in this case mediated through the diet and digestion of a species whose presence and territory extends beyond its body and biological substance.[13] At that point, I had never encountered one of Dixon's individual hogs in the flesh. But sitting in this person's driveway, it became clear that I was already *within* the industrial pig as a model.

The idea of this former activist looking out through the kitchen window still bothers me. I picture them gazing at their grain fields. They would see on the distant horizon the confinement barns that would consume every kernel. I imagine that it must be hard to sense in their property—and even in their own physical, laboring actions of planting and harvesting—the corporate hogs they fought for years. But my nonencounter with this former activist also suggested the need to think outside inherited scripts to write about what it means to live in this Porkopolis. The period of agrarian rediscovery and resistance to corporate agriculture was subdued long before I arrived in the area. The journalists and organizers had left. A book-length account of family farmers defending their tacit community values has become a hard one to tell ethnographically, in locals' own words, at least from this very specific part of the world. But other kinds of stories can and should be enunciated from this place, one where animal agribusiness is a tensely habituated fact of life after being active for almost thirty years.

What I am about to write may frustrate the kinds of readers who are versed in agrarian food movements. I also worry that these words will offend some of my most cherished friends from Dixon who lived in that region long before Dover Foods arrived, and who are normally granted exclusive authority by visiting writers to speak for the culture and values of the place as a whole. But after corporate pork production has been operating within swathes of the rural United States for almost three decades, we need new narratives that reject the hierarchical binaries that have structured some of this debate. We might try to imagine what possibilities emerge beyond the dyads of "natives and immigrants," "farmers and workers," and even "human and animal." Once there are relatively few individuals left that are positioned purely outside agribusiness, what remain are different intimacies and intensities of relation to industrial swine. Once the actions of even ferocious former activists are compelled to feed into industrial animal models, it becomes much harder to write with the clear moral crutch of either heroes and villains. However, what remains is something perhaps more honest: how people in this town, like so many of us, struggle within and against things they are a constitutive part of but do not know how to change. The rub is that after that failed meeting, I could not go anywhere without sensing traces of hogs entangled with rural aesthetics, landscapes, architecture, and bodies. Those confinement barns suddenly appeared porous. I came to see the routine actions of everyone in the region, in some manner, placed in working relation to hogs. Their lives were *converted into providing labor* to the industrial pig. If it wasn't for the hogs, after all, this would be a ghost town.

During the years that followed, other residents taught me their own ways of sensing intimate ties to living and dead hogs, as signs of industrial animality came to manifest within more than soils, grain fields, or gas station pumps. Some people can anticipate both subtle and intense waves of fecal stench as a dimension of local seasonality, distinguish among rendered substances in the slaughterhouse based on their scent, or develop anesthetic capacities to ignore all this olfactory surplus. Others have trained their senses of observation to perceive how accumulated residues of tens of millions of slaughtered hogs' diseases circulate through the landscape, infrastructure, and workers' homes (part 1). Some try to feel the dense emissions of porcine pheromones they believe provoke human desire, and I encountered workplace situations that reflect how human sexual hierarchies are being remade amid attempts to engineer hogs' reproductive instincts (part 2). Human racial and gender tropes were becoming naturalized into porcine musculoskeletal systems, and pharmaceutical regimentation of hog hormones had become tied to the kinship rhythms of daycare schedules (part 3). With time, I came to learn how remnants of dead pigs and repetitive motions are preserved in the muscle contours of workers' bodies and how doctors' offices have become pivotal sites for the profitability of capitalist pork (part 4). Even today—writing from the alternative food hub of Somerville, Massachusetts—living in Dixon makes me perceive traces of hog substance in my computer processor, on gelatin-coated pages of my essays and photographs on my wall, and in my medicine cabinet (part 5). I cannot write this book—it is possible that I cannot type this sentence—without touching dead traces of industrial pigs. The specific model of making and taking animal life developed in the United States means these factory farms are invisibly alongside us at all moments, and our routine actions are made to circulate through these Porkopolises in minute ways.

We might say that Dixon is already a ghost town—though a different type from the one meant by the motto. Since its founding, more than 100 million hogs have been conceived, born, raised, killed, and cut to pieces in this place. Each new piglet body born into this region carries records of those killed. Over the course of almost three decades, traces of now-dead hogs have been built up in physical landscapes, in microbial ecologies, in workers' muscle memory, and in ways of thinking about what the world can offer. This is a fragile place that is challenging the integrity of the porcine species through the historical weight of past diseases and rounds of engineering at the same moment that it is a test ground for replication elsewhere. These agribusinesses are at once spaces for making pork—for raising individual hog bodies—and for the ongoing development of durable models of industrial animality that are being refined with each and every butchered carcass. And those models, which remain largely unbothered and unchallenged by agrarian alternatives and urban food movements, are being exported around the globe in distinct forms to Asia, Latin America, and Eastern Europe (Dunn 2003; Lowe 2010; Schneider 2015).[14] It is possible that, years from now, the town of Dixon will host far fewer human inhabitants. But its peculiar histories and struggles over labor and life may still endure across the planet.

UNENDING UNIFORMITY

This would not be a popular thing to say in this conservative place, but it should be underlined: what the local motto elides is the way Dixon contains the husks of other ghost towns. Its agribusinesses first managed to run at capacity—that is, they were able to find enough willing people to populate working shifts—only after the American recession of 2008 decimated working-class communities on the coasts. More fundamentally, places such as Dixon are enabled by agricultural policies that prioritize cheap meat to subsidize the meager wages of post-Fordist urban service jobs and that, in turn, have led to the bankruptcy of thousands of farmers across the country (see Guthman 2011). Between 1992 and 2009, a period in which Dixon was increasing its inventory of hogs, the number of family-owned pig farms in the United States plummeted by more than 70 percent as the scale of corporate farms outstripped domestic demand for meat and the cheap price of overproduced animal bodies, matched with rising feed costs, made it difficult for smaller farms to subsist (see also McBride and Key 2013). Like other major and minor farm crises that evacuated the U.S. countryside over the twentieth century, this "industrial restructuring" is really a story of people being dispossessed of their homes (Dudley 2004). Dixon's concentration of swine life and death is therefore not just a technical and scientific achievement. It is also a product of a political-economic system built on cheap food that has allowed corporations to gain near-monopoly control over the porcine species.

Companies such as Dover Foods are a significant factor in farmers' dispossession and precarity across the United States. But its day-to-day operations are also, if paradoxically, a consequence and outgrowth of cheap meat. This corporation is one of a series of companies that are trying to create distinctions within industrial forms—unique kinds of "factory" farms—to lessen low profit margin pressures they themselves had a role in creating. While plotting this book, I spent a summer visiting potential research sites across the United States. I met with animal science professors and asked them where to find the most "industrial" of industrial pork. North Carolina hosts the world's largest slaughterhouse, with a dual disassembly line that butchers thirty-two thousand hogs per day. Utah contains one of the largest breeding farms in a single barn, giving it the most "concentrated" concentrated animal feeding operation, or CAFO (the government term for indoor confinement). Colorado, Kansas, Missouri, Nebraska, Oklahoma, and Texas had all seen CAFOS sprout up in the 1990s where few hogs had previously existed. Japanese- and European-owned farms offshored their production to these locales, and they are touted as owning the most advanced buildings, with electronic chips inserted in sows' ears and computerized hog feeding. Across the traditional hog-corn belt of Iowa, Minnesota, and Illinois, family farmers with growing animal herds were compelled to reorganize as limited liability corporations that pool resources and limit legal culpability for pollution of their communities (Ashwood et al. 2014).

What became clear is that there are many kinds of animal agribusiness operating today, each with distinct strategies for accumulating profits in the face of cheap meat. But they emerge from a common moment of reindustrialization. Scholars' accounts frame the rise of the pork CAFO as rooted in neoliberal corporate welfare schemes combined with environmental and labor deregulation policies that lured the industry away from its former nucleus in the Upper Midwest.[15] Local and state governments crafted special agricultural exceptions to environmental and nuisance laws, pushed right-to-work legislation to weaken the efficacy of labor organizing, and provided tax increment-financing incentives for corporations to relocate and build their infrastructure at reduced cost. Often articulated as an imitation of the chicken industry's restructuring in the 1950s and '60s,[16] meatpacking or feed milling corporations found a limited-risk entry into raising pigs by contracting with farmers who were struggling following the market collapse of other agricultural commodities (often tobacco [see Benson 2011]). These corporations provide "genetics" (semen or piglets), feed, technical advice, and purchase price floors to the farmers. The farmers are responsible for the land, buildings, and labor and for meeting the specifications of the contract (see Page 1997; Rich 2003). From 1987 to 2007, contracting shifted the pork landscape of the United States from a group of diversified small to midsize farmers who raised hogs outdoors as a buffer alongside grain crops to one in which only four corporations came to coordinate at least 64 percent of the national pork output (Hendrickson and Heffernan 2007).[17]

When Dover Foods entered the economically depressed region of Dixon in the early 1990s, it had its own strategy: it wanted to achieve the "full" vertical integration of an animal. Broadly put, and though it is hardly unique in this regard, this means that it wanted to directly own and engineer every stage of the pig's life-and-death cycle. It merged historically separate industries such as swine genetics, boar studs, sow insemination, hog growing barns, feed mills, slaughterhouses, and post-kill processing facilities. It has done so with few subcontracted farmers, unlike some other corporations, owning the vast majority of the land and buildings itself. Dover Foods now derives revenue from nearly everything that goes into or comes out of the porcine species while operating almost exclusively on the wage labor of thousands of migrant workers (and migrant managers from other parts of the country). Not only does this one corporation own 1,200 hog barns, scores of feed mills, and some of the world's largest slaughterhouses, but it also appears to be trying to construct a closed-loop system powered by porcine substances themselves. Dover Foods converts fat into biodiesel to fuel trucks; it recycles porcine blood into plasma for feeding piglets; and it captures energy from methane in hog feces to provide energy for barns and slaughterhouses. From the outside observer's view, the company has constructed a model for industrializing porcine vitality itself.[18] Dover Foods has used vertical integration to complete an odd sort of closed loop bioindustrial system that at once makes and is made from the stuff of porcine bodies, in ways far more extensive than meat. This is not simply a matter of natural pigs being inserted into the machine of the factory—as many popular critics frame agribusiness logic (see Imhoff 2010). Rather, to push the analogy in another manner, the machine of this factory is being constructed through distinct biological elements of the porcine species.

However, what was striking during interviews was how Dover Foods' own architects tended to grasp this system of production as a largely unfinished project, one whose potential was not yet realized. Their ambition is not merely to derive new profits from each discrete phase of the pig's life-and-death cycle. Many planners instead insisted their goal was to change the economic nature of the American pig now that they own the animals across that cycle. Depending on where these architects were located along the integrated chain of porcine life and death—from artificially inseminating sows for more robust litters to making lung-based pet food recipes—they had different sensibilities about how to fulfill integration's promise. As I heard the chief executive profess his goal was to "build a [human] culture of integration" laminated over integrated hogs, saw company architects developing 200-node computer profit models within the modern pig, and participated in classes where gurus taught post–World War II Japanese manufacturing theory to help rethink industrialized hog biology, I came away with portraits of a biocapitalist experiment that is ongoing. The idea of the "factory" within this factory farm variously emerged in conversation as a telos or inevitable endpoint of industrial capitalism, a company ethos, a prized aesthetic, an object of workers' resistance, and—especially—a matter of realizing (more) standardized life.

Cincinnati, the first place officially granted the label of global Porkopolis, was also known as the (plural) Empire City of Pigs (Wortley 1851). Its streets bustled with unique hogs. Residents going about their business would encounter an assortment of swine of distinct breeds, ages, sexes, shapes, colors, and temperaments (see, e.g., Bird 1856). Dover Foods' planners, by contrast, are searching for industrial knowledge and ways of seeing to enable a distinct kind of interspecies interface that would turn Dixon into what we might playfully call the (singular) Empire City of the Pig. Their goal is not only to generate millions of animals. At a moment when the profit margins of meat are very low—such that muscle sold in the United States, rather than circulating to higher-paying export markets in East Asia, is often treated by this company as a lost opportunity—the corporation is dedicated to increasing the value of the (industrial) porcine species through the unending pursuit of more bodily uniformity relative to its industrial competitors. Standardized life can reduce labor costs by enabling more machine-driven automation in slaughterhouses; its outputs can fetch higher prices on global wholesale markets; it generates biochemically consistent animals to build more commodities from their bodies; and it promises to serve as a model for replication elsewhere. Dover Foods is developing technics for turning diverse pigs into "the pig"; it is striving to transform actual hogs into tokens of an increasingly interchangeable capitalist animality. The goal of this ambivalent project—which is at once its source of current profit, ground for future competitive advantage, a source of interspecies violence, and an ecological threat—is to realize a capitalist species more homogeneous than any other in history and one that is capable of becoming unendingly more uniform over time.

....

At its broadest, then, *Porkopolis* is about the cultural politics of maintaining systems of industrial production in the United States, along with, following the lead of the anthropologist Cori Hayden (2012), the unending and never-quite-complete work of making things the same (Dunn 2004; Lampland and Starr 2009; Timmermans and Epstein 2010). In this sense, one might detect that the idea of a factory farm that I propose to develop in this book is more elusive than its standard liberal representation as a calculating site of short-term corporate profits, death, and exploitation.[19] It is some of those things. But the rush to itemize factory farming's socio-ecological harms can mask other tensions in American animal agribusiness. Within their boardrooms and at their worksites, many of these companies are motivated by an almost utopian sentiment to maintain pockets of intense static uniformity amid a broader planet that is increasingly restless—from erratic changes in climatic patterns and shifting borders and boundaries to capitalism's dizzying transformations of popular tastes and technologies (Berman 1983; Brown 2010; Morton 2013).

Moreover, at the planning stage, corporations such as Dover Foods are distinguished by a curious kind of reflexive industrialization. They are explicitly, literally, and often quite consciously trying to realize a "factory" farm. These organizations strive to translate industrial categories—such as "machine," "worker," and "manager," or buzzwords from the high industrial 1920s such as standardization and vertical integration—onto diverse workplace practices, pigs, and people (see Fitzgerald 2004; see also chapters 2, 4, and 8 in this volume). One project of such companies, in other words, is the construction of a (cultural) model. They are taking up seemingly outdated twentieth-century industrial stock images, organizational forms, and identities to help them grasp hogs and their human caretakers as potentially (more) standardizable beings.[20] Dover Foods is at once an odd and logical project: an unusual site of renewed grappling over inherited legacies of twentieth-century industrial capitalism and a speculative yet sensible outcome of cheap meat. The "factory" farm in this book is thus not a mere metaphor. These companies are plumbing industrial forms to overcome the cheap life that prior industrialization has wrought.[21] Moreover, this book's attunement to this kind of reflexive industrialization is not merely an intellectual pursuit that comes without political consequence, irony, or contradiction. It is corporations' legal regulation as "agricultural" operations subject to special exemptions on nuisance, air pollution, trucking, and labor laws—outside, at least, of the slaughterhouse stage that is legally regulated as "industrial"—that allows them to develop in the manner that they have unfolded in the United States over the past thirty years. The very category of the industrial emerges in these corporations as a matter of simultaneous desire and denial.[22]

In turn, at the level of execution, the worksites that compose mass-production are spaces where people are relearning the nature of domesticated American animal life. For the "things" agribusiness architects are trying to industrialize are not just the textures of hog muscle and fat in isolation. They include an expanding array of chemicals, minerals, microbes, machines, environments, nonhuman beings, and, especially, human labor practices that go into modern meat and make up pigs in the flesh. Standardizing pigs entails the concurrent standardization of all their relations.[23] While vertical integration is formally defined by corporate ownership and control of worksites, in practice it means an increasingly fine-grained division of labor across the porcine life-and-death cycle. Planners in these agribusinesses are engineering—principally by organizing human laborers' actions ever more finely through—the distinct muscles, fats, organs, bones, viruses, diets, semen, hormones, social hierarchies, instincts, perceptions (and so forth) of hogs. The industrialization of life and death is an ongoing process, shifting and responsive to the changes that it generates within porcine vitality itself. Indeed, we will come to see the American factory farm as a tense project in practice as well as conceptualization: its architects seek to create a uniform material and cultural world even as their attempts to manifest such aspirations within diverse pigs' biologies and behavior generates emergent forms of ecological flux, workplace strife, and intimate, even potentially radical, interspecies relationships. Achieving unendingly more standardized life—trying to further industrialize an organism that has been the subject of some two centuries of industrial transformations—is a project that is so totalizing and fine-grained that it creates its own instabilities.[24]

To put all of this in simpler terms, the (re)industrialization of pigs has come to require intimate and intense qualities of labor. At their most basic, the chapters of *Porkopolis* are about what it means to work (and be a worker) amid shifting worlds of industrialized porcine life. In other words, this book builds through analysis of the mundane things that people skirmish over in agribusiness workplaces.[25] They include many of the usual conflicts that one encounters in sites of industrial labor: control over the terms and process of work; wages, skill, and human dignity; the power-laden effects of adopting new technology; contested hierarchies of race, class, and gender; and what it means for diverse people to identify and act collectively as workers.[26] But there are limits to treating these sorts of places as industrial sites that are indistinguishable from any other. Following Timothy Pachirat (2011), it can matter that the objects (and sometimes subjects) of industrial production are not inanimate tires but living, sentient animals. Minimally, the politics of labor in these sites rarely tend to be about human labor alone—an egalitarian or even utopian factory farm in terms of worker remuneration or labor justice is still a fraught one (see also Wilderson 2003). They are equally about how the state of animal life conditions work. The chapters of this book thus ask whether inherited visions of transcending industrial capital via purely human-centered labor politics are adequate to agribusiness.

In addition to these endemic tensions of capitalist production, animal agribusiness entails topics that we rarely find attached to analyses of labor struggle: how people seek to achieve "the factory" and realize industrialism as an end; the ethics and limits of human labor itself; how to gain knowledge of nonhuman beings' nature; and how one might live as a more ethical person in spaces that are organized through the engineered vitalities of pigs. The vast majority of books on animal agribusiness suggest that one has to make a political choice between caring about the state of either "workers" or "pigs"—an anthropocentric or animal-centric epistemology (see Blanchette 2018). Part of this book's point is to show how the twenty-first century evolution of animal agribusiness has made that distinction untenable. As a more general reflection on industrial capital in times of environmental peril, *Porkopolis* articulates how struggles for labor justice and dignity are inseparable from the conditions of (nonhuman) vitality with which they are intertwined.

To reiterate my argument, in extended form, it is that agribusinesses have created a prolific yet fragile type of porcine life whose maintenance at massive scales has come to foment the transformation of facets of human existence in its image. This Porkopolis is a place where what it means to be a working human or an individual hog is inseparable from the broader state of industrial animal life that encompasses them both. Industrial animal biologies condition and mediate multiple dimensions of human life and labor, including regional class and race relations, forms of kinship, out-of-work sociality, working dignity, mental well-being, human bodily integrity, and ideologies of individual autonomy. This should not be read, however, as a unidirectional story of domination and degradation. Instead, as workers confront distinct types of industrial animals ranging from boars to carcasses—and across scales that extend from the care of one tiny injured piglet body up to the residual diseases of 100 million hogs—this very process depends on cultivating kinds of craft and care with pigs that are not so easily controlled by corporations. We might say that the political stakes of examining labor in the factory farm's worksites are about more than just developing a critique of the making of disposable meat, however problematic that may be. They are also locales of brewing struggle over and amid the shifting state of American industrial animality—including that of human animals—that has consequences for diverse communities as versions of this model are gradually being adopted across the globe.

AMERICAN ANIMALITY IN A BARCODE

"In a philosophical sense, full vertical integration would include everything from photosynthesis to the person eating the food." The speaker of this statement, sitting in his glass-walled corporate office hundreds of miles from Dixon, was named Drew Collins. He is best glossed as Dover Foods' lead architect of vertical integration. A tall, blond man in his mid-forties, Collins wore a pair of pressed khaki slacks and a blue Dover Foods oxford shirt whenever I saw him touring pork production sites in Dixon. He was politely reserved, with a calm emotional keel. Raised near farms in the Midwest, though without the capital to afford farmland of his own, he had saved up to purchase land after becoming an executive at Dover Foods. On weekends he retired with his family to their small corn farm. "I guess you might call that ironic," he said to me with a sheepish smile. Few would guess that this man's planning—more than that of any other person I have met—can reshape domesticated animal life.

Full vertical integration would include everything from photosynthesis to the person eating the food. Collins's wording is playful—an impractical, "philosophical" aside. Upstream, full corporate ownership of the hog would extend through its diet and metabolism into the processes that compose sun-infused plant life (Myers 2016). Downstream, it does not stop at the branded, braised piece of hog shoulder served on someone's plate. Full integration extends beyond meat into the very appetites and biology of the end consumer. Going to this outer limit involves the remaking of populations' desires in ways that are more amenable to corporate animal production and perhaps even capitalizing on human digestive waste. Collins's point was that "full" vertical integration of any animal species is a near-infinitely complex proposition, an ambiguously utopian and dystopian project. Yet his words are important because they underline how this agribusiness's commodity is not the isolated porcine organism. Collins is not working on the individual creature that comes to mind when I imagine a hog sitting in a barn. His planning centers on the total assemblage of things that make up present-day hogs in their actual flesh (see Guthman 2019; Haraway 2008). Collins is an engineer not of animals but of capitalist animality.

Collins occupies a unique position in the corporate structure. He is the only employee responsible for in-depth planning of production across every single phase of the pig's (pre)life and (post)death cycle. A slaughterhouse worker might make a similar slice of the right ham many thousands of times per day. Farmworkers in artificial insemination arguably have a more profound tactile knowledge of sow reproductive instincts and sentience than any animal ethologist. Others will nurture hundreds of thousands of animals aged from day one to twenty-one in farrowing barns, witnessing scores of variations of what it is to be a piglet—but seldom seeing a grown hog. Virtually every nonmanager's labor is embedded in one age grade, working type, biological function, or anatomical part of the porcine species. Even among those managers, fewer than a dozen oversee more than one short thread of life or death. And aside from one feed commodities buyer, some nutritionists, and the chief executive, few people beyond Collins cross the chasm from porcine life to death, or from death to life. If the classic image of the small farmer is someone who nurtures an animal across its entire life-and-death course, then Collins is one of the last people in this company who approximates that role. He is among the final farmers remaining in this system.

Collins would put his job differently. He liked to say that his role was to "find new money in our pigs." Passed down over the years, this catchphrase reflects how accountants conceived the operation. Armed with an excess of capital from other ventures, the company saw the American hog of the 1980s as an undercharted realm for revenue extraction. Collins identifies dimensions of the pig's life course, along with its post-death bodily substances, that might merit deeper investment. He once found, for example, a gap in the amount the corporation was paying for plasma to feed to baby piglets compared with how much others would pay the corporation for raw blood. He used the data to convince the chief executive to purchase centrifuges that allow Dover to recycle blood to nourish its own piglets.

Dover Foods recruited Collins in the 1990s after he developed a model to analyze how feed ingredients in a boar's diet affect the potency of its semen. While working at Dover Foods for more than a decade he expanded his program to incorporate more dimensions of the porcine species. As of the year 2010—and it is likely even more complicated today—the result was a roughly 200-node profitability model that analyzes dynamic parameters such as the prices of various feed ingredients and their substitutes, fuel prices, endemic diseases, drug usage, labor costs, and that week's ideal slaughter weight ("283 pounds"). The program treats the animal's life-and-death course—across boars, sows, piglets, hogs, carcasses, and substances—as one unified product. In other words, this is not a model based on the profitability of meat hogs' muscle substances alone. It operates at the level of the industrial species in its entirety; it incorporates cost variables across every type and stage of pig life and death that Dover currently owns, from genes to viscera.

"We are moving through the knowledge age of pork," Collins memorably told me one evening in a hotel bar, after our biweekly class in manufacturing theory, when "pork production is becoming transparent to all sectors of the food chain." Dover Foods' customers—and "customers" are not those who buy pork from grocery stores but wholesalers who process body parts into products such as branded bacon[27]—were demanding information about the technologies and events embedded into tenderloins but not measurable based on the sheer physical flesh quality (e.g., pH levels or water retention). I smiled to myself at the implication that even I, as an anthropologist, was being absorbed into a node of Collins's model; that how industrial hogs are discussed can affect their value.[28] I heard his statement partly as an acknowledgment that undercover videos of animal abuse and reports concerning animal farming's role in intensifying human antibiotic resistance were becoming risks to the corporation's ability to maintain profits. But his main point was to underline one of Dover Foods' convictions: that vertical integration, standardization, and direct ownership of the pig's existence is itself valuable. As the lead Dover salesperson once put it, integration is "what allows us to tell the Dover Foods story and give our customers a type of guarantee" that the company had directly dictated every single feed ingredient, drug, and event that affects the pork. The model itself was becoming a brand, and control—even if only partial—was emerging as a key source of distinction and value.

Recounting how he developed the knowledge age of pork while giving a presentation at a college, Collins slowly built up to his description of the pivotal slide of his lecture. But his PowerPoint image that purported to reveal the future of global animal agriculture was not, at first glance, a very captivating one. The next generation of animal flesh was a vacuum-sealed pork chop, with a sticker of a barcode affixed to its encasing plastic. Once scanned, he explained, this barcode of the future would describe "everything that goes into our product." Suffice it to say that this was not the type of hushed conversation that I pictured myself having in a dark tavern booth while researching American agribusiness companies. But I want to stick with it. The kind of thinking that underlies this barcode also underpins this book. This desired barcode illustrates the everyday managerial travails of agribusiness in late industrialism (Fortun 2012). And it provides a window into a politics of totality that rests at the very core of how agribusinesses are coming to remake places and people through the porcine species.

Perhaps the future barcode would include the hundreds of foodstuffs that a given hog ate, its various illnesses and treatments, or a range of genetic information detailing the qualities of its parent boar or sow. Maybe it could list the labor processes and the kinds of people that shaped the animal. Collins's barcode was part of a theory that total knowledge of porcine existence—a fully standardized and known life form, which one corporation had carefully overseen through its every expression of life and death—was becoming a route to value in terms of keeping customers' faith in the product and charging a premium. What is important to note is that Collins's barcode is not a register of the day-to-day life of any actual animal. The barcode's informatics would display a reflection of the experiences of a generic hog. Such a hog would embody the statistical mean of experiences, genetics, feed, or living conditions that adhere across Dover Foods' animal herd as a whole. This is one version—one reading, one way of materializing—the abstract capitalist animality that vertical integration portends but one can never see at any given site. The challenge of standardized life is to decrease variation around this mean; it is to more closely match the experiences of every single individual pig onto this abstract statistical animal. For instance, I doubt the barcode would include information on the time that I worked with a sow that was suffering from a bulging rectal prolapse that blocked her birth canal. We shot her in the head, tore open her uterus with box cutters, and "saved" her piglets with mouth-to-mouth resuscitation (see chapter 6). The barcode would not declare that a key ingredient in those pork chops is workers' breath. Its point is to imagine a system in which there are no such rare events.

The scanning of a barcode projects a sense that Dover Foods has deep knowledge of the porcine species while promising a future in which it will control the nature of the pig even more in the integrated system. Thus, the knowledge age of pork—signaled by scanning a barcode to encode all of industrial animality's 200 factors—is made imaginable by vertical integration, but it also makes evident the gaps in integration as a horizon of total knowledge. The challenge, of course, is not to "fully" integrate the pig, or to achieve absolutely perfect uniformity. It is to be more integrated and standardized than any other company. "Vertical integration is a mentality," I was often reminded by Dover Foods' senior managers. Many of their competitors own the farms, the feed, and the slaughterhouses. But they treat them as separate profit centers. Cardinal Packing's farm division will be encouraged to sell live hogs to a rival packing company if it can get a better price. Dover Foods' managers were adamant that this lack of an integrative ethos is not "real" vertical integration. "What I love about vertical integration is that I don't have to think in terms of my own little world, my single department," a transportation director told me in a trailer where he coordinated drivers. "Vertical integration allows me to treat our animals as a single unit."

I fixate on Collins's barcode for a few reasons. The first is because it is just such a managerial technology that allows him to grasp seven million hogs as a "single unit." Second, the kind of move that this barcode represents also underpins this book's ethnographic organization. Third, the barcode serves as a reflection of the state of animal industrialization in the United States. What the barcode underlines is how the project of American animal agribusiness has become the tangible realization of totalities. Dover Foods aims to own all of the pig, use all of the pig, control everything that goes into pigs, derive profit from every moment of the pig's life-and-death cycle, and know everything that can affect pigs' bodies in order to produce extreme uniformity. It is tempting to read this monopolizing ambition as a sign of this company's unmitigated power. But it also reflects how companies are trying to find "new money" in pigs when little obvious room for capitalist growth remains.[29]

The word "totality" in academic writing usually refers to the gathering together of apparently dissimilar things to find a synthesis that transcends what seems obvious. It has flickered in and out of debates that range as widely as Marxist revolutionary theory, the promise of so-called big data, and efforts to think within "systems" that overcome disciplinary thought.[30] In this book, however, I am less concerned with totality as an intellectual idea(l) than I am with how it is put into practice and struggle. How and to what effect are totalities done; how are worlds made porcine in practice? Why do we see these kinds of totalizing industrialisms emerging in an ostensibly postindustrial United States? What are the limits and forms of resistance to this kind of thinking and practice with animals?

In one sense, this book should itself be read as an exercise in totality making. It engages in the (impossible) project of knowing "all" of the industrial pig; it tries to move across every moment of the modern hog's existence. In another sense, each section aims to offer a maximally coherent articulation of the logic of the factory farm as a whole. Each section relatively privileges the practices of one workplace class—including senior managers, low-level farm managers, farmworkers, slaughterhouse workers, and porcine entrepreneurs— as they articulate their relationship to actual pigs, industrial animality, and standardized life. In addition to the Barcode, the figures used to illustrate these struggles over totality include "the Herd" (part I), "Stimulation" (part II), "the

Stockperson" (part III), "the Biological System" (part IV), and "the Lifecycle" (part V). These terms are all drawn from the long history of American pig farming and take on new resonance as managers and workers reinterpret them amid shifting industrial conditions of porcine life and death.

All of this book's parts can also be read as *counter*-barcodes, however, because they magnify the many gaps that belie the achievement of a completed porcine totality. At the core of this method is the pivotal distinction between animals (actual porcine organisms) and animality (expressions of the entirety of the pig as a "single unit") that emerges as a terrain of minor class, racial, and gendered conflict with the rise of vertical integration. The (corporate) ideal of integrated pork production is one in which each site, manifestation of pig, and labor practice simultaneously cites all the other moments without fragmentation.[31] Figures such as the barcode are thus aspirational class-based discourses with power-laden repercussions in terms of who can articulate an abstract "industrial animality" over tactile labor with individual, actual pigs. Yet each site on the route from pigs to pork is one where different visions of animality emerge and oppositional notions of who can claim privileged knowledge over actual animals begins to take shape. In this sense, each section depicts skirmishes over the very nature of building this unified agroindustrial complex.

But there is a final methodological reason that I spell out the minutiae of Collins's barcode. What we need to remember is that the barcode is an almost stereotypically corporate revelation. It is mundane, normal, and thoroughly *unexceptional*. I do not see the ambitions toward totality in things like the barcode as marked *only* by all-powerful corporate machinations. I think they are equally symptoms of how these planners are pushing against limits of our inherited systems of accumulating capital. They are about trying to maintain industrial capitalism's hold on an overindustrialized organism. This should affect how we write about them. In opposition to certain popular journalistic tracts that aim to confront industrial food systems, this book's premise is that the narrative conventions of the liberal exposé genre that shapes most meat writing are politically inadequate for our contemporary world. Many popular books—with a key exception being Upton Sinclair's classic novel, *The Jungle* (1906), that used the Chicago meatpackers as a vantage point onto our shared political and economic life—frame animal agribusiness as underpinned by nefarious behavior and moral deviance that is outside of all cultural norms. They insist that factory farms are so exceptional, and exceptionally bad, that their practices could be corrected if only they were "exposed" to the public. These factory farm exposés present themselves as radical interventions against power. But there is a kind of conservative tendency in this move. They assume that an ideal set of American moral norms and alternative agricultures already exist and use those images as a baseline for marking off corporate agribusiness's deviance.

Yet industrial meat *is* the American norm. And animal life has not been industrialized in the past thirty years; it historically has been a harbinger of industrialisms to come (Blanchette 2018). Henry Ford claimed to take his idea for the automobile assembly line from the Chicago meatpackers' disassembly line (Shukin 2009). Drug-aided human sciences of bodily growth and normative health are inseparable from efforts to industrialize animals' metabolism in the 1940s (Landecker, forthcoming). Ninety-six percent of American pork and chicken comes from an iteration of a factory farm, and these farms are globalizing at a rapid pace. What this book develops is an exposé of animal agribusiness not as an institution that departs from American cultural norms—as exceptionally bad and exceptional to regular, ongoing processes of industrialization in other places and industries—but one that uses the factory farm as a window to expose existing and looming American norms. I build across these pages not an exposé founded on identifying deviance but, instead, an *exposé of the normal*. These operations and their desire to realize lived totalities are what late industrialism might look like. Immersively tracing the lives and deaths of these industrial American animals, I suggest, can help us reflect more critically on the simultaneously powerful yet exhausted state of industrial capitalism more generally today.

This is also tied to the ethics of how one might represent the diverse kinds of people who have made their lives in Dixon and places like it. My frustration with the standard exposé genre is that it tends to position such places as a mere cautionary stop on the road. I think that is what people were telling me when they invoked haunting ghost towns. In exposé damage narratives, we gain fleeting glimpses of workers with repetitive stress injuries and stench-ridden environs that reduce these places to icons of pain and degradation.[32] Places such as Dixon, in turn, are then made to serve as negative narrative contrast devices for the visiting journalist's discovery of an inspiring, bucolic, and "normal" agriculture somewhere else. I share many of these authors' ecological, moral, and political concerns about the state of animal and rural life. I think that people's efforts to realize alternative American agricultures across cities and countrysides are courageous, important, and can make a profound difference.[33] And this book features no shortage of violence. But one of my gambits is that more immersive, highly-detailed portraits of life and death within factory farms can feed the critical imagination to spawn visions of other, as-yet nonexistent, American agricultures. Another is that, after decades of living and laboring amid industrial animality, people who dwell in Dixon can offer more than proof of damage. Sometimes these pages will feature people trying to practice and express—however fleetingly or subtly—alternative political relations to animal life and human labor. At other times, they follow how people try to find their own ways to make a decent and worthwhile life for themselves and others in spite of it all. Regardless, this book stays squarely within and against the many worlds that constitute animal agribusiness, narratively intensifying both their ongoing traumas *and* the possibility of new kinds of rural existence that may yet foment out from within them.[34]

FROM PRELIFE TO POSTDEATH

"Part I: Boar" is about how the industrial pig has come to require constant work. Confinement no longer contains this animal. Maintaining the genetic potency of industrial boars has made managers appraise how pig diseases are intertwined with wind patterns, terrain gradations, and humanity. One result is that corporations are enacting biosecurity protocols in workers' domestic homes, a move that frames human sociality as a reservoir sheltering porcine disease. Workers' social lives and kin networks are reimagined as a threat to the vitality of industrial hogs in ways that subtly alter the value of human autonomy in this region. This part inhabits the abstract technologies that allow managers to become attuned to the industrial pig as a fragile and world-defining species in need of new types of laboring subjectivity while tracing the politics of class in a zone reorganized around industrial animality. In turn, it analyzes how people can be seen to be engaged in the regulation of pigs' immunity in their routine actions outside work, whether while sharing some wine or praying in a church pew. This part begins to develop, in other words, the ways that industrialism itself relies on—and tries to co-opt—practices of care and animal intimacy.

"Part II: Sow" is about how senses of animal nature are wielded to devalue human labor. It enlivens the industrialization of porcine instinct, written with an eye to how instinct has long been central to grasping the industrialization of human bodies. It is based on my experiences working the artificial insemination line. Workers are tasked with "becoming the boar," enacting porcine instincts, by using their hands and bodies to imitate mating. These modes of building (human) labor practices through animality—of interpreting, acting out, and embodying sexual natures of swine—transform ideological impressions of instinct into terrains of gendered work and exploitation. Against theories that propose that the factory farm's task is to excise all natural "nature" out of production, then, I argue that each work phase is organized to magnify one expression of porcine nature at the expense of others. In particular, this part theorizes the kinds of interspecies and labor politics that are possible when people are intimate with only one dimension of pigs—in this case, reproductive instincts—and critically considers how companies attempt to manifest alleged *human* instincts to labor.

"Part III: Hog" examines how industrial pigs are overworked: both in that certain of their biologies have been engineered to work in overdrive and in that there is too much historical human labor coursing through their physiologies. It traces the labor of care and the politics of species as they unfold across the farrowing (birthing) rooms and growing barns. While the factory farm at this book's core exists to create a more standardized animal, refinements in sow genetics are creating litters that are too large to supply adequate nutrients to fetuses in the uterus. One result is litters that are emerging as runts. These runts are radically particular animals with ailments that workers must normalize within twenty days or the piglets will be euthanized. The part examines how "surplus" affect and capitalist intimacy is now required to save surplus pigs in ways that are both violent and redemptive for the people who struggle to find moments of craft and a broader way of life while working on these farms. To do so is both to take seriously workers' experiences and to query the limits of liberation via labor in this space.

"Part IV: Carcass" is about the vertical integration of human workers' bodies. It builds on a slaughterhouse manager's suggestion that, after two hundred years of industrial refinement, the disassembly line has reached the limits of the human body. It cannot go any faster without threatening acute injury, and the only path to increased throughput is a more standardized pig around which corporations could develop automated machines. In the year I arrived, Dover Foods added a health clinic for employees that ran intensive physicals in an attempt to test new hires' bodily condition and assign them spots on the disassembly line to minimize insurance claims. The clinic signals how the slaughterhouse manages discrete human biologies as a source of value in parallel and alongside those of pigs. This part thus articulates the joint commodification of animal biology across species while illustrating how factory farms are beginning to cultivate a mode of industrialization that goes far beyond labor theories of value that have classically underpinned this mode of capital.

"Part V: Viscera" is about how we are all recruited to work on industrial pigs. It is based on a series of postdeath ventures that derive value from the slaughterhouse's biological matter beyond meat in the form of bones, feces, fat, livers, lungs, and animals that are "out of spec." Total absorption of the animal's physiological substances is usually treated as a neutral matter of rationality and good environmental stewardship. My argument is that we should view it as deeply political. Using "all" of the pig depends on making us (and other species) subsidize the factory farm's model of animality ever more finely in our activities. The purpose of this section is not to exaggerate agribusiness power, even as industrial pigs' substances may coat countless items, including this book's surface. It is instead to point to the instability intrinsic to this model of industrialized animals: it depends on so many practices of consumption to sustain itself, more than can be supplied by human eaters alone. As the model of factory farm growth developed in places such as Dixon appears to be at its most totalizing and far-reaching, it is also at its most fragile.

A brief epilogue gathers together some of these arguments to articulate how American human beings are potent kin with American hogs, as two of the world's most heavily industrialized and overworked living beings, and calls for the very idea of deindustrialization to be critically reclaimed as an active and ongoing collective project.

PART I
BOAR

1.2 BOAR STUD LABORATORY
Laboratory workers sample
and pack semen into bags
for delivery to sow breeding
farms. The boars are kept in
a room behind the windows
on the back wall. Batches of
extracted semen are sent into
the laboratory through the
white pneumatic tube at the
back.

1.1 DRAWING OF A HOG (overleaf)
A worker's drawings of hogs
on the wooden railing of a
sow breeding farm.

ONE **THE DOVER FLIES**

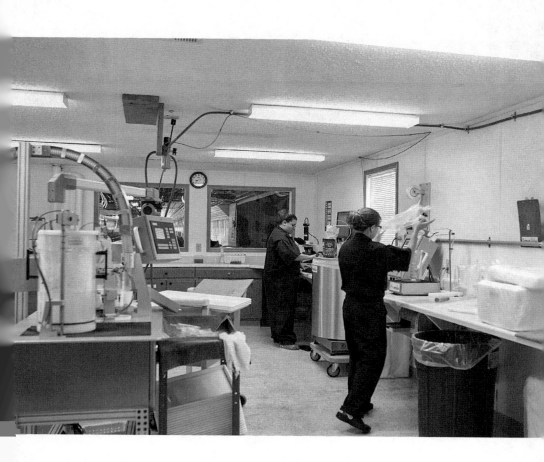

JAMES HODKINS, a retired wheat farmer, is a rare kind of acquaintance in this part of the world. He still fights tooth and nail against the merits of corporate hog production. Many friends remembered Dixon of the mid-1990s and its surroundings as a place of strife. Militant opponents of industrial hog farms drove across the countryside and shot rifle blasts through the corporation's feed augurs, attacking Dover via the proxy of its automated barns. Others are said to have clandestinely lined up mangy and diseased pigs on the perimeters of company property, attempting acts of bio-sabotage. After decades of living in the shadow of factory farms, people seldom issue existential critiques—let alone engage in militant action—against agribusiness. But even supporters of factory farms, defending them based on the idea that the paychecks support towns, would sometimes voice tacit fears about the ecological threat of being surrounded by a massive population of hogs.

1.3 **QUINCEAÑERA** Weekend events such as this party bring together workers from across the Live Side and the Plant Side of the corporation. They can thus be read as one of many bio-insecure spaces.

In 2009, a newspaper ran a report titled, "Experts Say Dover Bubble Not Real." James introduced me to the story, keeping a copy on his dining room table. The writer of the report enlisted meteorologists to try to discredit a local discourse that rain clouds were diverting in a circle around Dover Foods' farms and packing plants. Many argued their operations resulted in drought periods that require extra irrigation and affected cattle ranchers by desiccating their pastures. While a few meteorologists tried to claim that there were no statistically significant changes to regional rainfall since the slaughterhouse opened in the 1990s, friends I would meet around town insisted they were mistaken. For one middle-aged male bartender, "chemicals from those pig factories out there" were interacting with rain clouds around the slaughterhouse and biodiesel plants, causing moisture to dissipate. For James, it was the evaporation of "all that pig shit" in terms of the "methane gas, ammonia, and everything"—from the open-air pits of manure sitting on the company's 1,200 separate farms—that resulted in an understudied form of air pollution. The idea is that animal confinement leads to total biospheric reordering for all of the other forms of life that tenuously exist within this Dover Bubble, while expressing the haunting sense that manure—a material that was once prized in an agricultural community for its nutrients—is not the same substance it used to be.

The Dover Bubble, and the idea of an industrialized atmosphere that it brings into focus, suggests an anthropogenic yet unpredictably emergent ecosystem (see Choy and Zee 2015; Masco 2015). This Dover Bubble is a commentary on outsize industrial scale and the invisible reshaping of natural processes presumed to be ironclad laws in this rural community. It is a citation of the factory farm's power over the entirety of a regional biosphere, a force so omnipresent as to be imperceptible, yet one that creates new ways of interpreting one's surroundings. It depicts a unique place enveloped apart from others, a sort of digestive ecology infused with waste, where fecal chemicals cause divergence from historical ecological patterns. It is, above all else, a commentary on imbalance in the context of an agricultural economy, one where porcine nature is produced on such a massive scale—and set indoors, ostensibly seeking independence from the environment—that it depletes the life-giving rain required for other forms of regional agriculture, including wheat, corn, and pasture-based cattle. The Dover Bubble offers an interpretation of factory farming ecologies whereby one form of life—an agricultural monoculture— dominates all others in its orbit. It frames the region as a water-parched dead zone that is decimated by the excessive production of porcine life.

1.4 **ENTRYWAY INTO A CONFINEMENT BARN**
More than 1,200 of these buildings,
largely identical in architecture, dot
the one hundred-mile-radius region.

The critical theorist Walter Benjamin is a helpful guide for thinking through this particular sense of an industrialized nature. As Susan Buck-Morss (1989) reconstructs his unfinished *Arcades Project* (1999), Benjamin saw a reversal of common meanings of "Nature" and "History" in industrial capitalism. Prior to the industrial revolution, Nature seemed fixed. One might think of the peasant whose existence is tied to unchanging agricultural cycles and seasonality (Berger 1979). Benjamin, however, believed that industrial capital—at least in urban locales—upended this notion of Nature, replacing it with an alternative form of seasonality made visible by the changing fashions and trends of commodities on the city streets of Paris. Capitalism instituted a new form of (urban) Nature—by which he means a change in peoples' material surroundings—rooted in the interplay of commodities, science, and human-made landscapes. Tied to the industrial factory, this New Nature changed its face daily. As the urban dweller encountered a seasonal influx of trends and new clothing, gadgets, machines, or buildings, she was presented with a kaleidoscope of progress that masked the fixity behind it all: relations of industrial production. Capital's aesthetics confront the urban dweller as a shifting Nature while human History—hierarchical social relations, such as class, that we think as malleable or progressively improving—was solidified to a standstill in the factory (Buck-Morss 1989, 66–70).

Abstracting from Benjamin's Paris, we might say that Nature once signified preexisting and fixed laws of life that lay underneath the surface patterns of ecology. Such an orientation to the nonhuman world is surely waning in the so-called Anthropocene period, as Benjamin's reading comes full circle. No longer are the static social relations of factories only transforming Parisian built cityscapes. Instead, they are suffused into earth systems through traces of industrial labor, toxic chemicals, nuclear fallout, and greenhouse gases (Besky and Blanchette 2019; Masco 2015; Moore 2015; Murphy 2011). But this feels even more immediate in a corporate-owned bioregion, for in a zone where people try to see, smell, or touch how life is inflected with the omnipresence of mass-produced animals, nature feels like the New Nature.

If he read any of this, I am quite sure that James would tell me I am more full of excrement than a Dover Foods hog. But I found his ways of talking about factory farms to parallel how Benjamin discussed industrial capital. As we spoke over the course of an afternoon, James was trying to express a sense of unease about the shifting forms of life appearing around his property. As he peered out of his kitchen window, James saw ten metal-clad hog barns resting on the horizon. It was the surfaces of those structures that he had grown to

distrust as too regular and unchanging relative to the evolving natures appearing on his farmland.

James passed me a copy of a letter he had sent Dover Foods a few years previous that detailed how farms' fecal vapors were leaving his asthmatic wife bedridden. He recounted how hog barns had changed the place where he lived for eighty years. "I've seen about all of it, from the dirty '30s to the days of Dover," he tells me as we sip Cokes and stare over the horizon at the twin shimmering manure pits the size of football fields. "[There are] 10,560 hogs in there, in those ten barns. . . . You got two pits over there. There's only been one time since those were built that we've seen water up to the top of both pits . . . or 'lagoons.'" James believes Dover is allowing the manure to leach into the ground or evaporate into the air. He has been checking his water wells for fifteen years, but "so far . . . we haven't had high nitrogen content or anything like that. But we get it tested every year, just to be on the safe side."[1]

In his younger days, James welcomed the blooming effervescence as the season changed from winter to spring and brought the promise of another year's farm crop. Now the temperature shift heats up the liquid in the lagoons,

1.5–1.7 INDOOR CONFINEMENT TECHNOLOGIES The barns contain temperature-control devices, fans for propelling out gases, and automated feed machines.

resulting in waves of smell that take on an almost fog-like materiality. Rain, once prized in an agricultural region, brings the need to seal windows when the still surfaces of the manure pits are disturbed. The wind, blowing furiously across the flat grasslands, was once a burden as it drowned out outdoor voices and flung trash and branches across yards. Now James welcomes a pounding wind that will keep the air moving quickly, and brush out what he calls the "the wind": a slow-moving breeze from the west that drowns his property in thick clouds of odor. As we spoke, he struggled to describe the materiality of this invisible stench, describing an overwhelming tactility to the air that "just makes tears run out of your eyes." It permeates his house to the point where "you can have your head stuck in a plastic bag and you could still smell it," a deathly substance "that you could cut with a stick it [gets] so thick out there . . . it just makes you want to quit breathing." Indeed, that air is quite thick and complicated. In other places that more frequently spray fields with manure, researchers find that the contents of those lagoons can break up in the air into 331 odor-causing compounds, and a host of substances including methane, hydrogen sulfide, ammonia, endotoxin, antibiotic-resistant genes,

1.8 **LAGOON SIX** Clusters of indoor confinement barns flush waste out to open-air pits. The liquids evaporate or are sprayed as fertilizer on neighboring crop fields. This lagoon, the size of a football field, accumulates the urine and feces of 2,500 breeding sows.

and unmetabolized drugs (see Schiffinan et al. 1998; Spellman and Whiting 2007).

At least the deathly smell is explicable and even something James can learn to manage once he can predict its seasonality and, in this very limited sense, plan his daily routine around its waves. It is the invisible and insensible that haunt James. He is convinced that behind the surfaces of those barns something troubling is happening, though he can only sense its indexes and traces. He says that he sees more jackrabbits scuttling around his property and traces this back to when Dover Foods "hired a coyote exterminator and killed all our coyotes." He says, "They eliminated part of our wildlife balance, and now the rabbits are coming back," a muted reference to the hellish sight of thousands of jackrabbits swarming the Great Plains and Midwest along-side the storms of black soot during the Dustbowl of the 1930s (Egan 2006;

Worster 1979). He talks at length about how the barebones company-financed trailer parks on the outskirts of Dixon, the company cafeteria that deducts meals from paychecks, and the company-owned health clinics for workers mean that "it's getting more like the old coal mine things down in Pennsylvania. You work for them, you live in their house, and you bought the groceries from them. *And you never get away from it!*" In James's words, Dover Foods has not only created dead zones of stench around its properties—spaces uninhabitable and noxious to humans—but enacted a pre–New Deal regression to a Gilded Age period of total dependence on capital. He points to an orange fly swatter with a large black substance the size of a quarter smashed onto it and mentions the mystery of what he calls the Dover Flies, which now tend to swarm his porch:

> I've spent hundreds of dollars on big old cans of real powerful dairy barn spray, because [the flies will] just coat the inside of [the patio] to get out of the sun. You go out there, and you have to spray it to kill the flies. It'll keep them away for two or three hours, and then they'll come floating back. I

1.9 **WORKER HOUSING** The company sponsors housing for workers in a trailer park.

know they're Dover Flies because there's not anything out here that produces that many flies. They grow big flies. Your thumbnail, you couldn't see [it] if you had one land on it. They just appear, and they just stick to the walls. A lot of times they're so bad that you can't get out the door. You have to go out the other door . . . , and the freeze don't help at all. Maximum so far: it was minus 1.3 [degrees Fahrenheit] and we still had flies. You just can't kill them. Naturally, it used to be that when the weather got cold, they'd die. You never used to get flies in the winter time.

You just can't kill them. As James describes the Dover Flies, the porcine lives manufactured in the barns—alien to this part of the world—contaminate and animate other life-forms; the factory farm in-fills the Dover Flies with a supercharged vitality impervious to seasonality, weather, and the cycle of

1.10 **SHIPPING HOGS** A hog's snout pokes out of a truck as it travels on the route to slaughter.

1.11 COMPANY UNIFORMS
As part of biosecurity protocols, farm employees shower at each worksite and wear laundered uniforms. The company supplies boots and coveralls.

death. The Dover Flies are a postagricultural form of being, external to the seasons, not unlike the industrial pigs confined indoors in temperature-controlled barns. For James, the Dover Flies have mutated by taking facets of industrial confinement into their very bodies, surviving as if they were indoors in winter. He describes an airborne living ecology of excrement that is supported by studies that propose flies as vectors of antibiotic resistance, matching genes from manure lagoons to their intestinal tracts (Zurek and Ghosh 2014). His point, I think, is an important one that I develop in the next chapter: the factory farm renders industrial everything that it comes to touch. The industrial hog has become an atmospheric organism, making it impossible for anyone in its ever-expanding orbit to not be exposed (Choy and Zee 2015).

Yet, and despite my prods, James could not name a single thing that he had seen the company do over the previous decade that was unusual. Every day is the same, a clockwork routine of repetition. He watches a small crew of workers arrive at the growing barns across the road every morning. Transport semis occasionally come to the loading docks to collect hogs for slaughter. On some afternoons the "dead trucks" that look like trash compactors arrive to carry out the carcasses of animals from dumpsters and take them to the packing plant to be boiled down and rendered into inedible fat, bone meal, and protein. The workers leave at the same time each day. James just stares at those lagoons of manure that are as large as American football fields, asking why they always stay at the same level despite the thousands of animals defecating in the barns. James senses signs of vital seepage out of those barns, and they tell a story of a company and an economic experiment that is routinized but not secure. What James's stories share is a sense that the seemingly biosecure confinement barns are actually permeable, remaking bodies, ecologies, communities, and even the local biosphere along the factory farm's effluent plume. Indoor confinement, as a principle, suggests that the planet's natural environments are inadequate to house this kind of animal life. But now it appears that indoor confinement itself can no longer contain industrial hogs. James senses a barn site where internal stasis has transformed the ecologies that surround him, or one where nature is itself becoming a kind of New Nature.

TWO **THE HERD**

Intimate Biosecurity & Posthuman Labor

THE HUMAN VECTOR

In the late spring of 2013, porcine epidemic diarrhea virus (PEDV) arrived on the Great Plains as it swept through North American hog herds. Within a year, it had taken a toll of some seven million animals, or 10 percent of the pigs in the United States (Eisenstadt 2014). One of the disease's rumored ground zeroes was near the factory farms where I had, at that point, already conducted twenty-four months of ethnographic research. Moving across this multistate region on the Great Plains, the disease would hop over the Midwest's pockets of concentrated porcine life that stretch all the way from rural Missouri to Utah. I returned shortly after the outbreak as alarmed rumors were circulating around town that the Dover Foods slaughterhouse might shut down. In its first wave through Dover's animals, PEDV exhibited a piglet kill rate of nearly 100 percent. A friend who worked for the corporation grimly recounted how it had lost 190,000 piglets in one week. Across the United States, the number of diseased pig corpses became a source of environmental risk, the seepage from mass burial sites threatening groundwater (Strom 2014). Traveling via aerosolized manure over a still-uncertain number of miles, PEDV left few of Dover Foods' 1,200-plus confinement barns unaffected. In areas such as this one, contact with the virus was unavoidable. For example, a study describes how floors from fifty convenience stores in rural pork-intensive Iowa were swabbed for PEDV. They all returned positive for the disease (Thaler 2013). For those initial weeks of the outbreak, at least, PEDV changed the tenor of breeding farm labor from one of maximizing life to solemnly caretaking death. An acquaintance told me that her son, who worked in farrowing (piglet delivery), was returning home at night in tears. His days were a blur of pushing wheelbarrows of small corpses into dumpsters. As I visited breeding farms where I had previously worked, the acrid smoke of black incinerators saturated the summer air.

Yet the urgency that followed efforts to contain PEDV—initially framed by the pork industry as a foreign disease agent that appeared out of nowhere—elides quieter crises of reproduction that have long been endemic to the factory farm's routine operations. Prior to PEDV's appearance in the United States, far-reaching but mundane, almost unnoticeable biosecurity regimes were deemed necessary to maintain porcine proliferation. And these modes of corporate governance, developed through porcine vitalities, subtly redefine what it means to be human for those who work in a world saturated by concentrated animal life. In response, this chapter charts a political economy of speciation—a critical articulation of the making and ranking of species—to analyze how an ambiguously postanthropocentric politics of class and value is emerging in pockets of the rural United States organized around fragile capitalist life-forms. In so doing, my aim is to describe how we can grasp the factory farm as a project that, in spite of being built to take animal lives, comes to muddle the typical hierarchy of species and attempts to embed people in distinct and mutually isolated porcine worlds. The story begins near the end of my workplace-based research, when I first sensed the microbial textures that invisibly surrounded me, jolting my assumptions about the forms of routine labor and subjectivity that underlie the industrialization of the American pig.

I was standing with my coworker Cesar in the corner of a barn's concrete workshop as he took a cigarette break after working on the insemination line at a 2,500-sow breeding farm. This one barn alone births almost a thousand piglets per week for a pork corporation called Berkamp Meats, one of Dover Foods' regional competitors. Cesar balanced on the ridges of an open door frame while making sure his sanitized black rubber boots did not come into contact with the outside dirt surrounding the barn. His posture exhibited traces of the biosecurity-based discipline we learned in training, hinting at his tacit biological proximity to the animal (see Shukin 2009). As we discussed his life as a migrant to the United States, Cesar pointed his blue latex-covered hand at a white truck that veered over the gravel roads around the dozens of hog barns on the horizon. He guessed his father and brother were passengers. They formed part of an itinerant medical crew that visited dozens of barns every day, checking the status of automated feeders while injecting vaccines into growing animals after they left farrowing and nursery barns. Making idle chatter, I asked whether his whole family worked for Berkamp. He shrugged, "Me and my family, we have no choice because of biosecurity."[1]

Originally from Guatemala, Cesar migrated with his parents and siblings to the Great Plains around 2000, when he was in his early twenties, after hearing about gainful employment in slaughterhouses, on hog farms, and at feed mills. Sharing a trailer on the outskirts of town, the family plugged into the large K'iche'-speaking community and acquired work on Dover Foods' breeding farms. The family members worked on Dover Foods' sow farms for years, increasing their experience, until Berkamp Meats offered Cesar's father a supervisory position at the company. But there was a catch: when they heard this news, Dover's managers insisted that Cesar and his siblings either live separately from their father or all quit and find work with another company.

The managers were concerned that microscopic particles of hog saliva, blood, feces, semen, or barn bacteria from another company, or from another stage in Dover Foods' own meat production process, might be lodged in workers' ears, fingernails, and nostrils, despite worksite-mandated showering protocols.[2] The corporation's theory was that prolonged physical proximity among workers—across firms and across farms—could result in the transfer of disease over human bodies and then through untainted barns of swine. A few years earlier, they had allegedly started monitoring addresses on payroll forms to map overlaps between domestic living arrangements and the corporation's division of labor across its vertically integrated network of boar studs, sow farms, growing barns, feed mills, and slaughterhouses.

Intrigued, I inquired with employees in an ESL class and after church events in the town of Dixon. Many residents shared a similar story about how biosecurity disrupted their lives. A newlywed was disappointed that she had to abandon her job at a Dover breeding farm. She took pride in caring for newborn piglets, but she had to quit because her husband held a monotonous yet better-paid position cutting meat on the slaughterhouse disassembly line. Another maintained an old mailing address because he worked as an assistant manager in nursery barns for young pigs while his new roommates were in breeding. There was little overt outrage directed at these protocols. More often than not, people shrugged in befuddlement about why they existed. But these stories have stuck with me, for they imply changes in terms of how agribusinesses understand the nature and needs of the industrial pig. They suggest how the corporation is quietly beginning to see the porcine species as biophysically constituted via human kinship, sexuality, friendship, and social rhythms (Bear et al. 2015).

Even more striking was that senior managers were not immune to the social repercussions of their own biosecurity protocols. At an anniversary party for Dover Foods, a slaughterhouse manager felt frustrated because he barely recognized the faces of his colleagues from the "Live Side" of the company. He knew them primarily as names on a spreadsheet because, he claimed, principles of biosecurity suggest that the two sides should not socialize outside work except on these rare occasions.[3] Managers such as this one appeared to be living out protocols even stricter than those imposed on workers. The man was anticipating and modeling his sociality on an imagined future in which public space beyond the domestic household—such as bars, churches, or social clubs—is biosecure. The vertical integration of the hog—controlling all phases of the species' life and death while creating specialized sites and organization for each type and age of pig—was spawning forms of social reorganization as the corporation mapped out-of-work human relations onto the fissures of industrialized animal lifecycles, creating microbiopolitical ruts in regional circuits of sociality (Paxson 2008). Integration and waning states of porcine immunity were leading to efforts to create landscapes of porcine uniformity that extend beyond the barns and slaughterhouses where people work.

The result is a region where both managers and workers—albeit in profoundly unequal ways, each with distinct relationships to the industrial hog—are induced to consider their relation to a form of life that redefines humans, wind, and terrain as carriers of disease threatening the productivity of breeding stock.[4] Over the years I have read scholarly studies and pieces of journalism about factory farms that describe how manure-laden winds and nitrate-loaded wells degrade the quality of life in surrounding communities (see, e.g., Genoways 2014; Kirby 2010; Thu and Durrenberger 1998). The neighbors interviewed for these writings suggest that pork production remains porous, drawing our attention to the shared mediums—air and water—that continue to bind hogs and humans, despite the animals' confinement indoors. But biosecurity here requires another kind of attention to the invisible copresence of the pig in everyday life, a different kind of multispecies atmospheric attunement.[5] Since its founding as a global locus for hog production in the mid-1990s, this region is one where hogs have come to outnumber humans by more than fifty to one. In this context, Cesar's story hints at how a concentrated form of porcine life swells across the region, microscopically saturating human bodies while potentially buttressing novel forms of discipline and consciousness of one's relation to surrounding ecologies, kin, immune systems, and friendships. His story depicts a place where efforts to sustain the waning vitality of the industrial hog are provoking the industrialization of many other forms of social and biological life that exist in this animal's ever-expanding orbit.

Granted, industrial extension beyond the factory floor is not new.[6] Feminist social scientists have long shown the dynamic ways that domestic households and nonwage work are intertwined in the reproduction of capitalist industry. The household has always been essential to the (re)production of labor power and socialization, as well as to providing meaning for wage labor (see Federici 1975; Rubin 1975; Weeks 2011). Similarly, efforts to rationalize laborers' domestic sociality for the improvement of workplace morale date back to Fordism's founding moments. Henry Ford's Sociological Department infamously inspected employees' homes, hygiene, and spending habits in exchange for earning the (then-generous) $5 day (Meyer 1981). Yet biosecurity, in this instance, is not about biologically or socially reproducing human labor power. Nor does it form part of a humanist industrial morality, of creating the ideal worker who can stand on and withstand the assembly line. Instead, these interventions into human spheres are premised on reproducing the reproductive capacities of boars and sows (cf. Franklin and Ragoné 1998). They suggest an imminent orientation in which the value of routine action—from showering at home to sharing a bottle of wine in a park—could be indexed and appraised in terms of its potential effects on pigs' numerical proliferation.[7] People are coming to form kinship ties with the hogs they touch, as the state of hogs' immune systems is conjoined to the everyday lives of individuals going about their daily routine.

Much recent scholarship and political commentary probes possibilities for renewing life in damaged environments, for finding ways to value and engage beings beyond the human. On the one hand, we could continue to put into practice the fantasy of human exceptionalism by pretending that it is possible to maintain a pure separation between human and (all the other) "animal" worlds (Raffles 2010, 330). As Celia Lowe (2010) carefully articulates in a study of the viral (dis)entanglements of H5N1 (or "bird flu"), agricultural biosecurity figures as a central site for generating impossible anthropocentric ideals of rigorously ordered, perfectly planned, and purely human biosocial worlds. On the other, a broadly more-than-human scholarship has taken up the urgent political task of opposing such narratives of disembodied and autonomous human existence by articulating how species are relationally entangled at their core (Nading 2012; Porter 2013), living with and making each other up in interactive everyday flow (Haraway 2008; Kohn 2013) and shaping each other in codomesticated exchanges across deep history (Cassidy and Mullin 2007; Lien 2015; Tsing 2012b). But projects such as the factory farm—from outside, seemingly a straightforward site of human domination—suggest the need for another, ambiguous form of orientation: it is an anthropocentric project, in terms of satisfying human diets and livelihoods by taking the lives of other species (Wolfe 2012), that conjures fantasies of an ahuman landscape. Nor is it an idiosyncrasy of this site. Similar tendencies are perhaps visible in the body-breaking, pesticide-laden fruit farms of the U.S. West Coast (Holmes 2013), in Paraguay's deathly soy fields (Hetherington 2013), and at the factory farm itself as a key contributor of greenhouse gas emissions (Weis 2013). Industrial agriculture is manufacturing cheap food for human consumption by overtaking swathes of territory in ways that prioritize the value of its singular organisms over other forms of life.[8]

What Cesar's seemingly innocent family story suggests, then, is the ways that the working human, in all of its social and embodied aspects, is becoming suspect. This, too, is not necessarily new. The farm laborer's body has recently emerged as a site of risk in public health studies that fret about its ability to carry antibiotic-resistant bacteria off farms (Nadimpalli et al. 2014), or about how it could serve as a transmission point for zoonotic swine influenza viruses (Gray et al. 2007). But what is jarring about this postanthropocentric biosecurity protocol is its reversal of the typical or expected ranking of species. Human labor is framed in practice as a threat to industrial pork—albeit, at this moment, a necessary one, given that machines cannot raise hogs alone—and it is the industrial pig whose safety requires intervention. This constitutes the reverse of the standard anthropocentric fears of public policy, such that wild animals' suspect movements or leaky bodies will come to infect human populations through zoonotic illness (Davis 2007). The indoor confinement of farm animals is itself often justified in the face of the viral threat of unpredictable contact with beings such as wild geese, whose risky biologies make for key natural reservoirs of zoonotic disease (Fearnley 2015). Instead, this rural space, which is given over to making industrialized organisms, suggests how the laboring body and its unpredictable rhythms are engulfed by porcine illness in such a way that human sociality is now marked as one of the central virtual "reservoirs" sheltering porcine disease. This reversal marks a zone where the protection of porcine animality is broadly privileged over the cultural lives of the corporation's four thousand employees, despite individual pig bodies' being radically killable as a nondescript biomass in the slaughterhouse. Or, more precisely, such securities suggest an avowedly bio-capitalist landscape whereby individual porcine lives may be expendable as cheap meat, but intensifying the generative potentials of swine as a species—the vital processes of birth and growth (Helmreich 2008)—trumps classic humanist cultural ideals of autonomy, freedom, and privacy. This distinction between individual hogs and the porcine species, in turn, is the ground on which corporations are attempting to remake classes and racial distinctions among people, segregating them into novel kinds of relation with animals.

This chapter follows the foundational lead of scholars who have developed ethnographically specific ways to frame how vital governance extends across species and how people are made to "work on [themselves] in relation to" other, often anthropogenically weakened beings (Porter 2013, 144; Pandian 2008). What intrigues me about the factory farm's intimate biosecurities is how they mark an attempt to convert personal and private actions that seemingly have no bearing on others, such as looking for an apartment, into what we might label a posthuman form of labor in service of maintaining industrial porcine life. Such emerging subjectivities in the factory farm suggest a managerial-capitalist zone where the value of routine or previously unnoticed human activity is increasingly measured by how it is taken up by, and expressed in, other kinds of animals. By posthuman labor, in this case, I mean that pigs' life—their overarching vitality, capacities to proliferate, and immune systems—is turned into something workers perform. In turn, emerging dimensions of employees' everyday life become noticeable as work.

There are many ways that one might further develop the notion of a post-human labor, extending the discourse of posthumanism—which aims to de-center humanity as the bearer of autonomous value and exceptional unique-ness in the world (Wolfe 2008)—into a type of working practice. They might involve theorizing how nonhuman beings can also be said to "work" (White 1996; see also chapter 6 in this volume), a recognition of distributed worldly agencies such that humans never labor with just humans alone (Andrews 2008; see also chapter 5 in this volume), critiquing the exceptional value of human labor (Weeks 2011; see also chapter 4 in this volume), or paying attention to how artists and activists work to reveal interspecies entanglements (examples in Kirksey 2014; see also chapter 10 in this volume). But my aim is not to develop a philosophical posthumanism that critiques liberal capital-ism from outside. Instead, I trace how this sensibility—however disfigured or coopted—manifests in capitalist practices.[9] We might say that this site does not so much call for an effort to positively decenter the human as it requires us to grasp the work—especially that of managers—that enables hogs' vitality to centrally mediate a region. Not only might this enable us to see interspecies power relations anew, but it also has consequences for how we imagine industrial agriculture's founding myth as an efficient organizational form that uses less land and labor to "feed the world."

How, then, did the industrial pig come to embody a regionally exceptional status? How did this animal species become the central optic through which regional human action is appraised? How did the pig become such a fragile organism, in terms both of its physical frailty and of agribusiness's perception of its weakness, while simultaneously so privileged and worthy of protection? What, in short, is the shifting industrial pig (as opposed to the timeless natural, or individual organism, pig) as a form of life? Rather than reducing posthuman labor to an automatic outgrowth of biocapital's or the commodity form's inherent logic, the remainder of this chapter follows managers' social work that subjectively constructs the pig as a world-defining creature that quietly overdetermines the lives of regional residents (on overdetermination, see Sunder Rajan 2012). By a political economy of speciation, then, I am referring not to the classic taxonomical definition of species in terms of reproductive capacity and difference, much less searching for a stable essence of pig and human in a context in which these beings mutually (re)constitute each other.[10] Instead, for the remainder of this chapter I trace senior managers' ongoing efforts to know and inhabit the porcine species as a species. That is, I examine how they try to inhabit the porcine species as a totality—across types and ages, starting at genetic boars and moving all the way to 285-pound meat hogs—while, in turn, they rank and remake classes of people through the fissures of this pig.

THE EXPANDING BOUNDARIES OF THE HERD

Managers have learned to intervene in the Great Plains' saturated microbial ecology by analyzing how it becomes statistically indexed to the bodies of breeding stock, using an organizational technology they call "the Herd."[11] The Herd is invisible outside of spreadsheets, computer tabulations, scroll charts, and other abstract representations. Yet it productively mediates managers' experience not only of the industrial pig, but also of surrounding socioecologies, from trucking routes to wind patterns. In practice, the Herd operates as a kind of species-making device. It is a means for managers to abstract from the material, embodied expressions of individual porcine lives or types such as boars, sows, or piglets. Treating their pigs as a Herd, as I show, is how managers try to make themselves into proper managers of vertically integrated life. Senior managers are the only people in the company who plan across most manifestations of the (living) pig; the Herd is an organizational device that helps them take on the position of "manager" by working on—and claiming authority over—a larger proportion of the species than workers.

The Herd is a complicated icon for the factory farm as a whole. It is at once a rationalization for the rise of factory hog farms, a class-based mode of grasping the porcine species as a singular whole, and, in turn, a social technology that helps form regional classes of people through their relation to hogs. At its simplest, the Herd turns Dover Foods' 180,000 breeding animals, which annually produce five million 285-pound market hogs, into a statistically derived unit of life that is used to appraise the status of the total factory farming process at a given point in time. Such a status, expressed as the "herd health," is signaled through measures of the breeding animals' average productivity in terms of pig output. Depending on the position from which it is articulated—say, voiced from a growing farm versus a slaughterhouse—Herd Health might relate to either the average number of pigs or the pounds of meat produced per sow per year. Once they have formed this virtual mean-sow, the seniormost managers spend their days inspecting material and microbial factors in farms that are producing starkly less (or more) than the rest of the Herd. But the Herd, as I argue, is also a powerful means of forming species to achieve disciplinary control—and perhaps foreclosing more complicated ethics—not only over disease-ridden ecologies created by the factory farm but also over the moral character of farm laborers.

"The old farming mentality was to manage individual pigs," one senior manager named Barry memorably stated over drinks. "But our mentality is that we manage the Herd. . . . The old farmer used to like some boar or sow and he'd say, 'That's a good animal, I'm gonna keep it.'" Dover Foods does not favor any animals, he went on to explain, instead grasping high-performance sows as part of "natural variation." They cull and replace their genetic stock of breeding animals at regular intervals of age or litter numbers, regardless of a given animal's history. Rather than managing single pigs, then, they articulate themselves as managing abstracted genetics and probability across the whole of the breeding stock.[12] The Herd is a matter of managing the species as a single mean-sow that is conceptually standardized, even if individual sows vary in productivity. In this sense, we might read the Herd as an industrial abstraction, because it enacts a conceptual negation of productive differences across sows by making them disposable and interchangeable in farm practice (Braverman 1974, or, in distinct guise, Foucault 2003).

But while "the Herd" is a quantitative figure for making sense of epochal shifts in pork production, it also operated in managerial circles as a discursive term for establishing managers' own identity and, in turn, tethered regional class difference to how people relate to animals. Senior managers repeated an identical stock phrase whenever I asked them to define their role. "We work on the Herd," they would claim, "while hourly employees and farm managers work with the Herd." Such a proposition of identity does capture a felt reality, especially for senior managers whose daily experience with pigs is in statistical, sampling, tour-based inspection, or paper-based forms. But what interests me is the blurring of difference in the oppositional identity—a seaming of human labor and hog life—once senior managers narrate from the position of working on the Herd as a whole. "Working on" the Herd is best translated as improving the quantitative output of all of the breeding animals, irrespective of given animals' qualities. This can make everything from the animals' feed regimen to workers' actions into a legible input toward improving the total Herd. We can glimpse in this stock phrase how the boundaries of the Herd are open; the Herd is a mode of reading a territory through the lens of the porcine species in such a way that it incorporates everything from microbes and terrain to the behavior of human bodies. And without access to the category and attendant practices of working on the Herd as an abstract species whole across workplaces, workers can only relate to (or "work with") animal beings through experiences with concrete manifestations, stages, and specific types of hog life, such as boars, sows, piglets, grown pigs, or carcasses. In other words, local processes of making social class (and, as I will show, race) become mediated through the type and scale of animality people can sense and inhabit.[13]

Efforts to monitor the region's socioecological landscape through the Herd also differ from what biosecurity has tended to signify in anthropological theories and human-centered situations that problematize it as a virtual or future-oriented trope of governmentality, technoscience, and health planning (see Caduff 2014; Lakoff and Collier 2008). Biosecurity here forms a more banal, present-tense, enacted regime of corporate governance alongside a subtly inculcated ethic for living amid industrial animals. While its implied consequences may be significant, it is rarely remarked on in everyday life. Indeed, if a resident was not employed by these corporations, he or she might not know the protocols even exist. The Herd is a quiet matter of sustaining porcine life amid regional microbial degradation rather than a robust preemptive transformation of the social contract in anticipation of a catastrophic state of crisis such as a bioterror attack (see Cooper 2008; Lakoff 2008). And since the hog diseases that these biosecurity protocols address do not affect human health—and, unlike in Sarah Franklin's (2007, 174) analysis of the similarly innocuous foot-and-mouth disease, they do not affect international trade and the global circulation of meat (see also Smart and Smart 2011)—the state and its public health apparatuses' interventions into these illnesses are limited. For instance, there is no direct state pressure to cull animals with these illnesses. Indeed, while public health practitioners, under the auspices of a One Health approach, often struggle in the face of anthropocentrism to "incorporate the well-being of non-human animals in the purview of [public] health policy" (Lezaun and Porter 2015, 101; Porter 2013), the value of human livelihood in the factory farm is subordinated in some significant dimensions to the porcine species, and it is the unruly social lives of laboring humans that must be monitored to protect porcine proliferation.

Absent the all-or-nothing public imperative of protecting human life from zoonotic infection, these private biosecurity protocols are often framed by managers as mere economic inputs subject to ethically innocuous cost-benefit analyses as to whether they achieve returns in terms of breeding animal productivity.[14] But not everyone saw such protocols as justifiable or neutral ways to comprehend the "improvement" of animal life. Some managers at competing companies, such as Berkamp Meats, refused to enact the domestic protocols. As one explained:

> I favor a commonsense approach. I don't think we should be worried about what people are doing when they aren't at work. It's, it's . . . intrusive. I mean, we know that PRRS [a particularly rampant hog virus] can travel in wind for three miles, and we've got a lot of pigs here. What's next? Trucks spraying the air all over town? Will we put foot baths [iodine buckets] at every gas station entrance and make people disinfect their boots? Where does this end?

The manager is describing future techniques for disciplining the region's ecology, which requires expanding securitization of the Great Plains once managers open the Pandora's box of moving biosecurity beyond the barns. He makes a simple moral claim premised on a classic agricultural biosecurity that aims to exclude disease from barns (Allen and Levau 2015, 347). As private businesses, he states, pork companies should manage pig disease on the confines of their own farm property. He projects an imminent future of biosecurity interventions run amok, where working country and residential town collapse together via the circulation of pig disease. At the same time, though, this manager's refusal to enact the protocols at his company highlights that this is not a finished project, a totalized form, or an inevitable future. Great Plains biosecurity remains actual and virtual (Collier et al. 2004, 5). On the one hand, unlike large-scale, purely anticipatory biosecurities, it forms part of an everyday infrastructure—a routine regime, however incomplete. On the other, I noted that some workers refuse these biosecurity protocols, and some managers enact interventions more extensively in their own lives than they do in those of their employees. From church gatherings to birthday parties, from sharing a fork to sitting on a sofa with a coworker, there are as many potential bio-insecure spaces in this region as there are social relations. Yet as the manager here suggests, such is the power of the Herd's expanding boundaries signaled by things such as the domestic housing biosecurity protocol, for once they are enacted, they illuminate the multitude of bio-insecure practices that may affect the pig.[15]

GREENFIELD

The situation was not always like this. Elements of the Great Plains' natural ecology initially attracted companies to the region. They hoped its relative dearth of precipitation could mitigate the ecological concerns with respect to fecal and urine management that emerged in the 1990s out of North Carolina, the first region in the United States to experience the growth of new industrial hog farms. North Carolina was (and still is) inundated with hurricanes that caused dramatic overflowing of concentrated manure lagoons. Witnessing the public outcry that ensued, corporations—from North America, Western Europe, and East Asia—shifted their focus for new pork development to parts of the U.S. Great Plains and Midwest. They were drawn by the region's moderate temperatures; high evaporation rates, which decreased how often they would need to apply manure from the lagoons to surrounding fields; gusts of sharp winds that can help blow lingering smells from neighboring property; and availability of grain-based feed.

But a little-known fact about the rise of these so-called "(U.S.) American" factory farms is that they are part of a transnational account largely inspired by the success of an obscure pork operation in South America. Lacking experience in raising (and killing) pigs, multiple corporations—including Dover Foods, Trenton Produce, and others—sent their executives to visit sites in Denmark, Malaysia, and Chile around 1990 to consolidate emergent industrial global porcine knowledge. In Chile, a group of Dover managers discovered a corporation ironically named Super-Pollo (now Agrosuper) that they deemed the most organizationally advanced, which was allegedly posting production numbers that were unheard of anywhere else in the world.[16] This included figures such as more than twenty-five pigs weaned per sow per year, with stunningly low mortality rates that are largely unmatched to this day. A large percentage of Agrosuper's born pigs were making it to market slaughter without current forms of genetic-selection technology. As one Dover Foods geneticist put it, Agrosuper was "three years behind the new boar lines." The manager suggested that in spite of its lack of cutting-edge genetics, the Chilean company had a certain control over animal vitality that made the pigs like vegetal "cookie-cutters, peas in a pod." One of the factors behind Agrosuper's vital control was its ability to recruit cheap labor in Chile. This enabled more constant monitoring of sows' birthing activities, which ensured that weak piglets would receive immediate attention (see also chapter 6). But the dominant reason for Agrosuper's numerical success, at least as this manager put it, was that it operated out of a region of Chile that, at that time, contained few, if any, other pigs. The key hog diseases plaguing United States pork producers in the corn belt were largely absent from Chile's ecology.

The crucial attraction for corporations to the Great Plains and Midwest—at least outside the traditional nucleus that extends from Iowa to Minnesota—was its scarcity of pigs. In 1993, one of the counties that forms part of this book annually produced only a few thousand hogs. By 2010, it was raising millions of animals annually. The lack of hogs on the landscape was crucial for two reasons. The first was the nearly total absence of swine disease in the microbial ecology, an advantage that has clearly diminished over the past decades. But the second was the concurrent lack of independent hog farmers contracting to raise pigs, the standard form of risk sharing and integration in the corporate pork industry (Rich 2008). This enabled these corporations to attempt full vertical integration by purchasing the land and buildings themselves. As Dover Foods' chief executive recounted in an interview, the company was "a start-up, a greenfield," where "we could design a core system from scratch." "Greenfield" is business-speak for underdeveloped territory, marking a (neo-colonial) vision of this region as pure in its absence of pig disease, hog farmers, and preexisting claims on the land.

My own path to this area was carved out in the summer of 2007 during a visit to the office of Mark Getz, a professor of indoor confinement systems. There he described how companies in Dixon had achieved one of the world's most integrated forms of meat production. But what focused my attention on this region was this man's quiet tone as he described how he had become awed by the scale of Dover Foods. He did not mobilize the array of numbers usually taken to connote scale in this industry: the number of pigs slaughtered each day or the pounds of meat per sow harvested each year. Instead, he told me to go to see the operations through their roadside appearance. He said to pull into a gas station in Dixon, and count the trucks carrying animals that pass along the highway. Then, I would see "why locals call it the red meat capital of the world."

Perhaps I had a naïve idea of what a place that coordinates the lives and deaths of seven million animals would look like. But Dixon did not look like much of anything. It was similar to any other small midwestern town, albeit with a huge unmarked concrete box on the way out of town that did not announce that its purpose was hog killing. Faithfully following Getz's instructions, I pulled into one of Dixon's gas stations that line the highway running through town. My first stab at ethnographic research was reduced to an hours-long session of counting the semis that held cohorts of pigs, hoping they might yield insight as they rhythmically passed toward the slaughterhouse. They did not. With hindsight, however, I now realize that the substances of the pig—processed beyond recognition—surrounded me and made possible this first attempt at taking notes. Pig fat was blended into the gas station's diesel tanks, and bone protein was potentially mixed into the concrete below. Hog gelatin was likely glossing the pages of my notebook. The manufacturing process for the copper in my cell phone's processor may have involved porcine tissues (Meindertsma 2009). Most crucially, hog excrement was swirling in ultrafine invisible particles, blowing out of the trucks and threatening to infect other animals.

I did not realize it then, but Professor Getz was right: watching those trucks' tight intervals as they careered down the highway, I was staring directly at the vertical integration of life and death. Human bodies, truck motors, and porcine vision must be coordinated so that the loading, unloading, and sorting of pigs operates so seamlessly that its variation can be measured in minutes. I would later learn that Dover Foods shaved twenty minutes off its average truck loading time by training its drivers never to look at the pigs and to hold their bodies at an angle so as not to cast shadows—merging mechanical infrastructure with porcine perception. Hogs are prone to freeze and stop walking forward if they believe they are being watched or if they see bright colors or novel shapes (Grandin 2006). Trucks' rhythms coordinate the life-and-death cycle, and they themselves are records of the industrialization of porcine perception and sentience. We might say that there is nowhere to stand to gaze upon this book's subject matter. By this I do not (just) mean that it is a hidden abode, a secretive place that allows admittance only to those who work there (see Pachirat 2011; Vialles 1994). Instead, the forms of vertical integration that define the factory farm make it an interstitial space; this is a logistical project, following Deborah Cowen (2014), defined as much by the connections between nodes as by any fixed locale of work, such as an indoor confinement farm or a fast-paced slaughterhouse. Thus, while there may be no single place to stare directly at the vast, one hundred-mile-radius logistical complex that this book calls "the factory farm," it is also true that anything within its territory—including even that gas station parking lot—can be imagined as a site where hogs are raised.[17] As I came to learn from managers, industrial animality is itself being shaped and manifesting differently over truck routes that expose hogs to distinct environmental forms.

THE AGING OF THE HERD

On a midsummer Monday, I was waiting under the black 3:30 AM sky for my management guides to arrive in their company-branded van. For the past few months I had been periodically shadowing managers from various stages of porcine life across their routine working days and joining them in evening classes on Japanese manufacturing theory designed to rethink the "biological system" (in their own words [see chapter 8]) of pork production. On this day, we would be driving out to a boar stud facility where collections begin at 5 a.m. to ensure a steady supply of semen for morning inseminations on sow breeding farms. Since many of the most devastating pig diseases are communicable through the semen that underpins and conjoins (sow) breeding farms, boar studs are the most pivotal sites of biosecurity.

The industrial pig's chain of life and death actually begins many thousands of miles away, in another company's isolated genetic compound that crosses multiple historical breeds of hog to form its raw material. Vacuum-packed bags of these hybrid boars' semen are then shipped to a facility closer to Dixon—some four hundred miles away—where it will be crossed even further with a series of heritage breed sows imported by Dover Foods from around the world. Combining traits from each of these breeds, such as the leanness of German Piétrains, the corporation effectively alienates biological qualities from the history of human-hog relationships that cohered these types of bodies in place over century-long periods of interspecies engagement. The result is to replenish the company's collective stock of thousands of "genetic" boars and sows. These are the animals that will give birth to smaller litters of hardy, robust "commercial" sows. In turn, these commercial sows will be artificially inseminated—through a combination of "genetic" boar semen, human actions, and the potent pheromones of special Chinese Meishan-breed boars (chapter 4)—to generate massive litters of commercial hogs. These hogs, at last, are the ones that are slaughtered industrially for meat. The pork chop that emerges from the slaughterhouse is thus the product of the genetics, physiological behavior, and specialized "labor" of more than a dozen distinct hidden breeds and types of pig. The making of a standardized meat hog is based on an internal fragmentation of the species, along with the cultivation of specialist types of working hogs. There are multiple kinds of pig animating the creature that we most often think about as being the iconic, edible industrial pig.

Yet boar studs remain managed as if they are the places where life on factory farms begins. There are only a small handful of them, even in a large company such as Dover Foods, which births millions of hogs per year. Using fewer boars ensures greater uniformity across all of the animals. No more than eight people work in these sites at any given time, partly to decrease the number of human bodies that are carriers of outside microbes. There are two sections to an industrial boar stud, accessed through separate shower rooms. Employees in these sections never work in physical contact, separated as they are by glass walls and pneumatic tubes. On the "collection" side, workers gradually corral a rotating total of a few hundred boars toward a metal device with green pads that a boar can mount. This is called a dummy sow, and most boars will "mate" with it after some training. As the hog thrusts against the dummy sow, a worker squeezes and stimulates the boar's penis until the animal ejaculates into a one-liter plastic coffee mug-like container topped with cheesecloth for straining solids. The process takes about ten minutes per boar. This container is then sealed and put through a pneumatic tube into the laboratory. On the lab side, technicians sample the sperm for potency and motility on a computer and drop satisfactory batches into a large machine (see figure 1.2). This machine mixes the batches of semen with extender and automatically fills sixty milliliters into vacuum-packed plastic bags for delivery to farms. The extender solution enables more "doses" (as they are called) per boar ejaculation while preserving motility and other key characteristics of the sperm. Different grades of extender are used based on how far the semen is slated to travel. By the early morning, trucks will deliver these fresh bags of semen to sow farms across the countryside. On each of their inspection and touring days, senior managers essentially follow the movement of these genetics down the chain of life.

My twelve companions on these kinds of tours might be best glossed as pod managers. They were geneticists, nutritionists, veterinarians, and corporate executives who filled their working days on farm tours analyzing the most problematic strands of the Herd within Dover Foods' system, usually those undergoing some kind of disease event. Inspecting the interiors of barns certainly enabled forms of diagnostics—perhaps the farmworkers were being slack in cleaning farrowing rooms—but much of the pod managers' time was instead spent driving in a cramped van while diagnosing the external or environmental causes of symptoms witnessed on a given set of pigs. Their banter revealed a hard-earned familiarity with the ecology of the Great Plains as they described how terrain gradations around a site might explain disease rates or how an area's wind patterns could seam microbial networks across barns. They had learned, for example, that data on the spread of disease in wooded areas such as North Carolina did not apply to the relatively barren midwestern terrain. Where I saw flat grain fields, they saw traces of porcine life totally, yet differentially, spread over an uneven landscape.

Highly respected in the pork industry, this group of managers came together after working separately in corporations across the United States, Chile, the Philippines, England, and Canada. Graham, the head of live production operations, grew up in North Carolina during the first wave of industrialization in the late 1980s. A working-class kid unable to afford college, and not academically inclined—though gifted with what one of his subordinates called "a scary photographic memory"—he started out as an entry-level power washer in hog barns and jumped across corporations as he moved up the ranks. Barry, a senior regional manager, went to agricultural college in the 1980s, planning to take over his parents' beef cattle ranch. He soon found his family bankrupt in the midst of a farm crisis. After being recruited by a pork corporation, he became a global expert in emergent methods of artificial insemination. George was a British expatriate who was originally recruited by the company from the much less industrialized pig farms of England when Dover Foods was running trials with hogs raised outdoors. When those experiments were abandoned a few years later, George stayed on with the company to manage boar studs because his family had grown fond of the region and he liked the challenge of working with this scale of life. "There's nowhere else in the world that you can do these kinds of numbers [of hogs]," he told me. Gregory was the company's lead veterinarian. Although he initially was skeptical, he found himself enjoying the relative stability of corporate agribusiness after years of treating pigs in his private practice during perennial economic farm crises. He recounted walking into a private barn where emaciated, dying pigs had not been fed for days because their owner was too broke to buy feed.

These men entered the corporate pork industry under conditions not purely of their own choosing, but they also strove to create the most profitable and ethical pork corporation possible in an industry with very low margins of return. Although they had become tight-knit over the years, they were not unified in their beliefs. The pod managers—especially those trained in the veterinary mission—would often bicker over who was more "health-centered" versus "production-centered." During the 1990s, they mainly worked apart in different corporations during what they called "growth mode," when corporations rapidly expanded contracts and barn sites before states placed moratoria on new hog farms and competition started to bite into profit margins. The current goal, in so-called polishing mode, was to maximize porcine value in the vertically integrated system, searching, "now that there's no more low-hanging fruit," as they often put it, to find hidden new avenues for profitability within the porcine species.

Yet the grim sights on these farm tours hinted at the ways that vertical integration's promises of total control over porcine life remained unfulfilled, giving the impression that life constitutes an excessive entity that cannot ever be fully standardized (cf. Allen and Lavau 2015; Hinchcliffe and Ward 2014).[18] Growth mode ended at the same time that, as another manager put it, "the health system started to erode." One example of the many endemic illnesses afflicting the modern hog is porcine reproductive and respiratory syndrome (PRRS). It first emerged globally during the intensification of pork production in the late 1980s (Cho and Dee 2006); it disproportionately affects fragile lean pigs (Rich 2008); and it tends to get lodged in confinement barns (Harris 2004). The American industry frames PRRS as its most economically significant illness (prior to PEDV), costing U.S. farmers some $560–760 million per year (Johnson et al. 2006). Although PRRS weakens pigs' immunity, it seldom kills them directly. It causes miscarriages in gestating sows and decreases weight gains in market swine. It is an economic disease—we might call it a species or "animality" disease—because it throttles the Herd's proliferation.

Finally, a couple of pod managers lamented that the severity of outbreaks can increase as the concentration of animals deteriorates the ecology, resulting in what they called an "aging of the Herd" that worsens with time as strains of viruses mutate and compound with other illnesses. In these conditions, the demand to make the Herd's sows into corporate life-forms—expected to increase in numerical productivity each year, increasing in biocapitalist growth in spite of microbial aging—proves vexing even to the managers who ostensibly control the system. As one veterinarian declared in annoyed opposition to my insistence of his agency, "No. The Herd is everything. We are slaves to the Herd."

Such, at least, is the abstract Herd's-eye view of disease rendered into a shifting statistical portrait of its effect on animal reproduction. The daily tours of barns reminded everyone of a more visceral sense of pig disease as we walked past rows of animal cages, fixated on symptoms that might indicate PRRS or some other illness. One day the veterinarians would point at coughing animals or hogs' rumps streaked brown with "scours," or diarrhea. On another, piglets were emaciated with a condition called "suck-in," their stomachs taut against their ribs, or "thumping," a respiratory condition that makes pigs wheeze loudly. Low-level farm managers, working extra hours to handle an outbreak, would nervously recount how many "aborts" (miscarriages) they found on the floor during morning inspections. During one hundred-mile drives across barn sites, the pod managers often discussed animal scientists' research into the spread of hog illness, revealing how porcine materials saturate everything. For instance, Scott Dee and his colleagues (2002) have conducted experiments that demonstrate how viruses such as PRRS can blanket a region, creating an "area spread." It can infect pigs via wind transmission, mosquitoes, semen, blood, saliva, feces sprayed as fertilizer, rodents, workers' clothing, trucks that ship pigs, and delivery containers. As one Dover manager informed me, "We don't know how productive the genetics of our sows might be. We can't see the pure healthy animal."

Invoking academic research into disease, however, often led to disagreements over managers' own values of efficiency, animal welfare ethics, culpability, and limits to containing the Herd's degradation. In the mid-2000s, Dover tried to eradicate PRRS. Beyond the economics, most managers agreed that eliminating PRRS was an ethical prerogative given how it causes pig illness. They invested millions of dollars in cleaning barns, relocating farm sites, installing so-called bio-curtains of foliage on barns' air ducts, and initiating new biosecurity protocols. For three months there were no reports of symptoms of PRRS; it then broke in the genetic multiplier barns—the nucleus of vertical integration, where the commercial sows are conceived that bear meat animals for commercial slaughter. The vector of transmission was tracked to a hobbyist's show pig a few miles upwind. Once the genetic heart of the operation was infected, the disease spread through the downstream barns with crippling force because the new lines of hogs had no inbuilt immunity. Since that time, the pod managers, like those at most corporations, have pursued an endemic "PRRS-positive" production strategy. They manage and quarantine the virus as it appears in a barn, stabilizing its quantitative effects in terms of seasonal pig output and building immunity in the Herd as a whole.[19] Some suggested the veterinarians also became relatively more production-centered, perhaps qualifying the health-centered perspective learned in school. The totalizing quality of disease led to the adoption of a Herd-based cost-benefit approach to health, framing decreases in genetic productivity as the symptom.

MAKING BIOSECURE SUBJECTS

Amid this sense of invisible but densely encompassing porcine material, boar studs offer onlookers a much more disciplined aesthetic of life and labor. The boar stud is an icon of biosecurity; it is a destination for company investors and, especially, wholesalers hoping to witness a variation-free architectural image of precise control. The building is nested within a thirty-foot perimeter of gravel that tamps out plant life. It is isolated from human activity by twenty miles and the dividing line between two states, and there are no lights on the horizon save for the stars. Enclosing this dead zone is a twelve-foot-high, password-locked fence topped with barbed wire. Even the specially selected species of grass that extends beyond the perimeter is maintained to ensure that there are no weeds that might attract rodents.

Nonetheless, these aesthetics of security could be described as a spectacle—a performance—because the interiors of barns always teem with non-porcine life. Mice dart out to nibble at pigs' feed, and birds line the perimeters of the manure lagoons. Clouds of mosquitoes hover over the animals during warm months, leading to a measurable summertime decrease in slaughterhouse carcass yields from cutting out the bites on skin. I once saw a fire extinguisher encased in what appeared to be a centimeters-thick weave of grey cobwebs. I checked its date, thinking that it had not been changed for a decade. It had been inspected a few months earlier. This spectacular aspect, however, does not mean that on-farm biosecurity is futile. Its performativity is the overarching point.

As a United Nations Food and Agriculture Organization (2010, 3) publication for hog farms states, agricultural biosecurity is not only "the implementation of measures that reduce the risk of the introduction and spread of disease agents"; it also "requires the adoption of a set of attitudes and behaviors by people to reduce risk in all activities involving . . . animals and their products." These kinds of aesthetics are what we might call doubling biosecurities. They excise "disease agents" while demanding workers' psychosocial recognition of their corporeal and immunological intimacy with porcine life. This doubling mode of biosecurity becomes logical in sites where PRRS and other diseases are rampant, when the scale of production is so large—and human interaction outside of work is so unruly—that it leads managers to see working humans' socialities as reservoirs for animal illness.

Doubling biosecurities abound, from the tedium of power washing farrowing rooms and seeing the three-dimensionality of hog waste to the human food allowed in barns. The standard process of showering in and out at barn sites constitutes the prime example, a ritual that I would repeat as many as six times per tour. Workers undress on "the dirty side" and put their clothes into a bank of lockers. The first step is to take a regular shower, washing the body and hair using liquid company soap from a dispenser on the wall. The second is to scrub parts of the body that one might ignore during a shower at home, such as the fingernails, the ears' curves, and nostrils. Cotton swabs are available for drying these body parts on "the clean side" before donning the company's socks, brief-style underwear, T-shirts, blue coveralls, and rubber boots. This five-minute ritual made me question my actions during prior hours, recalling the animals and people I had met. I initially felt paranoid about whether missed flecks would be responsible for pig illness, once confessing that I had been with workers the previous evening.

Such accounting of one's corporeality is more pedagogical than enactive of actual biophysical security. It aims to turn workers into biosecure subjects who monitor their behavior despite managers' inability to watch their actions at all moments, such as when they are in the shower. By making workers fear their potential to harm animals, learned from past experiences of a disease outbreak in a barn, the shower enlists moral subjects to "work with" the Herd. Or, these biosecurities enable managers to maintain their identity as statistically production-centered by improving the output of the pigs that they confront abstractly—working on the Herd—while turning workers into health-centered subjects deemed culpable for the suffering of the pigs that they work with in a tactile manner.[20] Biosecurity protocols make subjective and tangible new kinds of workplace classes of people, tethered to concrete manifestations of the vertically integrated pig—boars, sows, growing hogs, or carcasses—and fixed in single barn sites, while letting pod managers dwell outside any single type of animal and work on the species as a whole.

Managers have developed a series of sensory technologies that enable them to experience a species—or animality—in its abstract entirety and that begin to make evident the need for the off-farm biosecurity protocols that initiated this chapter. On farm tours, as we departed the boar stud and moved across sites in the van, we were performing a (managerial) form of biosecurity, which I once heard someone call "walking the pods." Pod managers are the only people in the factory farm who can travel across distinct types of hog farms. A production manager, in distinction, might manage six sow farms but would not set foot in any growing barns. Senior managers work on the Herd because they are not locked into working with only one strand or type of pig; they practice a management of the pig in all of its possible expressions or manifestations, of *a species in potentia*. A pod consists of a lineage of all animals from boars to genetic sows (which make sows), commercial sows (which make meat animals), piglets, and hogs for the market.[21] The pod (also known as a genetic flow) is a genetic grouping or family of pigs that moves through predetermined sets of barns as the flow grows in weight and age.

Managers begin their tours at a boar stud because these sites sit at the apex of the so-called biosecurity pyramid through which pod managers organize their means of safely monitoring and physically entering a strand of the Herd without the risk of introducing new disease. Managers cannot have contact with pigs in any form lower on the pyramid—commercial sows, piglets, grown hogs, carcasses—for one to three days before entering a boar stud or genetic sow farm or before otherwise moving up. They can, however, move down the pyramid in a single day if they stay within the same pod (of which there are five across the company). The system is designed so that a given pod will (ideally) never make contact with other lineages of pigs, especially not in forms mediated by human bodies. The geographical set of barns through which a given pod moves (or "flows") can also be changed over time, such as when a barn or region of the Great Plains landscape seems saturated with disease.

These are technologies for translating statistical impressions of the Herd into embodied perception as managers "walk [down] the pods" by inspecting conditions across sections of a genetic flow in a day. When managers walk

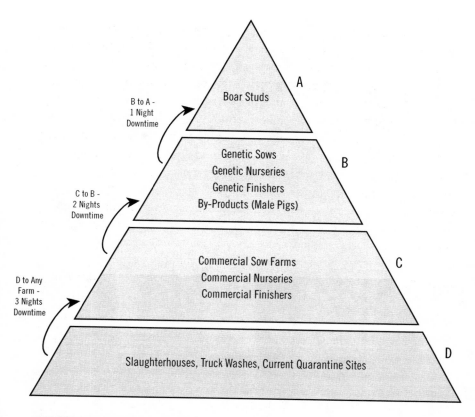

B to A -
1 Night
Downtime

A

Boar Studs

B

Genetic Sows
Genetic Nurseries
Genetic Finishers
By-Products (Male Pigs)

C to B -
2 Nights
Downtime

C

Commercial Sow Farms
Commercial Nurseries
Commercial Finishers

D to Any
Farm -
3 Nights
Downtime

D

Slaughterhouses, Truck Washes, Current Quarantine Sites

2.1 **BIOSECURITY PYRAMID** This example shows a planning document used to manage movements through the Herd. On any given week, it is updated to indicate the farms currently under quarantine. (Illustration by the author.)

the pods, they imagine themselves as moving down the spatiotemporal flow of life to physically witness all of the historical conditions that a lineage of pigs has experienced. The model itself requires standardized control of minute conditions over time. It presumes that young pigs downstream in a flow in growing barn #239 once experienced identical microbial and environmental conditions in upstream parts of the flow with their maternal sows in breeding barn #10. The essence of the pod is that it enables managers to isolate variables outside the Herd's genetics, focusing on all of the animate and inanimate beings that make up fleshly hogs in the everyday. The model maintains a sense of static temporality such that pigs in pod #4, growing at day 108 of their lives, are presumed identical to those of the same pod #4 at day 32. Since trucks move these pigs across similar spatial ecologies, geographies, and sets of barns, managers hypothesize that if a barn of pigs starts to exhibit poor performance numbers in terms of converting feed into flesh at day 92, then the piglets at day 14 will develop identical problems unless managers diagnose problems in the environment where these pigs will move on day 92.

The pod constitutes an organizational device to interpret the microbial ecology of the Great Plains because it potentially frames all external forms confronting pigs—barns, workers, wind patterns, terrain gradations, and even towns on trucking routes—as inputs affecting the lineage of pigs trickling down from the genetic sows. Everything in the region comes to matter and be defined in relation to pigs, instituting a practiced form of *porcine* exceptionalism. As a flow moves through space, managers can see it as filtering all the material things it confronts. Moreover, the need for the strict disciplining of all forms of life that orbit around the barns is embedded in this mode of multispecies organization. Conditions across the biosecurity pyramid and the flow must remain identical for managers to travel down pods and assume that pigs on day 14 will experience identical conditions on day 92, or that pod managers' bodies are not carrying new diseases from upstream farms into downstream barns. Standardized control over time—over life, material ecologies, and labor—is the condition on which the model stands.

These tethered sensory technologies—the Herd, the pod, and the biosecurity pyramid—enable workplace practices that materialize industrial animality as a form of life *in potentia*. Recall, as one manager put it earlier in this chapter—in distinction to old-time farmers who worked with individual animals—"Our mentality is that we manage the Herd." This abstract industrial animality temporarily manifests as forms of appearance in boars, sows, piglets, and grown meat pigs in a continuous flow of becoming that is potentially absorbing, like a sponge, the materialities of a region. One result of such embodied ecological perception of animal life is that it becomes clear that pigs are no longer raised in barns alone but across the region as a whole—including, perhaps, in gas stations' parking lots, churches, and even Cesar's family's living room. This is a particular kind of capitalist animal species. It undergirds regional policies, but it is perceptible only to those managers who (unlike workers) are not locked into working with a single type of hog. Its effect is to license managers to speak for the industrial species as a whole and to interpret a region through it. It illustrates the powerful and unequal forms of knowledge that underlie any act of trying to materialize, sense, and value a species in its entirety (see Chakrabarty 2009), for at the end of the day, the workers who do not have access to this model of pigness and animality are presented with only two choices: abide by the biosecurity dictates or potentially hold themselves accountable for harming the pigs in their care. This model of biosecurity is presented as a natural need of pigs in general, rather than as the very specific kinds of pigs that industrial concentration creates (see Lowe 2010).

PORCINE EXCEPTIONALISM

The standard notion of biosecurity is, at root, founded on a fantasy of separation—of "enclos[ing] humans and animals in specific, sterile, and segregated spaces" (Lezaun and Porter 2015, 100). I have suggested how the factory farm pushes beyond logics of hog confinement to the point at which managers feel they have to learn how to sense industrial animality as copresent with and defining every facet of a region, including workers' bodies. Unlike anthropocentric public health efforts that aim to control animality within human worlds— that police unruly animals' and insects' movements to buttress a hope for a purely human biosociality (for critiques, see Lowe 2010; Nading 2012)—what is striking is the partly enacted fantasy that underlies this corporate regime: it signals an impossible desire to embed humanity in strictly regimented porcine worlds, to contain workers' kin and social relations within one strand of a porcine pod. This process is not so much a matter of regional dehumanization as it is—in ways that remain hard to articulate, given the tendency to grasp capitalist projects such as the factory farm in terms of anthropocentric domination—a matter of reading and controlling territory and populations through the porcine species.

In closing, then, I want to return to the troubling core of Cesar's family story—that the industrial pig exists in his home—that jolted my settled sensibilities concerning agribusiness. In theory, capitalist agriculture is supposed to produce carnal abundance with minimal space and effort. Like all industrial projects, it concentrates labor and land use—even if, it must always be underlined, its externalities saturate the globe by polluting waterways and the atmosphere (Wallace 2016; Weis 2013). This "efficiency" is why it is deemed necessary to feed the world in the face of growing populations. This chapter suggests, in response, that the factory farm is not a straightforwardly anthropocentric project of reducing labor and land at the expense of increasing harm to animals and the environment. The species forms that managers are summoning in the wake of the waning vitality of the modern hog are better described as devices that *convert* human activities into labor and reveal how the industrial pig saturates an ecology. They mark the ongoing creation of a being whose sustenance requires emerging quantities and qualities of work by managers and workers. Once the human body becomes sensible as a reservoir of disease—a necessary threat to the porcine species—forms of mundane sociality, such as starting a new relationship, have the potential to be deemed bio-insecure, changing into labor in service of maintaining fragile animal vitalities. In turn, people are made to constantly work regulating pigs' immunities—immunities that the American system of animal agribusiness has made so fragile that they are potentially changing in tiny ways with each person's decision to, for example, sit on a couch with friends or share a bottle of wine.

Many ironies persist here: the anthropogenic creation of a postanthropocentric landscape; managers' species ontologies restricting their own autonomy; the industrialization of life maintained through increasing amounts and forms of (albeit unpaid and underrecognized) labor; and, most obvious, the fact that it is the individual killable pigs who are most burdened by their species' ascent to the position of a region's dominant organism. But one potent remainder lingers, for what remains most jarring to me, in retrospect, is how little overt outrage I heard about these policies from workers. People were, by and large, accommodating themselves to the stated nature and needs of this industrially incapacitated animal without much complaint (cf. Taylor 2017), effectively making room in their lives for this kind of vulnerable hog. Being vigilant of how one's surroundings, sociality, and actions can affect hogs is currently being coopted to sustain industrial capitalist animal reproduction (see Gibson-Graham 2008). But it necessitates that people act as if their community and kin are more than human, and it comes with the potential to reimagine life in common anew (Federici 2018). The willingness to accommodate vulnerable lives is, we shall see, a symptom of a politics of care and intimacy that is paradoxically fomenting within the violent conditions of factory farms.

PART II
SOW

3.2 **INITIALED SOW** Workers write their initials on sows after the first insemination so the company can track individual conception rates. The red slash indicates that the sow was still in estrous and inseminated again the next day. The black arrow indicates that she was found to be in her estrous cycle after being "heat-checked" by bringing a pheromone boar near.

3.1 **AI** (overleaf) Sows are stimulated at Blankenship Farm. Note the boar in a remote-controlled cage on the left side of the image, employed for his saliva pheromones.

THREE **SOMOS PUERCOS**

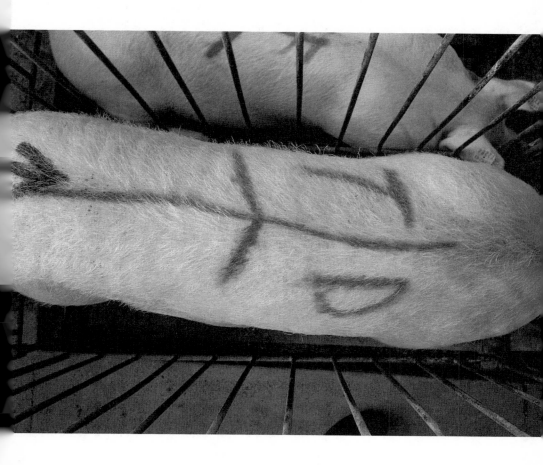

THE PREVIOUS CHAPTER traced the class contours of an agricultural company town where corporations are reappraising workers' social lives through the health and proliferation of breeding animals. Allow me to inflect the stakes of that situation slightly differently. We saw that managers' biosecurity regimes have the effect of defining human bodies as reservoirs that shelter porcine disease—that human labor is perceptible as both necessary and hostile to the pig. But there is another way to frame these bio(in)securities. Dover Foods is learning to grasp minute human actions—from feeding pigs in barns to praying in church pews—as potentially regulating porcine immune systems. Distinct pods of pigs' immune systems are distributed across an environment, including in workers' social lives and practices. These biosecurity protocols were designed to make laborers perceive themselves as entangled with and coconstitutive of pigs (Kosek 2010; Nading 2014). Workers are thus embodying *single* dimensions of porcine biology, even outside work. This and the following chapter begin developing what it means to be profoundly intimate with only one dimension of the porcine species, moving from immune systems into reproductive instincts.

What the manual worker—a person who, in managers' words, "works with" the Herd—becomes by the end of this process remains an open question, which I explore from different farm locations over the next few sections. The simple institutional definition of a farmworker in these agribusinesses is someone who works at only one production site or on one dimension of the pig, as opposed to the senior-most managers, who work across a life-and-death cycle. But the consequence of such a division of labor and animality laced through the fissures of the porcine species is that workers share little in terms of lived experience. In addition, if this biosecurity regime were to be fully realized, workers would maintain social ties only with others who are embedded in the same porcine phase. Underlying this is a politics of animals and entanglement that unequally takes hold of distinct human and pig bodies.

Or so I came to learn as I gathered on a snowy evening with my breeding coworkers in a farm exposition arena from the 1960s. The white paint on the barnlike structure's concrete walls was peeling, covered over with brightly hued ribbons, high school sports memorabilia, and old portraits of children posing with prizewinning animals. The aging arena had, for a long time, been a site of rural biosocial reproduction: generations of farm families had exhibited show pigs, sheep, and goats there as a means of modeling ideal values of husbandry and the improvement of self through arts of mating nonhuman bodies

3.3 SOW #6 WORKSHOP This is a place where workers store tools, take cigarette breaks, and jot down notes. The small picnic coolers are used to keep fifteen plastic bags of semen cool during transport into the barns for artificial insemination.

(see Ritvo 1987; Rosenberg 2015). When I watch these farm shows today, they usually give me the impression of quaint and bucolic tributes to a bygone agrarian era. But that is not quite right. Over the twentieth century, exhibiting animals was inseparable from industrial meat production. The carnal composition of each show pig was judged based on changing slaughterhouse parameters for shape and fat ratios; each generation of children exhibited and formed bonds with animals that embodied shifting industrial diets, tastes, and methods of killing (Coppin 2002). On this night, though, the arena was made into a banquet hall for Berkamp Meats' Christmas party, and it remained a site where rural people were being knotted with emerging formations of American animality.

Inside were fifty circular tables covered with white linens and surrounded by chairs for eight people. The floor was divided in half by two long wooden tables, which held platters of salad and carved roast beef au jus. In the front of the room a small stage was stacked with raffle prizes that ranged from $20 Wal-Mart gift certificates to forty-eight-inch television sets. Company executives would later thank retiring employees for their service, report on the

3.4 **BREEDING SOWS** Sows in individual gestation crates in Sow #6. These sows, no longer deemed adequately prolific, are about to be culled and sent to a sausage-making plant.

year's financials, and give plaques to exemplary workers. It was these types of gatherings—not beholden to other corporations' biosecurity dictates; open to everyone across production classes, from managers to farmworkers—that gave Berkamp Meats its local reputation as a company that cared about, and was a part of, the broader rural community.

It would be hard to find much in common among the coworkers who were seated around me, apart from the fact that we labored in the same barn— Sow #6. They all, in the abstracting language of managers, "worked with" the Herd. But despite the common label "farmworkers," it is hard to think of any of these people from the confines of a single predetermined class or subject position. Maria, for instance, was translating the table's discussion from Spanish to K'iche' for her husband. The two of them had moved here from an indigenous village in Guatemala a few years earlier, when they were in their late twenties. Maria showed a sense of curiosity about the unknown in hog barns, an eagerness to puzzle out their mundane happenings, and a very dry wit concerning the ambiguous sexualities of industrial breeding processes. At the same time, she framed herself in the language of a spectator in this country and these farms. She once mentioned that she had raised chickens in her village but was not interested in making moral comparisons about how animals are made to live in the United States. "It's different. This is [just] how they do things here," she once said, shrugging, as we filled gestation crates with sows. Her words reflected the narrow portraits of animal nature that migrants of color disproportionately endure.

Miguel was fashionably dressed in slim dark denim and Converse sneakers— an urban aesthetic rarely seen in the region. A thirty-something university graduate in his native state of Chihuahua, Mexico, he was well versed in continental philosophy, as I learned after he challenged me to analyze the barn while we sat on the backs of sows during artificial insemination. Miguel had worked in entry-level hog-breeding positions for six years, moving through a chain of barns in obscure rural hamlets that stretch from Texas to Minnesota—inhabiting a hidden industrial porcine geography—while accompanying his veterinarian girlfriend as she built her career. Angelica, who was around forty, was discussing renovations to her new home. This was an unusual sign of wealth, given that she had migrated from Mexico City just a few months earlier. She carried herself with gentility, but I do not think anyone disliked her. While drinking coffee in the barn's lunchroom, we would laugh every morning as she exited the shower room and applied copious amounts of moisturizer to her face and arms, as if she could shield her skin from pigs' effluent. Raul, a fifty-year-old Miami resident of Cuban origin who had moved

3.5 **FEEDERS** Feeders are attached to a central machine that fills and releases them. The red tabs on the top are used to measure the amount of food per feeding in terms of pounds, from three to ten. The round holes visible in the background feeders are used to add drugs and supplements to the diet by hand.

to the Midwest after Florida's construction industry collapsed in the 2008 recession, dominated the conversation, as always, with memories of his youth in Cuba and expressions of his strong desire to return from exile to one of his two homes, punctuated by dramatic expletives when he discussed Fidel Castro.

Cesar, one of the youngest of the bunch, was dressed in a shimmering black-collared shirt, as if he was about to go to a nightclub. His friend Felipe sat in stoic silence, the spitting image of a manly cowboy with his thin mustache, crisp jeans, and pointy, black ostrich skin boots. Blanca, who was seated to my right, was probably the most talented hog-farm worker that I have met, building on a decade of experience in barns since she had moved from California to the Midwest. She once told me in an interview, with shades of sadness and deep pride, "This barn . . . sows . . . it's all I've ever known my whole adult life." Senior managers, when explaining how to effectively carry out needle injections or piglet castration, would tell me to mimic Blanca's rapid and precise movements. Infinitely more knowledgeable than most others about the random contingencies that can arise from the mass-production of life—what managers, in the idiom of their post–World War II manufacturing philosophy, call "profound knowledge" of the workplace—she remained stuck in her position as a manual worker. She did not speak English well, and the senior-most Berkamp managers, born in the U.S. Midwest, did not know very much Spanish. This made her unable to become a farm manager like our boss, Francisco, who acted as a nodal point for translating information from rural barns to town offices.

In this half of the banquet room, hog-farm workers were seated in a combination of out-of-work kinship networks and workplace affiliations—Sow #3, Boar Stud, Genetics #2, Feeder Barn #12, the Medication Crew. Amid differences in national origin, education, gender, socioeconomic class, language, age, legal status, and subculture, the only obvious point of unification on this side was that those gathered around the tables were born in various parts of Latin America (or were, in the local Anglo parlance, Hispanics).[1] And some—especially the men, such as Felipe, who had grown up in small villages in Mexico—likely longed to sit on the other side of the arena.

Berkamp Meats was sharing the rental of the hall with a feedlot company. On the other side were beef cattle workers. While feedlots are legally classified as CAFOS—a "factory" farm like any other, in the eyes of some—the experiential differences between working in confinement hog barns and beef cattle feedlots are significant. Feedlots are set outdoors, and they are inseparable from the pasture-based cow-calf ranches that birth the cattle for subsequent fattening in the feedlot (Hoelle 2015; Pollan 2002). As the Western poet John

3.6 **COWBOY HAT** The well-used hat of a cowboy rests on a chair after the day's chores are completed.

Ericksson (2004) puts it, some might argue that these people are a diminished form of the version that once roamed the plains during cattle drives—"feedlot cowboys," he calls this iteration. But, he notes, this is perhaps better framed as a matter of ongoing cultural tenacity than as one-sided degradation. Feedlot cowboys retain a sense of shared identity, local pride, affective ties to the landscape, trained mannerisms, and uniforms. The other half of the room was overwhelmingly white. The people sitting there ranged in age from twenty to seventy; they sported cowboy hats and brown boots, faded Wrangler jeans, and stiffly starched shirts in plaid patterns. The (male) swine managers and (female) white office administrators from Berkamp were also conspicuously seated on the feedlot company's side of the room.

Working with cattle, steeped as it is in the lore of rodeo legends, is a local badge of male identity in this region of the Great Plains. Work in feedlots also pays a much higher wage. A beginning feedlot cowboy earns about $14 per hour, while a hog-barn worker might make $9–$10 (in early 2010s dollars; it is closer to $13 today). During an interview, a feedlot human resources manager tried to justify this income discrepancy across animal species. She claimed that cowboying is skilled work because employees ride horses around pens and corrals, and they must hold driver's licenses. "Cowboys would never carpool to work," she said, laughing and shrugging, "and for safety's sake, we need people who grew up around horses." Yet the inability of hog-farm workers born in Latin America to ride horses or drive cars was contradicted every morning that I pulled into the gravel parking lot of Sow #6. The back windshields of my coworkers' pickup trucks were laminated with decals of surnames over pictures of bucking horses, denoting a family's stable. They reflected other forms of rural collectivity on these plains, where semilegal horse racing takes place on weekends in a clandestine location in the countryside, funded by work in hog CAFOS and slaughterhouses.

A couple of people left the Christmas party to drink beer in the parking lot, because alcohol was not permitted at these events. Baptist morality tended to dominate public gatherings, although most people in the room would have identified as Catholic or Methodist. The rest of us sat quietly for a while, gazing at the other side of the hall. Rocio, another Sow #6 worker, finally broke the silence by shaking her head in amusement while muttering, "Somos puercos" (We're pigs). I did a double-take, thinking I had misheard her. "What?" I asked. She looked at me as if I was an idiot, raising her eyebrow and sweeping her arm across the right (and overwhelmingly white) side of the banquet hall while others sitting around the table cackled at how matter-of-factly she was breaking local racial silences, despite their obviousness, to a white guy. Rocio quickly changed the subject by rolling her eyes and informing me that if my name was drawn for the forty-eight-inch TV, she would get to keep it.

"Somos puercos." These are two small words that index deep and swirling histories of violence and exclusion. So many events had to cohere, far beyond that room and even American agribusiness, to make Rocio refer to herself as industrial swine along with, importantly, how the pig itself became this kind of pig. Even scratching the surface of the racial arrangements in the banquet hall might require attention to the history of capitalism's wage segregation at work (Roediger and Esch 2014), or how the U.S.-Mexico border became a political-economic technology designed to cheapen the labor of people who were born to the south of its gates (De Genova 2005; DeLeon 2015). Rocio's joke is weighted with more than three hundred years of experimental efforts on colonial plantations and farms to simplify nature—or, at least, to make it appear simplified—using the work of nonwhite human bodies (Carney 2001; Mintz 1984; Tsing 2012b). Agricultural colleges' efforts to immobilize and simplify pigs' nature using confinement technologies is but a recent example of

3.7 CHAMBER OF COMMERCE
Old rodeo memorabilia
line the walls of the town
of Dixon's Chamber of
Commerce.

such processes. It is tied to mythologies of white settlement, the U.S. west, and its cattle culture, invoked everywhere from political campaigns to cigarette advertisements (Sayre 2002). And it is inseparable from the history of racialized agrarian political economy in the United States, such as how farmworkers have long been subject to laws that limit their capacities to organize or receive labor benefits enjoyed in other sectors (see Wozniacka 2019), along with how those same workers must shoulder the effects of today's neoliberal policies that prioritize cheap food (Guthman 2011).

"We're pigs." Amid these wider histories, Rocio's joke still hums with the historical weight of dehumanization and white supremacy; it is laced with how the animal other has long acted as a resource of colonial cultural politics in the racial othering of those deemed less than human (Moore et al. 2003; Pandian 2008). Animalization is never innocent (see Weheliye 2014). No one wants to be called a pig, even in a region where traces of industrial animality are omnipresent. Rocio's words echo how Western symbols of hogs—as filthy, low-class creatures—historically have been made to leach onto those who dwell among them (McNeur 2014; Mizelle 2012). Thinking about it now reminds me of when Felipe dejectedly came into the break room from the barns, his arms materially and symbolically caked with the shit of Berkamp's hogs. He washed in the sink for a long time, a matter of minutes, until the water ran clear. "The life of the poor," he sighed as I watched, declaring that this degraded and degrading version of an agricultural job does not define him—that he *could* wash clean—even if he otherwise took pride in agrarian proficiency.

In the banquet hall, differences among people drawn from many backgrounds seemed effaced by the fact that they touch pigs. Still, as Anand Pandian (2008, 93) reminds us in a study of colonial Indian governance, there are contextual valences of animalization, and it can matter what "*kind* of animal one might embody." As he puts it, "Bestial images and metaphors are best understood . . . in relation to concrete practices of engagement, labor, and struggle between our kind and others" (Pandian 2008, 93). It has taken a lot of technical engineering to produce the sow as a mundane creature—as a simple animal that requires little skill to work with relative to the culture-laden cow; as an entry-level sort of species that makes and is made by entry-level manual laborers. Rocio's joke inflects differently in a context in which people who are locally glossed as "immigrants," even if they have lived in Dixon for a decade or were born in the United States, work in the invisible spaces of pig barns and slaughterhouses while those called "locals" care for cows in the shimmering sun. Mass-producing

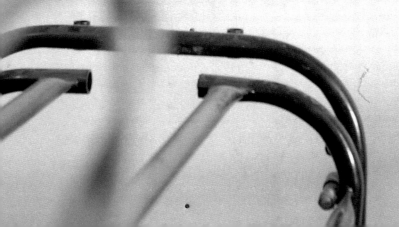

3.8 **FARROWING ROOM**
These cards are matched
to the number stapled
into the sow's ear. They
give information on the
sow's history in terms
of health, litter sizes,
number of pigs weaned,
number of pregnancies,
and other figures.

hogs is treated as a physical undertaking; the relatively more industrialized space of the breeding farm is treated as one of iterable pigs and people.

Take artificial insemination (see figure 3.1). It is the product of an enormous amount of scientific knowledge and work in agricultural colleges. And given that its primary purpose since the 1990s has been to devalue the work of specific people and pigs, I think that it can also justifiably be called a racial technology (see also Murphy 2017). Fewer than 10 percent of North American pig farms used artificial insemination (AI) in 1990, and those that did were show pig and genetics companies that aimed to produce singular exemplar animals (Johnson 2006; for its development in the United Kingdom, see Brassley 2007). The barn where I worked, Sow #6, was designed as late as 1993 for what is now called "natural mating" in the pork industry, with central open "HQ Pens" that allow boars and sows to physically mate. The industrial utility of AI is twofold. As we have seen, it cultivates genetic uniformity across the herd by allowing corporations to dilute a boar's semen into multiple "doses" (as they are called), which also decreases the number of (large and expensive to feed) boars a corporation must maintain. Second, it is faster than natural mating, reducing labor costs and obviating the animals' willpower and whimsy (Flowers and Alhusen 1992). To achieve consistent AI, scientists created a vast inventory of knowledge on porcine reproductive physiology, instinct, and sentience from the 1960s to the 1990s (Stratman and Self 1961). They tested conception rates and litter sizes while studying sows' reproductive sensoria by experimenting with oxytocin injections, playing recordings of grunting boars, positioning images of boars in the sows' field of vision, and spraying concentrated pheromones (Flowers 1998; McGlone and Pond 2003, 62–63; Vander Wal 2000). These sensual substitutions of boars—akin to extracts of embodied boar essences—were designed to make the sow exhibit "the classic standing reflex," or "lordosis behavior," without the physical touch of an actual boar (McGlone and Pond 2003, 62). "Lordosis" refers to the moment when the sow's legs lock, and it freezes prior to the moment "in nature" when the boar would mount. The worker is then made to imitate scripted and standardized boar behavior in her rubs and presses (see chapter 4).

Forms of Manichaean difference were on display in that old farm exhibition arena—skilled versus unskilled, mental versus manual labor, mind versus body, whiteness versus nonwhiteness, native versus migrant, universal versus particular (cf. Fanon 1963). They appeared to be unfolding under the dyad of cow versus pig. But my point is that Rocio's quip was inseparable from the fact that the pig is an industrial animal. And what exactly that means—the

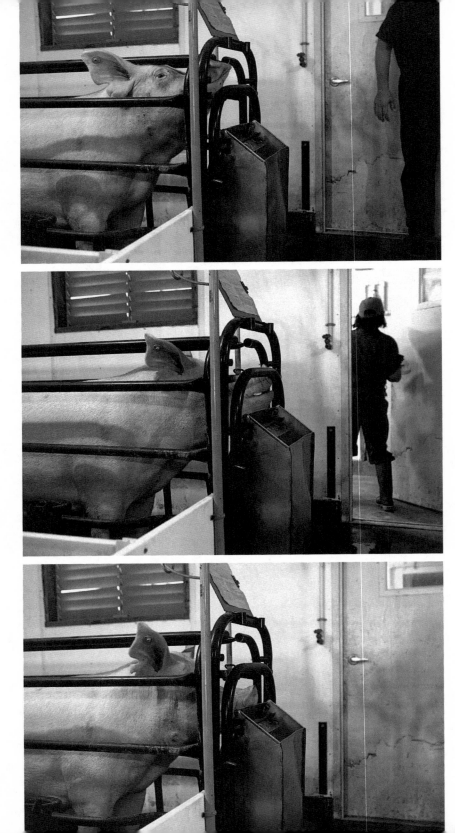

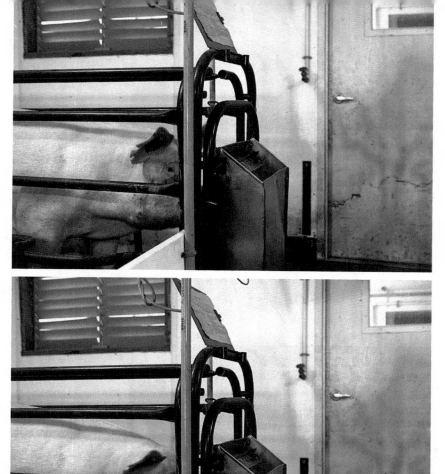

3.9–3.14 **SOW IN FARROWING CRATE** A sow in her farrowing crate. She is ready to farrow three months, three weeks, and three days after conception.

nature of swine that Rocio bitterly claimed to be—is, I argue across the next chapter, not only inherited through buried histories of racial violence. The industrial sow is also a subtle and ongoing site of struggle over forms of life on the AI line that goes beyond the technics of reproducing piglets. Types of animals make and manifest types of workers, and vice versa (Salzinger 2004). This is an act of corporate domination in the practices that define the industrial animal and, in turn, of the labor that goes into its production as people wrestle with a form of capitalist animality that defines the worth of their embodied actions. It is one that depends on a (neo)colonial hierarchy of some people having to work with these animals *for life* in a region where raising and killing pigs is often the exclusive source of employment for people who are not locally admitted to shifting categories of whiteness.[2] That banquet hall was undergirded by a politics of American animality that turns racial formations into animal flesh, emplacing race into capitalist meat, for we will see that there is nothing "simple" about industrial pigs. Relating to industrial sows is a hard-earned skill. But what that banquet hall suggested was how U.S. American sensibilities and ideologies about the nature of swine function to cheapen the exploitation of energy extracted out of workers who are drawn from across the Americas and beyond.

FOUR **STIMULATION**
Instincts in Production

SITTING ON SOWS

Over the course of a month, I spent eight hours per day gazing around barns and reflecting on scenes of mass-produced porcine life with Felipe, Miguel, Maria, and a couple others as we straddled the backs of breeding sows during artificial insemination (AI). Our bodies were meant to act as mere weights, imitating the back pressure of a boar's mounting until the sow's uterine muscle contractions draw the semen in through a catheter-like spirette attached to a plastic bag. Managers claimed that injecting the semen into sows was less effective, resulting in consequential decreases in conception rates and litter sizes when measured in the aggregate. They argued that AI required the merging of boar aesthetics—sight and smell—with specialized forms of human touch. Agency was ambiguous. Sometimes it took two minutes. Other times—particularly with unbred gilts that had not undergone the process—it could take as long as thirty minutes as we tried to activate the sows' instincts. Just sitting on sows was quite slow, and experienced workers had other tactile modes of enacting porcine reproductive natures.[1] We each did this roughly one hundred times per week as we tried to breed an average of 122 different sows in the 2,500-head breeding barn that Berkamp Meats called Sow #6.[2] From this perch, my actions were partly (and indeterminately) responsible for the conception of more than two thousand piglet fetuses.

This chapter describes labor, gender, and sexual politics as they unfold on the artificial insemination line, as workers are made to conjure and inhabit American animal natures. It is about the industrialization of porcine instinct and drives, and it is written with an eye to the long history of how animal instinct has also been central to the industrialization of human bodies engaged in manual labor (Frederickson 2014; Taylor 1911). From the archive of industrial labor studies I take the sensibility that capitalist labor, machines, and technology are always sites of conflict as different classes vie for control over the terms, pace, and value of their work (Bell 1947; Burawoy 1979; Noble 1984; Salzinger 2004). From animal studies, I take up a critique of the idea of "the animal" itself as something that effaces difference between and within species while threatening to double back to affect human populations (Derrida 2008; Kosek 2010). This tradition has been premised, in part, on relating to nonhuman beings anew; it is based on escaping blinding neo-Cartesian notions that reduce all animals—and potentially humans—to mindless, reactive, machinic, and instinctual things consumed by reflexes (Haraway 2008; Kohn 2013; Shannon 2013). My claim in what follows is that, on factory farms, these distinct ideas must be linked. When agribusiness tries to turn pig instincts into capitalist technologies and working terrains, the value of labor becomes inseparable from the ability to conjure, perform, or inhabit porcine reproductive natures otherwise.

This chapter also begins to tie a conceptual knot that has always been treated too vaguely by critics of factory farms. Dating to Ruth Harrison's classic *Animal Machines* (1964), writers have lamented how agribusinesses treat animals like machines (see Singer 1978). But it is rarely clear what this means in practice, beyond critiquing the callous ways people talk about pigs as mindless. Moving across a twisting terrain that arches from the minutiae of labor on the insemination line to manufacturing theory classes in hotel conference rooms and South American horse blood farms, this chapter traces the hard social work, research institutes, and scientific knowledge necessary to keep animals reduced to something akin to reactive bio-machines—based, in part, on the production and manifestation of instincts within both hogs' *and* human workers' embodied behavior.[3] Instinct, seemingly fixed and in the nature of swine, is made in practice at the intersection of species. The broader point that I underline here is that, from the space of artificial insemination, industrialization is not just engineered into pigs' genetics or environments. Industrialization is a social relation that is continually being (re)enacted between species. To make industrial sow instincts, workers must become ambiguously instinctual.

INDUSTRIAL PHEROMONES

As I settled into the back patio of a bar on the Friday evening following my first week of work on Sow #6's AI line, pigs were the last things I wanted to think about. My week had been a blur of sense impressions, most of them tactile: pressing down to put pressure on the dry, straw-like fur of sows' backs until my wrists ached; wrenching the scratchy rope harnesses of the recalcitrant six hundred-pound boars whose saliva infused the air with pheromones (and who were, in turn, interpreting my bodily posture for the right moment to strike at my knees); and, most vividly of all, using a long metal stick to scrape and grind fecal matter off concrete slats until it loudly splashed into the pool of effluent whose odor was thickly wafting up from under the floor.

I found myself sitting at a table with Janine, a former clerical employee for a major pork corporation in her mid-thirties. She was eager to know about my experiences of working in a concentrated animal feeding operation (CAFO). I could not yet describe the undigested impressions. Thinking back to something from a few months earlier, when I had been shadowing managers, I mentioned that the gendered division of labor in the breeding barns was odd. There were many exceptions to the rule. But women tended to help deliver the piglets 114 days after conception, while it was usually men who did artificial insemination. A few workers had also mentioned—matter-of-factly and without elaboration—how this human sexual division was laminated across the fissures of the porcine species. To my speculative ears, it carries a suggestion of how the mass-production of life is underpinned by two forms of sex work: at once the industrial reproduction of piglet bodies mediated by human touch, along with the ardent reproduction of a sex/gender system of binary identity and heterosexuality that is made to extend even across mammalian species (cf. Rubin 1975).[4] Most managers were puzzled by my questions about this division of labor, and some denied that such a division even exists. But a few offhandedly tried to rationalize (and naturalize) the distribution. For example, one claimed that "feminine" women naturally gravitate to the "nurturing" work of piglet care (see chapter 6). Another said it is hard for relatively short women to sit on the sows, as is part of the mounting and back pressure protocol for artificial insemination.

Janine, however, claimed to hold the authoritative answer. She explained that the interspecies sexual division of labor was a matter of risk: it was safer to have a single-gender majority in each department, especially during the (undersupervised and understaffed) weekend shift. At some point in the mid-2000s, she asserted, a manager friend of hers who was working overtime caught two employees having sex in a barn room during a weekend shift. I blurted out an unprintable expression of shock—initially because of the site of the act, but also because such an embarrassing, but ultimately inconsequential, incident would merit a wholesale shift in corporate policy. I had missed the point. "It's all the pheromones in the air," Janine clarified. Allegedly, some managers speculated that hog pheromones in the barn's atmosphere, concentrated by the use of specially selected Chinese Meishan "heritage" boars, were arousing workers. She framed the industrial generation of porcine semiochemicals as imperceptibly leaping across species, and as an occupational hazard.

I do not know whether this story is true. When I mentioned it to some managers, they rolled their eyes. It slipped from my mind shortly thereafter. Years later, however, I began thinking back to the idea of pheromonal pollution. Porcine instincts overtaking human agency is a subversive reading of the labor process of AI. Janine's story frames the factory farm not as a unidirectional zone of human domination and domestication,[5] but as a place where exposure to the invisible substances of hormonal attraction infects human work. Across this chapter I recount less dramatic or titillating instances of how animal automata affect, and remake, the politics of labor. But the story's insight lies in how the mass-production of pheromones transforms instincts and animal drives into something workers must traverse, however unequally, within an economy of meat.

For example, a much more staid pig production textbook, written by the animal scientists John McGlone and Wilson Pond (2003), suggests still other ways that porcine instincts can condition the character and practice of labor on farms. It provides the basic rationale for what is a form of imitative substitution of boar presence and behavior that managers tend to call "Stimulation." McGlone and Pond (2003, 62–63) write that during insemination,

> The sow often does not experience [boar] courtship and mounting. These components are thought to be necessary for maximum reproductive rates, but not for average or minimal reproductive rates. It is beneficial to maximize AI reproductive rates, so it is important to consider ways to replace the courtship and mounting experiences. Handlers can replace mounting by applying back pressure on the sow, which causes the sow to show the classic standing reflex [lordosis]. Application of back pressure may also improve reproductive performance. . . . Producers know that . . . an experienced human can provide a more complete courtship experience to the sow.

The ambiguity embedded in this excerpted rendition of Stimulation—that is, whether the "more complete courtship experience" is read as either a replication or an intensification of what happens "in nature"—will later emerge as a dimension of labor politics. But for now, this framing hints at the terrains of interspecies sociality that employees must navigate on the factory farm. The simple fact is that pigs in industrial confinement never reproduce outside a form that is mediated through human touch. After the early 2000s, when most of the world's largest pork corporations adopted AI, human action became a key physical replacement for boar touch. In these operations, Stimulation is an imitation of sow-boar reproductive signs; it is a tactile series of codified actions extracted, abstracted, and condensed from decades of scientific observation of porcine mating. To manifest high piglet-reproduction rates, farm managers are tasked with having workers reliably replicate the "instinctual" mating actions of boars in their presses, tugs, scratches, and rubs of the sow's back. The basic labor process of artificial insemination on factory farms is thus predicated on inhabiting and performing a kind of porcine nature.

From one angle, then, we will see that managers are attempting to standardize (and deskill) the labor process by authoritatively scripting the key signs and actions of boar-sow mating (cf. Braverman 1974; Uexkull 2010). Instinct—which, in its classic definition, might be described as a fixed and unchanging "stereotyped sequence of premodeled action executed by reflex in the manner of an automatism" (Massumi 2014, 13)—is a crucial resource for planning standardized and predictable labor practices precisely because it is supposed to, in theory, *always be the same.* But from another angle, Stimulation and the embodied human performance of animal instinct opens a space where cross-species intimacies—and the question of who can ably inhabit and translate animal natures into their actions—can erupt as minor skirmishes on the line. Artificial insemination is thus not just a fraught site for the mass-reproduction of killable porcine bodies but also one that simultaneously and subtly remakes gendered practices of labor and animal nature.

Instinct is a pivotal yet arguably still underexamined figure—at least, outside the Freudian tradition—in the history of social theory and anthropology (but see Bateson 1972; Frederickson 2014; Hrdy 2000; Lampland 2009; Van Dooren 2013; Massumi 2014). Instincts and their whispers of biological determinism have long been abused as tools to make existing social relations appear fixed and unchangeable. Instincts have also proved a violent figure in attempts to naturalize intractable differences among "the human," lesser humans, and "the animal" (see esp. Glick 2013; Kosek 2010; Moore et al. 2003). Much writing has theorized the stakes of the ideological divide between "the animal" as a bio-machine directed by totalizing instincts versus animals as complex persons with worldly agencies, alive to their surroundings (e.g., Haraway 2008; Kohn 2013). Scholars have built on such discussions to argue that nonhuman beings are more open to the world than we typically give them credit for (e.g., Despret 2016; Raffles 2010). But anthropologists, perhaps marked by the battles over sociobiology and other conservative social theories that reduce humans to purely reactive automata controlled by evolutionary drives, have often made it a goal to simply question the instinctual as an explanation.[6] Instead, we might explore why instinct seems to be such a recurrently popular idea, along with the different kinds and uses of instinct in the world. In short, I am less interested in exploring what instinct *is*—how to define such a thing, whether it emanates from bodies—than I am in exploring what instinct *does*.

The machine has long been a productive metaphor for thinking about industrialization (see, most famously, Marx 1964). Less notice is paid to how instincts have underpinned the very idea of "manual" labor and the factory system. Tracing the instinctual in nineteenth-century children's books, for instance, Kathleen Frederickson (2014, 83) notes how "insects become such compelling figures for [imagining] workers in the nineteenth century precisely because their mass collectivity and instinctive work fit so well with the emerging models of factory labor."[7] These models of "manual" work—that is, of purely embodied labor—were deemed mindless (see also Peña 1997). Instincts are also present as a curious ideal in American industrialism through figures such as the founder of scientific management, Frederick Winslow Taylor (1911). He infamously claimed that "trained gorillas" were the best living candidates to execute his repetitive piecework, to perfectly replicate his instructions, because they allegedly and unthinkingly would always do the same thing. As Antonio Gramsci (1971) critiqued this image of manual workers as trained gorillas, industrial capitalism's instinctual ideal man was one who could endure the monotony of the assembly line on autopilot once the factory system was cleaved into his muscle memory.

In light of this history, at a moment when farms are *trying* to become "factories"—and former farmers are enacting themselves as "farm managers"—it is perhaps not surprising to see the instinctual become a figure of organization within agribusiness. Instincts offer an alluring basis for managers' planning, especially against emergent and worldly aspects of porcine life such as individual proclivities, sentience, and memory. A hog locked in its own instinctual world—fundamentally extricable from its environment—would constitute the possibility of regimenting and making uniform the process of insemination using the animal's internal nature. Frederickson (2014, 24) describes how scientific practice of the mid-1800s first framed instinct as an entity unto itself, something that "acts immediately, forcefully, and unavoidably, without paying attention to setting or context." Instinct would appear to present the possibility of a workplace where humans engage in routinized acts with the sort of extreme regularity and lack of difference that has long been projected onto animals. The instinctual becomes about more than neuronal reflexes in swine or metaphors for animalized "manual" workers: it can be seen as a symbol of agribusiness's ideal of standardized life, in which human action perfectly mimics a set of animals with such predictable behavior that there are never any (unique) events.[8]

Granted, flourishing instincts and a system built through animal natures are not the images that come to mind when one walks into a hog CAFO. Sows will never see daylight except through tiny windows on the barn's periphery, hazily covered in cobwebs and fecal dust. Breeding sows, confined in two-foot-by-seven-foot gestation crates for their truncated lives, are unable to turn around. Once she reaches breeding age at six months, the average sow might walk ten more times: to and from another cage to farrow her litters. Immobilized on concrete floors that crack and ulcerate their hooves, sows, often prematurely stricken with lameness, are reduced to an essence of reproduction. In a confined barn of metal and concrete, scores of evolutionarily ingrained behaviors—rooting in soil, making foliage nests, maintaining cleanliness, or running over long distances—are blocked from expression for most of the millions of pigs that are annually killed for meat in the United States.[9]

It would thus seem hard to disagree with critics who claim that the factory farm's primary goal is to excise all forms of natural nature (see the examples in Imhoff 2010). But in the breeding phase of the factory farm, there is a twist. Gestation crates and indoor confinement do suppress most instinctual behaviors, but they do so *in order to* magnify the expression of one form of behavior: reproductive instincts. Less a simple matter of nature's negation, one kind of reproductive instinct become mass-produced and magnified to the point at which it forms an ideological and material terrain that both workers and managers must now navigate in the workplace. Labor in this phase of the factory farm is not experienced as reproducing piglets so much as it is experienced as reliably manifesting neuronal reflexes. This is an illustration of a mode of capitalist intimacy and detachment—of a kind of vertically integrated intimacy—whereby workers come to gain historically unprecedented familiarity with one (yet only one) dimension of sows.[10]

STIMULATION VERSION ONE: "YOU HAVE TO BE THE BOAR"

The daily routine rarely changes, although how I perceived it would shift over time. During the fall and early winter of 2010, I joined others as they left their homes and tiny towns across the Great Plains and Midwest before dawn, grabbing burritos from food trucks and turning off highways lined with grain fields and beef feedlots onto dirt roads. On my first day of work, I was embarrassed when I was an hour late after getting lost in the expanse of the countryside, where rusted silos, bridges, distant windmills, and subtle twists in the road are the equivalent of road signs. Equipped with scant instructions, I kept pulling into hog barns along the way to check their signs but could not find one marked Sow #6 for what felt like ages. I finally pulled into a gravel lot with about ten vehicles lining the side of the metal barns connected by passageways. As I rang Sow #6's doorbell and a militaryesque siren chime rang out, I did not realize that even parking here temporarily a few times would make me permanently identifiable as a sow-farm worker to most Dixon residents. Four-foot-wide exhaust fans propel odorous fumes out of the barn and onto surrounding vehicles. These odors would occasionally reemerge from my car's upholstery for the next five years when the sun heated the interior fabric's foam.

A forty-something-year-old man named Fernando, also a new hire, opened the door and nodded at me with a stern look. I entered the metal-sided barn; dropped my packed lunch through a hole in the wall, as I had learned to do while shadowing managers; opened the door of a gender-coded shower room; undressed; and took a shower. Although the faux-wood-paneled room was empty due to my tardiness, coffee mixed with hot chocolate usually made its rounds there each morning. The manager—Francisco, a short, thin man around forty-five years old who was drowning in his coveralls—was seated in the kitchen. "We've been waiting for you," he said with a warm smile. A former schoolteacher and health inspector from Guatemala City, Francisco had migrated to the region a decade earlier and worked his way up to his position as general manager of Sow #6. Respected by workers, he invested the barns with a gravitas and sense of responsibility as he gave speeches that ranged in topic from caring for animals to feeding the world. He did his best, in other words, to humanize this kind of work.

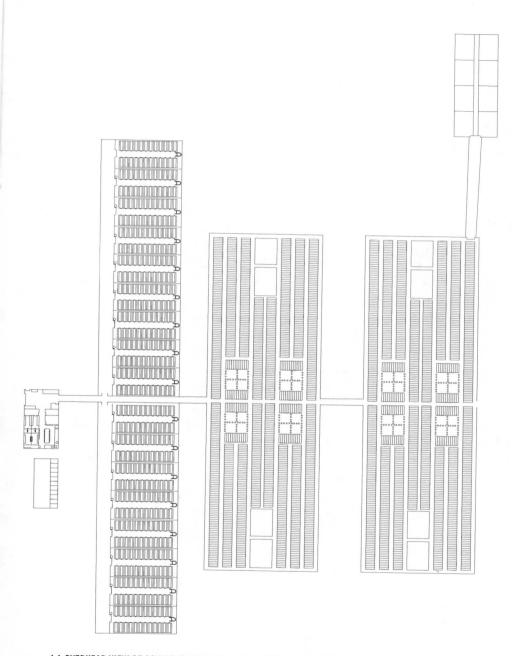

4.1 **OVERHEAD VIEW OF SOW #6** An interior view of Sow #6 (only approximately to scale). At the left is the lunchroom, parking lot, and workshop. The long middle structure holds the farrowing (piglet delivery) rooms. The two barns on the right contain gestating sows in individual crates. The open spaces in the middle are "HQ Pens" held over from when this barn used to practice "natural mating" by caging a boar and sow together. The top structure jutting out at the right is where replacement sows (unbred gilts) are raised until sexual maturity. (Illustration by the author.)

In my time in the barns, the lingua franca ebbed and flowed alongside regional migration patterns. When I was shadowing managers in Dover Foods' barns in May, the omnipresence of K'iche' spoken by migrants from Guatemala made workers' banter impossible for me to overhear. In Sow #6, Spanish was the norm for my first four weeks of work, until Raul was hired. The people who spoke K'iche' as their primary language could not understand his Cuban Spanish, and I, too, struggled with it, so most agreed to speak a slowed patchwork of Spanglish. Regardless of a given moment's lingua franca, however, the technical workplace terms for mass-producing life would puncture sentences and deliver reminders that the system was conceived and controlled by English-speakers—"los feeder," "los runt," "los scour," "los wean," to name just a few. This alienation from the idiom and infrastructure of the workplace would sometimes manifest in ways that initially surprised and perplexed me. For example, despite the fact that I was shorter than three other men, Cesar would ask me to deliver the daily scoops of powdered drugs into the side holes of sow-feeding machines suspended six-and-a-half feet above the ground. I thought he was making me do a task that he felt was irritating, as the bitter medication often sprinkled into my mouth and eyes. When I asked, he pointed to the height of the feeders, insisting that the barn was designed for white people, though the last time anyone remembered a *güero* (light-skinned person) working in Sow #6 was a veterinarian apprentice in 2003. She lasted three days.[11] Perhaps it is different with nonmechanical things. When I struggled to get the sows to draw in semen, jokes about how pigs were not attracted to white people rang through the barns to riotous laughter.

By 7:55 a.m. everyone had removed their slippers and moved into the twenty-foot-by-thirty-foot concrete workshop. This room, where we snuck breaks, was overflowing with welding tools for fixing the bars of broken crates, clipboards for recording data, parts for replacement feeders, vials of drugs, tubes of lubricant, and plastic and foam spirettes for artificial insemination. Rows of bulk liquid containers lined the floor under the tables: Squeal Clean Sow Wash, Chlorhex-Lube, Synergize Barn Cleaner, Aspen Gentle Iodine 1%, and Jaguar Bait Chunx. We would assemble our tools for the job, which included knee-high rubber boots, earplugs, wads of latex gloves, notepads, spray bottles of iodine for confined sows with scratches or with bedsores from lying on the ground all day, and thick crayons that were used to mark the backs of sows with our initials after they were inseminated.

One last morning pause would ensue as the twelve or so of us gathered around Francisco. He passed around flat, heavy brooms and gave directions

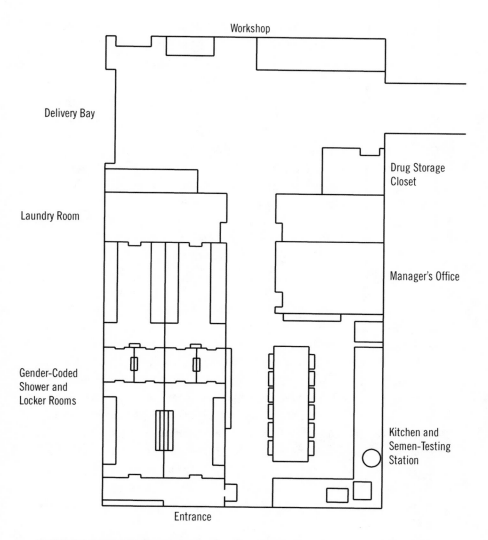

4.2 **SOW #6 WORKERS' QUARTERS** Details of workers' shower, break, and tool storage areas. (Illustration by the author.)

as to who would be tugging levers and checking feeders located in the center, south, north, east, and west of the barns. We would then walk down the 120-foot tin-clad hallway in silence and pass through two insulated metal doors with "Sow #6" scrawled in random places with black magic marker, untouched since the building's construction twenty years ago. Each morning we would burst into a scene of 2,500 shrieking animals that create an enormous intensity of squeals and banging cages that, a safety manager informed me, would reach 105–115 decibels—as loud as a rock concert—when the hogs spotted entering humans and realized that it was feeding time. Exposure to this soundscape for more than fifteen minutes would constitute an Occupational Safety and Health Administration violation.

I wedged soft yellow foam disposable earplugs so tightly into my ear cavities that the hogs' screams became background hums drowned out by the dull pulse of my steps, the scraping sensation of my broom on concrete, my heartbeat, and my breath. The earplugs also block audible communication among workers, making hand cues the early-morning language. We raced through the barn, pulling levers that release feed to rows of ninety sows, and in ten minutes the barn went dead quiet except for the odd bang of a cage or a shriek from across the barn by a sow whose feeder release valve had malfunctioned. It did not take long to grow numb to the sensory overload in the barns. On that first week I lined my pockets with blue latex gloves, replacing them every time they showed signs of tearing from metal bars or pricks of sow fur. I grabbed the long undershirts and made sure that the sleeves covered my arms all the way and tucked my coverall pants into my rubber boots. The effect of this was to reduce my body to two routes of exposure: the eyes and— at least until my olfactory sense went blank from extreme overstimulation, which happened within a half-hour—the nose. After about a week of working in these barns, I no longer jumped when animals shrieked. I started to take off my long undershirt and felt the humid heat of 2,500 sows. Dried brown muck caked on my arms looked like dirt until I reminded myself that there is no soil in the barns.

On my second day of work, as I was starting to explain my research to coworkers over lunch, Francisco exited his office and waved his hand to indicate that I should follow him to the barns. He walked past rows of animals to one of the central HQ Pens where a sow was standing on the concrete square outside her cage. This solitary animal was a "cull sow" (see figure 3.4). A sow is culled when she is older than three and too large for her gestation crate; is no longer producing litters larger than eleven piglets "born alive"; or cannot nurse more than ten piglets because her teats are injured. A couple of days after Francisco marked her back "XXX" with a black crayon, the cull sow was shipped to a meatpacker, likely in the U.S. South, to make spiced foods such as sausage (see chapter 10).

Francisco opened a gestation crate to release a boar, and he came over to lean next to me against an empty bank of crates. "These pigs"—the P-Boars— he said, "are special animals. They are very smelly." The P-Boars are Chinese Meishan pigs, a gray-haired breed that, when cross-bred with Durocs, resembles a massive wolf. Meishans excrete strong concentrations of pheromones in their saliva (Johnson 2007). During AI, P-Boars are moved in rope harnesses or remote-controlled cages in front of sows to help produce the lordosis reflex and, as Francisco put it, increase "Stimulation." Sow #6 had five P-Boars, and they were the only animals who were given proper names and ascribed personalities: "El Perro" (the passive dog), "El Peludo" (the hairy one), "Enrique Iglesias" (a boar that seemed attractive to sows), and "José" (a boar with only one testicle, named after a former employee who allegedly had similar anatomy). The P-Boar that was standing in front of me, an aggressive animal that had developed tricks to bite workers as they guided him in front of sows, was "El Cabron" (the asshole). Later he was renamed "El Chapo" after the Mexican cartel leader.[12] P-Boars are working animals, assisting the efficacy of human actions by contributing one olfactory part of themselves to American meat.

Francisco partnered Meishan P-Boars with in-heat cull sows for "natural" mating once a week to maintain the animals' pheromonal intensities (see Rix and Ketchum 2010). Workers monitor them during mating activity, as boars can be violent with weak cull sows. Indeed, AI is now described as an ethical benefit on CAFOS, as I learned when Francisco discussed how the "natural mating" era was marked by injuries to sows and as he admonished a coworker for an animal welfare violation after she left a sow and a P-Boar to mate alone. Francisco recycled this moment of monitoring as a training model in AI for new employees. "Just watch the boar; look carefully at what he does," he instructed as El Chapo mounted the sow. We stood there watching the pigs mate for fifteen minutes, gaining a lesson on the relative "efficiency" of AI. Francisco would pause to gradually construct his portrait of a standardized animal by isolating discrete moments in El Chapo's subtle "Stimulation"-building activity. Though the boar was doing many things, Francisco would note when El Chapo shifted his weight onto parts of the sow, rolled his snout across the back, or draped his hooves against the sow's sides. As he would later pause to observe AI, he would often remind us, "You have to be the boar" (a stock phrase in the pork industry [see Johnson 2007; "Sow and Pig Care to the Max" 2011]).

A curious logic emerged from Francisco's apprenticeship in animal mating. He presented AI technique as a matter of mimicking the instinctually timeless repetition of the boar, his standardization of farm labor practice emanating from the demands of nature. Nature, in this scripting of porcine mating, was always already industrialized. By making workers inhabit the semiotic signs of animal mating and codifying action around them, Francisco's lessons reduced modern hogs' reproductive life to six discrete kinds of pressure.[13] Performing these standardized forms of touch would, in turn, obviate the need for skilled workers by rendering them interchangeable, as the whole process could, in theory, be reduced to six simple movements. Anyone could be taught to "be the boar."

El Chapo finally dismounted as four other workers entered the barn. Francisco instructed Maria to tie El Chapo in front of a row of sows. "Now it's your turn," he said, nodding, treating this job with the utmost seriousness as he opened up the back of a gestation crate and nodded at me to get in with the sow. I entered the narrow two-foot-by-seven-foot space, wedging myself against the side of the crate's metal bars as I felt the 350 pounds of the sow softly press into my knees as she shifted her weight from hoof to hoof. Not knowing where to rest my hands, I laid them atop the animal's back. Francisco directed me to rub the sow's back. My hands scraped against the animal's dry, straw-like fur as I tried to reproduce El Chapo's initial movements with his snout. "Soft back pressure": I pushed the palms of my hands deep into the hard backbone directly in front of the stub of the sow's tail, mimicking the boar's early mounting. "Flank it! Reach around and pull up on her stomach": I pulled on the flesh on the left side of the sow's udder, trying to imitate El Chapo's motions with his hoof. "Now get up on the sow's back": As I "mounted" the sow with the assistance of the gestation crate's bars, the full weight of my knees digging into the small of its back, the sow's ears shot up. Her body froze in the position she was in, legs firmly on the floor, with her head cocked to the left side between us and El Chapo, as the boar lay on the concrete in front of the gestation crate.

"Ella esta lista" (She's ready), said Francisco, as an experienced worker, Felipe, jokingly echoed, "Yes, she's horny. . . . Ooooeee!" while pointing to the sow's erect ears. Francisco prepared the clear spirette, or *popote* (straw), by squeezing a circle of lubricant jelly from a 300 milliliter (ml) tube around the green foam tip that locks into the sow's cervix. He wiped the sow's vulva with a tissue to clear it of feces and dust from the barn and guided my arm forward by the elbow to properly position the popote six inches deep, until there was a feeling of pressure and it became harder to twist. Following his instructions I hoisted myself onto the sow so I was straddling her and facing away from her head. Francisco snapped off the plastic tip of a 60 ml vacuum-packed bag of semen and affixed it to the top of the popote. On this first occasion the bag drained quickly, perhaps within the span of a minute, leading Felipe to flash out a grin and sarcastically suggest I was a natural. As I climbed off the sow, Francisco handed me a red crayon, and I drew a long line that extended from the sow's neck to her tail, with my initials, "A B", scrawled on each side. Francisco grabbed the sow's card from the front of her cage and wrote "610" in the corner. The number "610" indicated the collective genetics of the semen boars that were the source of the semen in a barn some thirty miles away.

In Sow #6, artificial insemination always refers back to the scene of standardized natural mating. As we worked, our every action was theoretically informed by the memory of Francisco's distillation of El Chapo. The trouble, however, was that despite being one of the most faithful practitioners of Francisco's distilled and simplified boar, I was always among the slowest of workers on the AI line. Despite coming to make my actions hew closer and closer to the distilled six practices of that boar, the outcome of the process was not uniform. Inseminating each sow would randomly take anywhere from two to thirty minutes, and the six instinctual actions that I repeated would feel less like the "one best way" (Taylor 1911) than like an act of standardization for its own sake. Being perched on the back of sow for twenty minutes, idly waiting for the sow to start contracting the semen, was a slow and boring reminder that we were touching other animal worlds that escaped our grasp—or, perhaps, that this factory farm's architects discouraged yet also depended on other kinds of engagement with breeding animals.

THE SOW IS A MACHINE!

"P . . . M . . . M . . . M . . . WHAT?" shouted a tall man in a black suit as he paced in front of the tables in a hotel conference room. Without hesitation the twenty senior corporate managers seated around him, ranging from khaki-clad executives to the Wrangler-wearing bosses of the slaughterhouse, answered with a resounding "E!" The man in the suit was named Jim Goodman. He was locally known as the Doc. He flew in from his midwestern office every two weeks to lead three different three-hour sessions in post–World War II Japanese manufacturing theory with twenty students in each. Executives had brought the Doc, a guru who teaches statistics-based continuous quality improvement (CQI) programs (also known as total quality management), to Dover a decade earlier to teach them the industrial philosophies of Walter Shewhart (1986), Kaoru Ishikawa (1985), and W. Edwards Deming (2000; see also Gabor 1992; Tsutsui 2001). The classes were designed to build a common language across workplace divisions. Continuous quality improvement was meant to buttress a "cultural" form of integration that extends beyond formal ownership of every moment of the pig's existence. All senior managers had to attend, whether they worked in human resources, in farming, on the kill floor, in maintenance, in rendering, or in biodiesel.[14]

The idea of the classes was thus to enable managers to find a way to communicate across the distinct material processes of, say, artificial insemination and organ rendering while also helping them explain their work regimens to wholesale customers in East Asia. I often heard Dover Foods' chief executive state that his priority was to cultivate a "culture of integration" across workplace divisions, especially between the so-called Live Side (birthing and raising hogs) and the Plant Side (killing and processing hogs). Employees from these two groups were rarely in the same room, but they would bicker about why they held such different capitalist philosophies. As one veterinarian told me, "We fight to keep the pigs alive; they try to kill them as fast as they can." Others elaborated more complex theories of practice, materiality, and space. For one Live Side manager, the Plant Side (literally) could not think outside the box. He proposed that employees on the Plant Side were limited in imagination because the Plant Side could always see the killing of pigs. Moreover, he claimed, the slaughter was so fragmented after two hundred years of industrialization that the Plant Side could think only about shaving off a few seconds instead of conceiving entirely new paradigms for killing. "They're too close to their processes," he insisted. By contrast, those on the Live Side—who could only rarely be present on any given farm—had to be able to coordinate across a thousand farm sites and develop statistical forms of managing distant workplaces. As the man said, "We've integrated the pigs. Now we need to integrate our people."[15] The first step to integrating themselves was to come to an agreement over the very nature of industrial hogs.

On the first day of class, after showing videos from the 1980s on business applications of Thomas Kuhn's scholarship, Goodman argued that his approach was designed to lead to "paradigm shifts" in what it means to manufacture life. He relished the opportunity to act as a "rock in the shoe" of managers who believed it was impossible to translate industrial manufacturing methods into what they called the "biological system" of pork production; he claimed his role was to instill in his students the belief that life can be built to spec. Mocking the hesitation of pupils, the Doc insisted that the high variation inherent in biological processes—whether of sow insemination or biodiesel transesterification—should be viewed instead as an opportunity for improvement and competitive advantage. Variation was not grounds for a form of paralysis that would make managers gravitate to methods of pig farming or industrial slaughter they had learned while growing up in Iowa.

"PMMME"—which stands for persons, machines, methods, materials, and environments—was his favorite slogan. It forced managers to gain a sense of distance from their work environments and develop ways to measure pig production statistically by dividing "systems" into "processes." The Doc used PMMME as a means of abstracting rationality from industrial schemas and mobilizing it in other contexts, from manufacturing car tires to nursing piglets. To illustrate CQI's universal pretensions of measurement and show how it could be applied to any situation, he drew on the amusing example of "efficient" nose picking, transposing the processual categories this way: the person is his brain; the machine, his finger; the method, his hand movements; the material, the contents of his nasal cavity; and the environment, the conference room.

"Quality" in CQI means nothing more than statistical decreases in process variation. What makes something high quality, in this program, is that it has low variation. Quality is premised, Goodman argued, on isolating and standardizing every input in a broader system. Training in CQI was designed to help managers see factory farms as fractal.[16] While the entire process of producing pigs from life to death can be broken into a system composed of five PMMME components, each process that makes up that system (e.g., artificial insemination or a sub-step of AI, such as sow estrous detection) is also divisible into five components—hence, the "continuous" element of CQI. Improvement in quality is an infinite horizon that gradually shifts to finer resolutions of engineering.

In a sense, it is the existence of exactly this kind of training that made me move to the town of Dixon in the first place. When I started researching this book, I was interested in the basic question of what it means to industrialize life. While "factory farm" has become a household phrase in the United States, it is often used in popular media as little more than a term of critique. Outside of rural histories from the early twentieth century (see Fitzgerald 2004), remarkably little research has been conducted on how industrial ideals, methods, and aesthetics are still being taken up in animal agriculture. The classes illustrated one obvious way in which these agribusinesses are what we might call "meta-factories": they index how managers sought to achieve the aesthetics and rationalities of historical factories, often as ends in and of themselves. In other words, the "factory" farm is not just a metaphor. It is a kind of rationality that planners were trying to achieve.[17]

Dover Foods uses CQI training to bring about shifts in managerial consciousness. These developments of discourse—the Herd from chapter 2 being only one example among others to emerge from such classes—provide a conceptual bridge to unite the distinct material acts of raising versus killing hogs. I glimpsed one such moment when a group of midlevel managers realized during a coffee break that, in CQI, breeding sows are really Machines for manufacturing Material (piglets). Such an observation put the Doc's figurative rock in my shoe. I protested to classmates that, ethically, we should not describe living animals as if they were inanimate, mechanized objects. The statement seemed to reverberate with every nightmare of a neo-Cartesian science that grasps animals as unthinking and machinic automata without sentience or feelings (see Desperet 2016).

While I admitted that we could playfully read sows as machines during a later disagreement with the Doc, he was adamant that "pigs have always been Machines" across the history of American farming. This was a statement not about the nature of pigs but, instead, about the context in which pigs are mobilized in agriculture. The power of these categories, he went on to claim, is that they allow managers to reorient themselves toward what capitalist farmers have been doing tacitly for hundreds of years. Such consciousness-raising moments are not designed to lead to direct transformations in production regimens but to gain an intellectual grip on the biological system as it exists in practice. Only at that instant, the moment of achieving an abstracted conceptual equivalence between so-called manufacturing systems and biological systems, can one to begin to reanalyze sows as sharing characteristics with other kinds of industrial machines.

Such ideas resonate with, and complicate, proposals in animal studies, particularly the work of Edmund Russell (2004) and his colleagues to articulate a new evolutionary history. Russell notes that scholars have long ignored the ways that biological beings have been industrialized—say, horses whose bodies are bred and shaped for war or cows whose udders produce exponentially more milk than they did just a few decades ago (Greene 2004; Orland 2004). Pushing against tacit assumptions concerning divisions between nature and culture, Russell proposes that we should analyze farmed organisms as "workers," "machines," or "factories." This heuristic idea is insightful in its collapsing of conceptual barriers, but it is also problematic in its assumption that there are preexisting, ahistorical, or singular things called "the worker," "the machine," or "the factory."

While robust debates are underway in animal studies about how to define and analyze an industrialized living being, we should not forget the very long history of debate—especially in the Marxist tradition—of what constitutes an industrial machine in the first place. Indeed, I came to this chapter's focus on instincts only after noticing the ways that CQI programs are themselves in a curious alignment with the Marxist reading of mechanization. Much like the Doc's concept of the machine, Marx's version was not predicated on the materiality of objects. It did not necessarily refer to concrete mechanical technologies, such as an assembly line. It was part of a general social process of exploiting additional surplus value from laborers. The shift in CQI, in a sense, worked on me: as I returned to work the day after these classes, I was thinking about sows as machines.

In a middle section of *Capital*, Marx argues that "the machine" comes into being only with its insertion into the social space of the large-scale factory; it emerges only once capitalist-controlled objects coordinate the labor process. In what he calls the manu-factory period, capital controlled the labor process subjectively using embodied managers who tried to coordinate the division of labor, but this still relied relatively more on workers' cooperation. But in the machino-factory, capital (or "dead labor") appears in the form of a machine. As Marx (1992, 508) writes, "Large-scale industry . . . possesses in the machine an entirely objective organization of production, which confronts the worker as a pre-existing material condition of production."[18] In other words, it puts the worker to work. As the science studies scholar Donald MacKenzie (1984, 487) reframes the industrial machine—such as an engine-driven (dis-) assembly line—after a century of empirical scholarship on the issue, it is a tool for control over the labor process. As he puts it, "It undermined the basis on which manufacturing workers had resisted the encroachments of capital." The machine transformed society and the experience of human labor by extending the working day, breaking workers' guild collectives, socially devaluing labor, and creating a rigid form of discipline over laborers in the workplace by setting the pace and terms of how labor is executed. This is, in other words, remarkably similar to how animal instincts unfold and are enacted on the insemination line. Rather than protesting the abstract ethics of calling animals "machines," the remainder of this chapter examines on-the-ground struggles that reduce (or do not reduce) sows to machines whose natures set the terms and pace of human labor.

STIMULATION VERSION 2: "HOGS ARE HOGS"

"Hogs are hogs. But employees change," declared Graham, the head of Dover Foods' live production operations. I first heard him use this phrase during a meeting with twelve interns from an agricultural college. The motto reflects how he tries to conjure porcine natures. Sow instincts at Dover Foods manifest differently from those at Berkamp Meats; Graham's workers are made to press distinct kinds of industrial archetypes into sows' backs. Graham was trying to script modes of touching sows in ways that were designed to make distinct sows *become* a generic "sow." Five months before I ever touched a sow on the artificial insemination line at Berkamp Meats, Graham had introduced me to Blankenship Farm, an enormous 12,500-head sow barn that alone births more than 300,000 piglets in a year.

Near the middle portion of a six-hour inspection of Blankenship Farm, Graham motioned me over for a demonstration of Dover Foods' AI practice. A P-Boar was in a remote-controlled cage called the Robo-Boar on tracks in front of a bank of sows (see figure 3.1). A group of workers, who would collectively conduct 1,500 "services" of sows that week, used a handheld device to move the boar in front of uninseminated sows. Aside from briefly rubbing the sow's back from tail to neck using the identical motion—about four light circuits to quickly check whether the sow was responding to the P-Boar's pheromones—these workers never touched the animal. After inserting the spirette and the bag of semen into a sow's uterus, they placed a weighted white band over each sow's back and moved on to the next one. The process was given a veneer of automation, with all of the "Stimulation" emerging from a forty-pound weight and the labor process built around the gestation crates and the remote-controlled Robo-Boar.

The back weights effectively black-box forms of difference across pigs while ensuring that workers touch every single sow in the exact same way. As we silently watched this scene play out in the barns for a half-hour, Graham carefully monitoring workers' movements to ensure that they were identical, I asked Brian, the company's head geneticist, what was happening during this moment within the sow. His reply was an accurate reading of the multispecies social scene that was emerging in front of us, painting the sow as an inherently biomechanical being: "Oh, you know, the pressure on the back is triggering the brain, which sends a signal to the sow's body that it should contract."

This scene represents one archetype of manufacturing the sow as a timeless and instinctual animal; it is an AI technique built out of the idea that "hogs are hogs" and systems of human labor can be built around their ontological sameness. The pig that emerges from this scene is purely reproductive. Much like the cyclical concept of the Herd and "genetic flow," it is impossible to paint this as a moment of "production," when human labor and agency bring something new into the world. Instead, it is a human-assisted moment of reproduction in the unfolding of the pig's fixed nature. Companies such as Dover Foods codify labor and interspecies touch *as if* the pig is a fixed machine.

Five months later, when I recounted this to Francisco, he was incredulous: "I don't know why people use those things. We tried to use those back weights, but they gave us lower conception rates—like, 4 percent lower." Graham and a Dover geneticist did not disagree, acknowledging that back weights could lead to lower conception rates. Graham explained, "Sure, that might be true. But we have lower labor costs. You won't see ten people working the breeding departments on one of my [small] sow farms. What matters to me is that it is predictable." In other words, the back weights enabled the deskilling of workers and ensured that labor practices across Dover Foods' dozens of sow farms were identical. The back weight AI technique simultaneously brings into expression one type of pig, an interchangeable worker, and a standardized factory farm. Francisco's response was telling: he declared that the back weights "provide no Stimulation; only pressure." Trials had been run, he informed me, and if you "follow the sow . . . you'll see the difference." Berkamp averaged .5 fewer piglets born alive when using the back weights as opposed to "Stimulation" with workers' hands and bodies. Stimulation as a concept allowed Francisco to articulate a sense that labor mattered in the proliferation and reproduction of the porcine species, creating conditions of possibility for the articulation of other kinds of interspecies engagement.

STIMULATION VERSION 3: "ALL SOWS ARE DIFFERENT"

For a long time, I had a tendency to write something like this: after a month of sitting on sows' backs, creatures immobilized and coursing with reflexes in gestation crates that could never quite drain their individuality, *my actions* became responsible for the conception of two thousand fetuses. But this sentence is best read as a reflection of the ideology of (male) agency cultivated by artificial insemination. This ambiguous paternity is part of what it means to "become boar" on the factory farm, of acting out the instinctual heterosexual behavior of an animal that most of us only fleetingly encounter. Paternity is written into the affective masculine animality of the insemination barns, where the workforce is 80 percent male (as opposed to the "nurturing" space of delivery that is 80 percent female). In this space, it is always the boar that stimulates and the sow that is stimulated. Men are made to imitate male pigs distilled by male managers. The five boars—the Meishan P-Boars—are the only animals on the farm that can interact with workers; are not reduced to an indistinguishable mass; are named; and invite cross-species identification.

"Stimulation," in Francisco's ongoing lessons, would emerge over time as a more ambiguous word than it appeared to be in his initial training; it came more into line with our earlier textbook authors' ambiguity in terms of what constitutes the "more complete courtship experience" (McGlone and Pond 2003, 83). Perhaps Francisco's divergent instinctual philosophy reflected his own position as an ascendant manager—and a former worker—who was dedicated to the task of standardizing labor as an ideal but also saw skill buried in this form of work. One can read, as I did earlier, his lessons as matter of predetermined *stimulus*—a miming of weights, presses, and tugs as the human body becomes a mere conduit for a fixed animal nature. Alternatively, the longer I worked in Sow #6, the more I perceived the idea of Stimulation as practiced by some of my coworkers (and buttressed by Francisco's lessons) as paternal *stimulating*—an ongoing, human-centered intensifying of instincts beyond what animals are capable of producing "in nature."[19] These forms of Stimulation can potentially improve conception rates and litter integrity beyond what happens in moments when actual boars and sows physically mate. Stimulation allowed Francisco to articulate the value of both standardization *and* (human) agency in terms of regularizing and intensifying the vitality of porcine reproduction, creating the conditions of possibility for the embodiment of skilled instinctual behavior in workers' bodies. It created the possibility for a humanistic notion of labor within these barns that is creative and that leaves its trace on this world by making new things (see Terkel 1974; Weeks 2011).

In my second week of work, as I was sitting on the back of a sow going through the six motions, Francisco rounded the corner and began a motivational speech. "What you do right now will matter for the rest of these pigs' [the piglets] life," he declared. "The more you Stimulate, the more [the sows] will contract." Crucially, Francisco's elaborated notion of Stimulation here figured as not just a matter of achieving high conception rates. "Good Stimulation," he insisted, "*might give us an extra pig, and good pigs*."[20] If the logic of species is one of reproductive capacity, what do we make of these paternal claims of an industrial meat pig(let) that comes into existence only through Stimulation and whose body reverberates with traces of human touch? Laboring on sow instincts is here an intervention into porcine reproduction such that alienated records of human touch can come "alive" in the extra piglets of large litters and inside the very corporeal quality of animals. Industrialized porcine life is not only anthropogenic in quantitative terms of litter sizes. Taken to its terminal end—*the good pigs*—the textural quality of each and every hog's slaughtered carcass, ten months later, might be anthropogenically indexed to traces of workers' motion at this moment of conception. These presses would animate hogs and reverberate through the biophysical substance of their bodies. Nodding his approval at my behavior, Francisco paused on the other workers before he left for another part of the barn.

His lecture was intended for Felipe and especially Maria. Maria was standing next to a sow, looking bored as she gently patted the animal's back as if it was an injured cat, waiting for the semen bag to slowly drain without mounting the animal. She rolled her eyes as he walked away. Felipe, by contrast, was furiously cycling through a blur of motions, jumping up to dig his knees into the sow's back, concentrating and putting the whole of his body into every movement. His gaze was fixated on the animal's upper back while he flicked his eyes to see whether bubbles of semen were moving down the straw. Neither grasped artificial insemination as a matter of laboring across universal species—of "humans" without (gendered) difference working on identical pigs without individuality.

Despite being initially dismissive of my presence, Felipe tried to take me along as his apprentice over time. I came to see Felipe's blur of movements as signaling a tactile interrogation and critique of some managers' ideas of universal animality, as he tried to come into contact with and inhabit other sow natures. In down moments, he would demonstrate an inventory of breeding techniques and forms of touch for me. Sitting on the sow, using his interchangeable body weight, was only one of these forms. Others included pushing and tugging on the fur in dozens of different places, flanking the animal in distinct ways, varying the speed and intensity of his motions, talking to the animal in different pitches of voice, and other Stimulative tricks and techniques. "Back pressure," for Felipe, was not just a matter of weight. Some techniques, such as twisting and tugging on the animal's stub of a tail, would do nothing to one sow but cause the semen bag to instantly drain with another animal. This was not just a random quirk of Felipe's. When I asked Miguel why he also employed a variety of techniques—for it was much harder work than just sitting—he shrugged and said, "All sows are different."

Felipe (semi-jokingly) liked to explain his craft through an odd form of paternal instinctuality that was nonetheless sharply attuned to the site. He claimed that his ability to marshal deep-seated masculine affection granted him intimate forms of access to the sow; that there was a cross-species masculine essence that enabled him to do better than merely "becoming the boar." He would insist that efficacious action on the insemination line "is like making love to a girl [*chiquita*]. You need to watch the sow, look at what she is doing." He framed the sows' postures, foot positions, and contraction patterns as all carrying subtle traces of meaning—that he was communicating in some way with the animals—and as forming the ground for interspecies sexual signification. If the bubbles on the straw move up and down rather than descending in a steady pattern, he insisted, "you're not stimulating her enough." As Felipe would later put it as he loudly talked to the animals, made noises at them, and he tugged on different spots of their fur, "The sow will [draw semen] if you put on the right type of pressure, but it is a bit different for every one."

Felipe's technique drew blushes from others, part of the risqué scandal being his invocation of a hint of sentient desire in what is supposed to be a purely instinctual zone of mechanistic reflexes. And his craft pride was of a decidedly measured sort. It was not hard to see alienation lurking behind much of this: intimately heterosexualizing the sow achieves *detachment* from factory farms by insisting that neither he nor his skills are defined by this job (see Candea 2010). This pan-species (hetero)masculinization of breeding was a refusal to "become boar" on managers' terms.[21] Or maybe it was just his favorite joke, one that makes sense in this space of industrial reproduction and succeeded in making us all uncomfortable. At the same time, by invoking workplace skill as founded on a cross-species essence that enables only heterosexual men to gain instinctual animal proximity, Felipe's quips had the effect of masculinizing the breeding space, worker solidarity, the capacity to express skill and self-worth, and the agrarian ability to engage other forms of life. While listening to all of this, Maria rolled her eyes, as she tended to do, and kept petting the sow.

In Felipe's strained efforts to articulate a form of skill he was trying to enunciate a sense of laboring self-worth by invoking himself as instinctually connected to animals beyond what managers are capable of scripting. And he was touching *something*. As Felipe proudly, if sometimes jokingly, performed his alter-instincts, he was the fastest person on the line, never taking more than five minutes per sow. I initially interpreted his actions as a matter of labor communication—as past workers who had moved through the barns had "trained" the sows to respond to forms of touch—making the "instinctual" a form of socialized labor. Cycling back through memories of reading old romantic tracts on humanist collective creativity through work (e.g., Crawford 2009; Terkel 1974), I imagined a relationship of labor histories and skill held together within the memory of sows, animal minds serving as repositories for working-class tactile connections and shared forms of craft. But Felipe's explanations seemed adamantly to push against this cute humanist story. He insisted that each sow is different because the animals are born with individual proclivities, and he would point to the gilts to make his argument that more complex natures were unfolding all around us. When inseminating gilts—sows that have not yet been bred—he would take five minutes while others took thirty. Felipe's craft could be interpreted as a masculinized matter of skilled searching across the possible range of sow predilections that can emerge over the species as a whole. Less a matter of assuming that the pig was an industrially standardized creature or some kind of reactive biomachine, Felipe's embodied tactile archive—formed through years of contact with animals—enabled him to interact with many different expressions of a vital animal nature.

BLOOD MARES AND THE HUMAN "INSTINCT" TO WORK

Years later I still find it hard to write about these kinds of scenes. There is simply no safe place to stand on the insemination line, nowhere that does not—in various ways—reproduce this sexual economy of meat. My point in spelling out these minor sexual and labor struggles in detail is not to romanticize Felipe's strident and uncomfortable efforts to become attuned to animal natures in this space of violence. But it is also not to belittle them. The outcome is paradoxical. Managers—in pursuit of standardization and predictability across people and pigs—encourage workers to work *less hard*. Francisco's ideal is that workers just sit on sows, even if he turns a blind eye to practices such as Felipe's either because it is undoubtedly faster or because he has a certain respect for his craft. Workers such as Felipe and Miguel (often clandestinely) *work harder* than is officially sanctioned. Felipe's efforts to enact and inhabit alter-instincts—other animal natures—through hard labor reflect how difficult it is to achieve dignity and worth in factory farms.

But it was not until I first read about the blood mares with whom we were unknowingly colaboring that I came to realize that these struggles are not only about hog instincts so much as they are about managing deeply inculcated ideologies of *human* nature. In early 2017, the European animal welfare organization Tierschutzbund Zurich (TSB) released an update to its two-year undercover investigation into South American horse blood farms. The organization's findings not only provide a disturbing glimpse into the hidden violence that underlies global animal agribusiness and its cheap meat; they also suggest ongoing trials to further naturalize human labor as the key locus of value within a capitalist world system. Blood mares point to how emerging dimensions of animal life are becoming newly subject to necessary labor, and, in turn, how some life forms are remade to put humans to work.

While documenting the importation of horse meat into the European Union, TSB learned that pharmaceutical companies were engaged in a more lucrative trade with farms in Uruguay and Argentina. Or maybe "farms" is not the right word for these odd places, which operate in a regulatory lacuna outside rules that guide the generation of flesh from domesticated animals. Thirty years ago, companies began renting privately owned forests and populating them with thousands of semi-wild mares that are left to fend for themselves, thus avoiding the cost of feed and veterinary care. On these blood-and-timber plantations, there are only three direct stages of human intervention: impregnation, weekly blood extractions over the initial few months of pregnancy, and then abortion. Only 70 percent of the bony mares survive being drained by long brown hoses, and they are then returned to the woods to begin the cycle anew. In the first half of 2017, just one of these sites alone exported some $10 million worth of processed blood, in the form of 1.3 kilograms of pregnant mare serum gonadotropin (PMSG). In turn, PMSG has become an indispensable tool in the artificial insemination of pigs on North American factory farms.

The TSB report shook me, partly because I remember injecting this horse blood into sows' necks. But back then I knew PMSG only by one of its brand names: Merck P.G. 600.[22] It was just one of the many small glass vials of clear hormones that line storage closets in confinement breeding barns, whose purpose is to temporarily manifest animal physiological states that enable laboring interventions into porcine biology (see chapter 5). The serum is designed to bring sows back into estrous immediately after a litter is weaned. It cuts down a few, as the pork industry suggestively calls them, "unproductive days" when sows' vitality is not directed to work on gestation (see Beldo

2017). Second, PMSG synchronizes the expression of estrous in a barn of sows. It allows breeding-farm workers to show up in the morning and be put to work immediately inseminating an entire section of a barn; mare serum is used to compress sow reproduction into an 8–5 industrial working-day window. In other words, the whole point of the drug is to keep human hands "productive" for the entirety of this paid time as we rubbed pigs' backs down a single-file line of gestation crates that *felt* industrial in its repetition. This mare serum indexes a vast cross-continental movement of biology and exploitation. South American horses are kept impregnated with little human work—and then their blood is processed by scientists in European labs to make workers born in Central America more intensely weave their labor through animal biology—all to ensure that corporations' North American sows are constantly pregnant. This is a drug of capitalist ideals: it is a substance that makes sows better approximate a "machine" that extracts consistent effort from workers.

What none of us in those barns could detect is how much human knowledge, science, and energy is expended to keep us all working and to find a few extra pennies of profit in a pork chop. As I reread this chapter, drafted as it was years before I learned about the blood mares, it dawns on me that the question of who is being drugged during an injection of PMSG is actually quite ambiguous. The drug comes to act on the injectors, not only because it puts us to work, but because it "Stimulates" *humans* in its psychoactive effects. While rubbing and pressing sows' backs during insemination, I was always convinced that my labor was the central agent in the barns, that my effort and skill alone would determine rates of conception. Pregnant mare serum gonadotropin creates conditions that make human work feel like the effective prime mover of the world.

Since its founding, capitalist public culture has treated work as a privileged and uniquely human matter of shaping, authoring, and animating the world (see Federici 2004; Vogel 1988). Work has been a central site for refining the doctrine of human exceptionalism and its insistence that our species uniquely stands apart from all other forms of life—buttressing the idea that it is our nature (and duty) as human beings to transform the natural world through labor. While earlier forms of Marxism saw dignified work beyond capitalism as a path to realizing collective human liberation (Braverman 1974), capitalist labor in much of the world has been reduced to something that many of us must do to have any dignity at all. As Kathi Weeks (2011, 7) puts it, "The social role of waged work has been so naturalized as to seem necessary and inevitable, something that might be tinkered with but never escaped." The very existence of PMSG, and drugging of animals to create conditions that make human labor possible, are political matters because they make inherited industrial ideas of human nature *feel* natural. It is worth questioning just how much scientific and intellectual effort is expended to maintain these kinds of ideologies of the human. So much collective energy and resources are marshaled through the global movement of horse blood, all just to have human labor affecting yet another dimension of pigs. It takes a great deal of interspecies engineering to create human work on factory farms. Given that the collective social good of these pharmaceuticals can likely be measured in a decrease of a mere penny per pound of pork, it is hard to treat this as a matter of rational economic "efficiency." It is at least equally plausible to frame things like PMSG as ideological drugs that manifest industrialism in the world by making humans and hogs into "workers" and "machines."

Perhaps, then, the political practice that was most critically attuned to instincts in this place were really Maria's actions on the insemination line. Palliative touches such as anesthetically petting the sow's back can be read as a form of distancing that offers something different: a refusal to become part of this highly Stimulated instinctual machine; a refusal to work on reproducing models of sows and killable piglet bodies (cf. Weeks 2011). Whether it takes two minutes or two hours for the semen bag to drain, Maria simply petted sows as multiple dueling paternities and forms of human Stimulation swirled around and summoned her to author porcine life. Refusal of work, in this context, should not be thought of as a *lack* of work. Maria's practice, in retrospect, must have been a hard form of labor to sustain. In the time that I was employed at Sow #6, she had to endure constant scolding by both managers and workers alike. But her practice matters because it is the only one I encountered that directly questions human volition and agency on the insemination line. By partially suspending the work of reproduction, her seemingly lazy and uninterested strokes of the back might be critically interrogating the value of human labor, and the limits of labor politics, from within this kind of place. Touching sows in ways that do not generate yet more killable bodies at least offers forward the *possibility* of knowing hogs in forms that are not overdetermined by instinct.

For what remains most striking in these excerpts is not the tactile humanist skirmishes over labor and gender hierarchies playing out through hog bodies. What is remarkable is the degree to which the sow itself has disappeared from the picture—amid a constant invocation of animality, instinct, and nature. I remain struck by the fact that, despite touching hundreds of sows, I cannot confidently state that I emerged with any kind of positive knowledge of this animal outside of the ways that is manifests in confinement. What I know about with an extreme depth of intimacy is reproductive instincts: one single facet of hogs. Contemporary industrial pigs are the product of hundreds of such single-trait intimacies—all slightly different, honed into distinct physiologies and biologies, all compounded and forgotten in American meat. The following section explores other political possibilities latent within these vertically integrated intimacies.

PART III
HOG

5.2 **SOW ID CARD**
Sow ID cards list the animal's reproductive history in terms of animals born alive, number of piglets weaned, number of piglets fostered by the sow, and causes of piglet death.

5.1 **FINISHING BARN** (overleaf)
A man inspecting the condition of hogs at around four months of age.

FIVE **LUTALYSE**

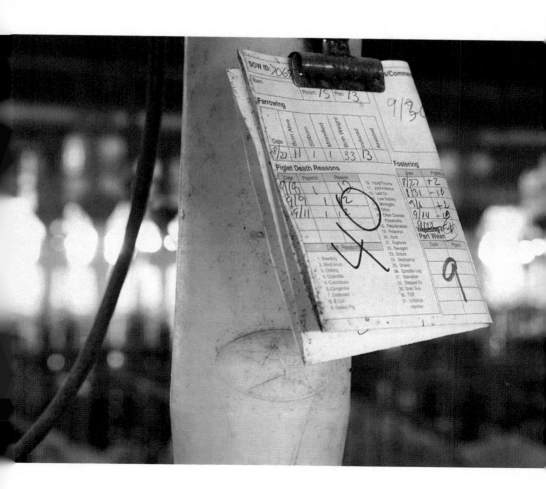

AS PART OF SOW #6'S TRAINING PROGRAM, I learned most of the assigned tasks on the farrowing side alongside Raul, a wiry and wisecracking man around fifty years of age. This was his second job since he had undergone a self-imposed exile to the Great Plains a year earlier. He was trying to keep the mortgage on his home afloat after he lost his income during the collapse of Miami's construction industry during the recession of 2008. Refugees from Burma, Ethiopia, and South Sudan were drawn to the region in search of work largely through church networks, while Cubans such as Raul were mostly recruited at job fairs in Miami. Grensome Meats, a packing plant located a few hundred miles north, had flown Raul to the area. The company put him in temporary housing, gave him a $500 advance to get settled, and required him to work on the cutting floor for at least one year.

The second he could escape *los mataderos*, Raul moved south with friends. "My body's too old for those slaughterhouses," he said, flexing his right hand at the memory of pain in the smallest of muscles from repetitive motion with a knife on the cutting floor. He did not speak enough English to be employed in retail or in an office job. "The only work they'd give me was on sow farms," he said with a shrug. During my time at Sow #6, four people arrived for one day of work, never to show up again, as they were overwhelmed by the odor and heat of thousands of hog bodies. But as I got to know Raul, I realized he derived an ironic satisfaction from being surrounded by pigs. Like a lot of my coworkers, he genuinely liked the animals. But he also told me that he had saved money for one year in rural Cuba to buy a single cow and that it was his proudest possession. "One cow, one cow," he chanted, looking around and cackling about his former sense of value as he dripped milk into a piglet's mouth amid hundreds of animals.

Nursing weak piglets is a grating task reserved for new hires. Each morning, Raul and I grabbed four blue plastic baby bottles from the workshop and filled them with a scoop of sugary powdered milk and water. (I tasted the liquid after a shrieking piglet gurgled it back in my face.) The job is perhaps better described as "force-feeding" than "nursing." Our coworker Blanca gave a demonstration. She picked up one of the runts and gripped its neck under the base of the skull using her thumb and index finger, its screaming mouth facing the ceiling. The tiny piglet shrieked so loudly that my ears rang, and I involuntarily caught myself cringing; she then silenced the animal with a squirt of milk. After a few seconds of gurgling, with half the liquid running

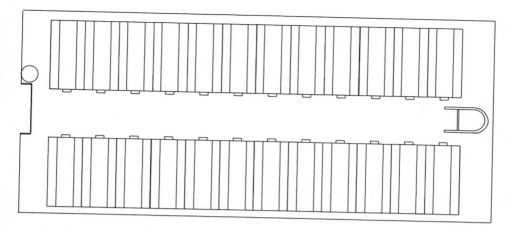

5.3 OVERHEAD VIEW OF FARROWING ROOM The room contains twenty-four farrowing crates ordered in a clockwise manner. The crate at the top left is #1 and the one at the bottom left is #24. The circle at the left is an iodine bucket for disinfecting boots. Sows are fed by hand at this stage using a wheelbarrow. (Illustration by the author)

out of its mouth, the piglet swallowed. Blanca repeated with a few more drops until the baby animal started drinking from the nozzle. Francisco, our manager, later walked by. "Pigs are like children. They claim all the teats and won't let the little ones have one," he explained as we watched a dominant baby animal bite the neck of a tiny one that had jumped for an unoccupied teat. The crates held fourteen or fifteen piglets while most sows have only twelve to fourteen working teats, meaning that piglets' natural social hierarchies can deteriorate the runt's fragile condition.

For ten days, until someone else was hired, Raul and I moved through the farrowing rooms in a circle, taking turns refilling and warming bottles, returning to clammy and milk-stained piglets every fifteen minutes with more liquid in an often-futile effort to keep them alive. I felt the hours tick away amid a blur of piglet shrieks, sticky residue of powdered milk, cold bodies, and back pain from sitting on the narrow plastic edge of farrowing crates. I was surprised to find that work in these rooms—places of abundant life, the ostensible opposite of the slaughterhouse—is experienced as a constant confrontation with near-death. But what I did not realize at the time was that Raul and I were among the first generation of workers to be formally assigned to act as human nurses. While powdered milk has been kept on confinement farms for decades to deal with the rare situation in which a single piglet is too weak to get sustenance, it was only in the late 2000s that "runt feeder" was turned into a routine task or job title.[1] This repetitive job is a product of systemic genetic changes—of transformations that made litter sizes swell larger than can be sustained biophysically by sows. Nursing runts of the litter is one small example of this part's basic argument: that human laborers are being turned into external prosthetics for hogs by taking on physiological functions that used to be autonomous. The biology of the industrial pig is not contiguous with its body. It requires expanding arrays of labor to survive.

One morning as we were making our rounds through farrowing rooms, the squeals of piglets were suddenly drowned out by a huge BANG! that sounded like an aluminum baseball bat slamming against concrete. Startled, Raul dropped his piglet. I thought something had gotten caught in the exhaust fans on the wall. As I glanced over, Raul was scanning the temperature systems and heating ducts that line the center of the ceiling. He located the source of the noise first. A four hundred-pound pregnant sow at the far end of the room was repeatedly weaving and knocking her skull against one of

5.4 **FARROWING CRATES** Rooms are kept dark and warm for the piglets, as one manager put it, "to imitate nesting." The humidity and smell in these rooms makes it hard to stay in one for more than ten minutes. Another manager once claimed, "It bugs me. . . . It gets under your skin. It's hard to breathe."

the metal bars of her farrowing crate. BANG! BANG! BANG! The sound was so loud, ricocheting off walls. We both ran over and stared, frozen, at the sow for at least thirty seconds. "What's she want?" asked Raul as we walked around the crate. We tried to keep our distance from the seemingly erratic animal. BANG! BANG! BANG! We positioned ourselves on the sow's right side, trying to follow the leftward direction of her head to see whether she was pointing us toward something. Thinking she was hungry, I ran to get a scoop of feed, but the sow did not acknowledge me. Raul checked her water nozzle. It worked fine. The rhythmic skull smacking was inexplicable. A red welt was starting to form on her forehead.

Raul and I sprinted down the long hall outside the farrowing room, our coworkers giving us puzzled looks as we passed. When we found our manager, Francisco, taking inventory in the workshop, Raul shouted, "There's a crazy sow!" Without thinking, I blurted out, "Please go check on it! I think it's trying to kill itself!" After returning, Francisco solemnly, even sheepishly,

5.5 **SUCKLING PIGLETS** These suckling newborn piglets still have tails, indicating that they are between one and four days old.

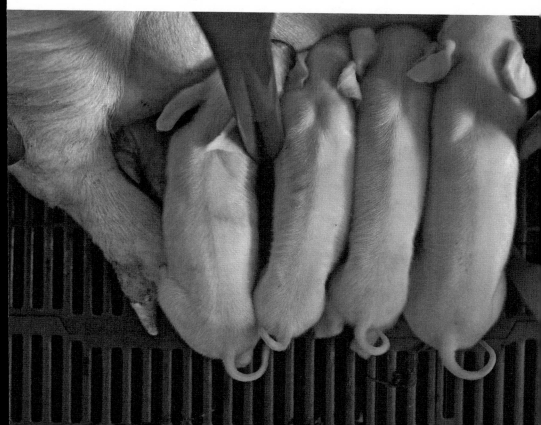

explained to us that this is a rare behavior. "This is what happens when we give the Lutalyse," he said. "The sows try to nest, but they don't have that here. They can't nest."

That sow weaving her head against confining metal bars can stand as a profound symbol of the factory farm, though it is more than just that. It is a reminder of how agribusiness magnifies some evolutionary behavior—such as reproductive instincts—only to radically deny others. The many factors and underlying practices that forced this sow to unwittingly injure herself get at the core of this part's concerns. Across the pages that follow, I suggest that this evolutionary-instinctual protest was a sign and symptom of the modern hog's changing relationship to human labor. Industrial hogs are becoming *overworked* in two senses. First, each type of hog is being refined to do only one thing—emit pheromones, ovulate, gestate, or metabolize feed—with increasing intensity. Second, prior historical rounds of engineering and histories of human-hog working engagement now require new intensities and intimacies of human labor to be sustained. Let me take this step by step.

DIVISIONS OF LABOR AND ANIMALITY

It was the execution of the photograph that begins this part of the book that forced me to rethink the human-hog relationships that underlie standardized life (see figure 5.1). The image is a series of one thousand different frames that have been digitally stitched together. The image's execution required the human subject of the photo—a forty-something-year-old man who spends his days driving around the countryside, inspecting animals in different growing barns for illness—to stand in one place for ninety minutes. When my photographic collaborator, Sean Sprague, needed to adjust the lighting in the barns, he gave the man a short break while I acted as his body double. I was shocked to find that I could not last more than two minutes. The hogs would circle me, nip at my knees, and knock me over. I did not have the bodily habitus to interact with these two hundred-pound hogs that were four-and-a-half months old and collectively penned; I could not hold my hands in such a way to corral the animals, stop their nipping, make them circle rather than charge me.

Conversely, one might also say that these pigs could not figure out how to interact with me. They had not encountered a person who held his body in this manner. This was jarring because, after working at breeding farms, I

5.6 ONE-MONTH-OLD PIGS
IN GROWING BARN
These recently weaned
pigs are in the early
stages of growth.

thought I knew how to act around hogs pretty well. It dawned on me that I had knowledge of pregnant sows and baby piglets as they live in individual crates—I could enact forms of labor that allowed us to get on together—but I knew little about how to behave with open-penned, nearly grown meat hogs. Meanwhile, there are many workers who have perhaps never encountered a boar, sow, piglet, slaughtered carcass, or rendered fat. Some have gained rich expertise and bodily habitus with open-penned four-month-old pigs. But due to concerns that pig diseases can transfer across workers' bodies (recall chapter 2), their labor is embedded primarily in this stage of porcine life.

This moment opened up ways to think about the conjoined division of labor and animality. In his study of the modern honeybee, Jake Kosek (2010, 670) writes: "What it means to be human is a product of the shifting cartography of what it is to be animal." Read from the American factory farm, the geographer's cartographic reference is helpful: as new components are added to this corporate *map* of economically significant dimensions of industrial animality, they are gradually converted into forms that are mediated by human labor. The underlying proposition of the factory farm is that more profitable pork will be attained only via the ongoing laboring mediation of animal biologies at deeper and more specialized facets of existence. From this vantage point, the story of industrial agriculture is not one of "dominating nature" but, instead, a matter of exerting social energy to make forms of life require new qualities of human labor to be sustained. The American factory farm is not a project of detached human mastery over hogs so much as it is one of reengineering human communities and embedding their labor in novel ways through the porcine species' changing life-and-death cycle.

Yet there may be irony in anchoring a book on agribusiness in the politics of work and the remaking of human being, because most commentators tend to define factory farms by their *lack* of human labor. From one side, agribusiness sympathizers claim that industrial pork is an efficient way to make meat. By this they mean, as we have seen, that agribusiness requires less in terms of labor (and land) costs than does any other farming system (McBride and Key 2013). These authors, often those who are fixated on lowering the market price of meat, are not altogether wrong. Labor costs per unit of pork chop have dramatically decreased in the national aggregate over the past fifty years. There are, after all, far fewer people employed in agriculture than ever before (Leonard 2014; Paarlberg 2010; Paarlberg 2016). But such abstract statistics in the aggregate tell us relatively little about the increasingly small

5.7 EATING IN A NURSERY BARN
At this point, pigs should grow at a fairly uniform pace, though minor differences in bodily form and temperament will accrue as each pen forms a hierarchy of dominance. The result is that some pigs will get less food. Note the scratches on the ear from a recent fight on the rightmost pigs.

handful of communities and workers who must endure elevated concentrations of swine. Those statistics are born of political economic processes that unequally concentrate the weight of an entire species on the exploited backs of a hyperproductive few. Moreover, they do not account for the unpaid labor provided by human workers and hogs, work that has become necessary to sustain the anthropogenic fragility of the species (see Moore 2015). Maintaining this scale and degree of uniform hogs over time has led to an explosion of new qualities and quantities of undernoticed work: paid and unpaid, inside and outside of formal workplaces, within Dixon and even around the planet. Indeed, the notion of an industrial pig—or an industrialized nature, more generally—that I develop in this section is an organism that is riveted with contradictions in that its biophysical survival has come to require human work, even as that labor can be seen as hostile to the species as it sustains conditions of life that are deleterious to animals.

LUTALYSE

Of the many drugs that we injected into hogs, the clear vials of Pfizer's Lutalyse (dinoprost tromethamine, a prostaglandin) were the only ones that elicited a strong reaction from my coworkers. Lutalyse is a birth induction drug that ensures sows will farrow no later than 114 days from the moment of conception, timed to take place during the regular working day. Piglet mortality is reduced when workers are present to pull animals out of the birth canal with their lubricated arms every twenty minutes during farrowing—a task called "sleeving"— especially at a moment in time when new generations of sows are having an

5.8–5.10 FOUR-MONTH-OLD HOGS IN GROWING PENS At mid-weight, growing hogs are again moved to "finisher" barns. At this point, mortality rates decline significantly. As one manager described this point in the process, "The barns raise the hogs now."

overabundance of offspring, with massive litter sizes and blocked birth canals (chapter 6).

Lutalyse was a complicated drug on the farms. Pregnant women, such as Maria, were expressly forbidden from entering the drug storage closet. Senior workers refused to touch the drug, claiming that mere contact with the vials made their throats constrict. However, it was also amongst the most "moral" of porcine drugs. Berkamp Meats—deemed the most community-centered of the area's factory farms—might have used Lutalyse at a higher rate than the others did. Managers were proud that they could ensure their employees would have a regular 8–5 job, Monday through Friday, while other corporations' work regimens were structured around the temporal unpredictability of their sows' uterine contractions and extended into evenings.[2] Many coworkers left other companies for this one as they were starting families because they wanted to know in advance that they could pick up their children from daycare, participating in the kinship rhythms of standardized industrial time. Whether through bearing similar mammalian bodies or competing temporal interests, Lutalyse was distinguished for creating types of farmwork at the same moment that it manifested hormonal states in animals; the induction drug materialized moments of cross-species proximity and competition. Seaming livelihood and ways of life across species, Lutalyse at once intensified labor in the working-day window, while providing an escape from labor on an animal that now seems to require almost constant supervision. A means of coping with the growing demands of the industrial pig, Lutalyse is a precarious tool to maintain industrial time amid an industrial animal biology that now exceeds it.

STEREOTYPIES

The sow weaving her head against the metal bars of a crate was a rare expression of stereotypical behavior, defined by ethologists as repetitive actions that are invariable in form and serve no obvious function in terms of play, work, or bodily reproduction. Left to their own devices, sows will make a nest out of foliage before they settle down to give birth. When they are locked in a metal-and-concrete farrowing crate without straw, their nesting instinct—exaggerated through injections of prostaglandin—can occasionally transform into behavior such as head weaving. Working in factory farms means confronting a display of subtler stereotypies, such as rooms full of sows compulsively biting their bars, or others seemingly oblivious to the world as they repetitively chew the air or root their noses raw in the concrete floor. Stereotypies are potent reminders of the many other ways of life and times suspended in limbo in the projects of capitalist modernity (see Pandian 2009).

Applied ethologists explain the stereotypy either as occurring because of an environmental blockade to evolutionarily ingrained behavior or as the behavioral product of an environment without any stimulation. The animal welfare scientist David Fraser (2008, 142–44) complicates these definitions of the stereotypy. He suggests that other scholars overlook the function of a stereotypy: rather than being useless noise, stereotypies can reduce an animal's level of emotional arousal, acting to calm pigs in stressful situations. But regardless of whether it is grasped as a matter of being frustrated, "bored," or a defense mechanism, the stereotypy is, in this context, a potent manifestation of a being whose evolutionary behavior has been estranged as human labor. This is a species that is left with very little to do except repetitiously metabolize, gestate, give birth, and nurse.

In recent years, scholars in anthropology and geography have initiated an important dialogue on the relation between nonhuman nature and capitalist work (Beldo 2017; Moore 2015; Tsing 2015). Resisting the chauvinism of prior Marxian theories that posit human work as the prime mover of the world (see, e.g., Vogel 1988), as the singular source of worldly creation, or *poesis*, these authors argue that capitalist value depends on the unpaid work of nonhuman beings. That pigs give capital these kinds of "free gifts"—or that capital appropriates the unrecognized work of nonhuman others—is a compelling way to think about factory farms (cf. Tsing 2013). Pheromones, gestation, and digestion are all biophysical porcine processes that are not solely "authored" by wage labor, even if they are necessary for wage labor to accrue value (see

5.11 **A PORTRAIT OF A HOG**
A four-month-old hog "poses" in the finisher barns.

33

also Beldo 2017; Kosek 2010, 669; Labban 2014). But the factory farm is also constituted—as the source of standardization and of some of its violence—by an attempt to reject some of these "free gifts." The ideal of factory farms, however impossible this might be to realize in practice, is one in which every biological function of the porcine species is tinged and adjusted through human work. The logic of standardized life, in a nutshell, is of mediating human work through hogs' physiological processes to cultivate uniformity. We might say that agribusiness has its own theory of animal labor: all pigs work, but not the same way. Standardized porcine life is being embodied, enacted, and buttressed by human workers as much as it is by industrial pigs.

HORMONE WORKERS

Yet to frame the industrial animal as constituted by, and dependent on, standardized (and standardizing) labor might be counterintuitive, given that we rarely hear about the diverse hands that underlie meat. Many instead describe how the indoor life of the American hog is riskily sustained through the use of antibiotics mixed into feed, which keep confined hogs uniformly growing despite cramped conditions (see Blanchette 2019; Kirchhelle 2018). The pig is routinely fed and injected with a cocktail of lincomycin, zinc bacitracin, tetracycline, sulfamethazine, and penicillin, matched with dozens of vaccines, vitamins, and beta-agonists such as ractopamine that promote muscle leanness. Such drugs maintain the industrial species in a dual sense: they sustain its raw life in barns teeming with illness and regulate its carnal composition with semi-predictable rates of growth and fat-to-muscle ratios.

But while such drugs for life garner much media reporting due to the risks of generating antibiotic resistance genes that can move through microbial communities off of the farm, relatively little attention is paid to another, ubiquitous class of chemicals: the drugs for labor. These scores of injections are omnipresent on factory farms. Like the plantation horse blood discussed in chapter 4, they are designed to synchronize hormonal statuses across groups of animals. Enacting a chemical massification of hogs, hormonal drugs compress biological time into industrial time while temporarily manifesting the ideal porcine state of the factory farm: a herd of identical sows.[3] As a farm worker, I would rarely encounter antibiotics except during a visit to a feed mill, where fifty-pound bags are stacked on pallets against the walls, ready to be mixed and pelletized into feed. Occasionally we would inject milky-white liquid penicillin or clear "linco" into breeding animals with leg lameness as part of a last-ditch effort to heal their infections. But many mornings were, instead, consumed by carefully managing animal hormones with plastic syringes, disposable needle tips, and 30 ml vials of liquid drugs in hand. We would slowly, slowly move behind animals in their gestation crates so as not to provoke a sudden reaction. We would cover the glint of the needle, which tends to scare the animals, with our latex gloves. Alarming a given sow at this crucial moment can result in her forever reacting with rage when a human worker enters her gestation crate, permanently rendering her untreatable. Animal welfare researchers have also found that sows who are scared of human workers may also gestate smaller and less robust litters (Hemsworth 2003).

Some drugs are used to ensure, for example, that sets of sows—particularly unbred gilts—enter into estrous on the day that they are slated for insemination. Others, such as injections of oxytocin, intensify sows' uterine contractions so they deliver all of their piglets within the supervised nine-hour working day. Exaggerating mammalian processes into tight temporal windows, these labor-saving *and* labor-intensifying drugs have the effect of coming to act on the injectors to compel workplace action. They exposed us to animals

5.12 **GROWN HOGS IN A FINISHER BARN** A "load" of hogs in finisher barns for final fattening. These animals are almost 285 pounds and will likely be slaughtered within the week.

that can be worked on within industrial time while ensuring that many porcine behaviors—right down, notably, to the stimulation of hormones—were mediated by human action.

The sheer number of injections to which the modern pig is subjected is stunning; as a result, abscesses and broken needle tips lost in hogs' flesh have become a large economic concern within the industry. Some companies have even taken up old Soviet needleless injection systems that were never put into use for mass-inoculation on humans, repurposing the technology on factory farms. Dover Foods injected hogs thirty-two million times in 2009.

But what I want to emphasize is that the very existence of someone in a workplace who can, on a given day, be called "the hormone worker" is itself a reflection of how the human division of labor has been cleaved into the fissures of the porcine species. In a quite tangible sense, *the pig* as a unified single organism no longer exists in this system. Much as we read in the previous chapter on instinct, each worker spends chunks of the day tending to increasingly delimited and specific porcine components such as hormones, nursing, perceptions, or bedsores. The idea that there is one person who serves as the hormone worker is an illustration of how formerly autonomous porcine qualities, which once "belonged" to and were generated by the porcine species, are becoming alienated from pigs' biology and transformed into terrains of alienable human labor.[4] This relationship of alienation, in turn, is the ground on which new forms of human-animal intimacy are arising.

SIX **STOCKPERSON**
Love, Muscles, & the Industrial Runt

THE RUNTING OF LIFE

On January 19, 2015, the *New York Times* set off a firestorm after publishing an exposé of an obscure U.S. Department of Agriculture (USDA) farm animal research laboratory in rural Nebraska. The author of the investigation, Michael Moss, worked with a veterinarian whistle-blower to reveal how taxpayer-funded government scientists were conducting experiments to recreate mammalian natures for agribusiness's benefit. The center's founding director encapsulated its mission in a 1981 article, lamenting the "inefficient" state of farm animal vitality. How could science accept fixed reproductive limits to cattle, he rhetorically asked, when species such as catfish give birth to one thousand times their weight in offspring (Moss 2015a)? Over the decades that followed, scientists at the U.S. Meat Animal Research Center (USMARC) would work with the goal of increasing the litters of pigs, cows, and sheep to generate more profit per animal.

Using Freedom of Information Act requests, Moss unveiled scenes of suffering that, according to another commentator, reflect an "American horror story" (Bershadker 2015). Weak unviable lambs were abandoned by their mothers and left to starve in fields unassisted by researchers. For thirty-one years, efforts to make cows systematically birth twins and triplets led to deformed calves. Moss witnessed piles of dead piglets, crushed by their maternal sows. In the face of outcry against genetic violence, USDA Secretary Tom Vilsack ordered a moratorium on new experiments at the center (Moss 2015b). Six months later, operations resumed with minor changes following a report by auditors that the experiments fell within the ethical norms of industry standard practices (U.S. Department of Agriculture 2015).

While it is tempting to cry foul, we might instead sit for a moment with the implications of the auditors' findings. The practices of the center are perfectly normal. The USMARC is indistinguishable from many other pivotal American and international sites that are dedicated to actively remaking animal natures. Indeed, what I find perhaps most jarring about sites such as the one above is how they might reflect an unspoken consensus in global agribusiness about the future of domesticated animal vitality. Elite agricultural actors—scientists, economists, and public relations pundits—seem to believe that the gradual increase in reproductive capacity is inevitable. After ten years of research, I remain struck that I have rarely read a pork industry commentator forecast a future scenario in which sows' litter sizes could decrease; it appears to be near-impossible in the industry to encounter a conceptual or ethical limit proposed for sows' biological reproductive capacity (Eckblad 2011). The idea that litter sizes must interminably grow has become so taken for granted that even animal welfare scientists—those most concerned with the pig's bodily integrity—have taken a central measure of humane farming conditions to be whether the sow reproduces at high levels (McGlone and Pond 2003). Within the cultural norms of many of these elite American agricultural engineers and scientists, interminable proliferation seems to have become the unstated essence and telos of animal life.[1]

By this chapter's end, I aim to illustrate how the fallout of places such as the USMARC is being carried on migrant workers' shoulders. But for now, consider an esoteric fact: for the past fifteen years, piglets born in the United States appear to have been shrinking. This is perhaps one of the less glaring transformations of animal nature to take place over the past century. Sows went from roaming pastures and rooting in soil to being confined in gestation crates. They were bred for quite radical forms of docility, such that they can survive in tiny crates without exhibiting behavior that is excessively debilitating. A variety of breeds suitable to different climates were replaced with a pool of regularly updated "models" generated out of isolated compounds in North Dakota and Manitoba. In spite of these many waves of industrial restructuring of hog nature and farming, however, one thing that remained a constant was that a healthy newborn piglet would weigh three to four pounds.

Although it went unnoticed by even agribusiness's most ardent critics, these basic dimensions of porcine vitality—what constitutes a normal pig at the moment when it enters the world—had started to shift by the mid-2000s.

Institutes and genetics companies, primarily in Europe but also in the United States, were using selective breeding to develop what pork production magazines now call the "hyperprolific sow."[2] These creatures ovulate 300 percent more eggs than previous generations of hogs. The goal of this single-trait selection was to generate a substantial increase in litter sizes, enabling corporations to create more animals using less space and feed to house sows. Indeed, it would appear hard for companies *not* to try adopting sows with hyperprolific qualities. Unlike in typical industries, where human labor is the primary cost, the main expense in animal farming is feed. An average of one extra pig per litter in corporations that own 100,000 sows—which would allow them to house fewer sows—means that they can save $25 million per year.

All of this boils down to a figure that is omnipresent in pork industry discussions: 30 P/S/Y. The number refers to the average number of pigs that a farm's sows bear in a calendar year. In the 1990s, 20 P/S/Y was an achievement reserved for the top 10 percent of all U.S. farms. Soon thereafter, an influential veterinarian declared the statistical mean of 30 P/S/Y to be "the new goal. It's in our sights, it's no longer a dream" (quoted in Vansickle 2009). For pork industry observers and forecasters, 30 P/S/Y has become the new status to which all farms and sows must gravitate; it is deemed the measure of porcine output required for future corporations to remain competitive as profit margins tighten due to low market prices and feed-grain costs. Nor does it appear like it will stop there: some European farms are claiming that they can successfully reach 35 P/S/Y across a herd, and individual animals are touted as being capable of reaching 40 P/S/Y (Vansickle 2009).

Only recently has the ideology of infinite proliferation shown flashes of tension. As genetic "improvement" has made litter sizes increase, ovulation rates appear to be starting to outpace the sow's uterine capacity—leading to the runting of piglets, while also resulting in an unbalanced sow that is no longer able to nurse all of her young. Over the past twenty-five years, the average litter size in the United States has increased by 30 percent. Between 1989 and 2014, litter sizes swelled from 7.86 to 10.31. Even these generic numbers from the USDA's farm surveys are deceptive, for they include small farmers. Swine Management Services, a benchmarking program that anonymously includes 757 corporate farms, placed the average litter size of corporations at 13.16, with those in the top ninety-seventh percentile sustaining an astounding 15.11 pigs per litter in 2011 (Miller 2011b). On average, sows have only fourteen working teats, meaning that single-trait selection for ovulation on some farms exceeds the species' biological nursing capabilities. A large proportion of farmworkers' days, as we have seen, are now spent nursing piglets with powdered milk.

While we typically understand industrialization to be premised on the reduction of labor, 30 P/S/Y seems to be having the paradoxical effect of requiring new intensities of human-pig entanglement in order to be sustained. On the one hand, acts that used to be performed autonomously as "free" biological action by pigs—nursing piglets and muscle development being examples—are now assisted by humans. On the other, farms with highly prolific sows are increasingly being advised to dedicate more of their labor time to monitoring the birth of these weaker piglets (see, for instance, Gadd 2015). Even with constant supervision of these pigs that are engineered to be frail, death losses are rising. Some 12.6 percent of piglets on the largest farms—those most likely to host sows with hyperprolific qualities—died before weaning in 2012.[3] Yet farms are still gaining more overall living pigs per litter with hyperprolific sows while reporting a reduction in expenditures per pig.

This industrial proliferation is also, paradoxically, leading to a strange sort of de-domestication or postmodern type of feral life.[4] While the fact that larger litters result in lower birth weights and less stable pigs is well documented, there is (as yet) relatively little published research on the physiology of this phenomenon. What is clear is that runting is not universal in its effects on populations of pigs. It exposes pigs to multiple traumas and has the effect of making bodies less predictable than previous generations. The problem of the engineered runt is thus not just a temporary one of beginning at a small state (see Foxcroft et al. 2006). Intrauterine growth retardation results in an animal that develops at a slower rate across its lifetime (Smith et al. 2007). To name just a few of the runt's traumas: its number and type of muscle fibers are severely impacted (Foxcroft and Town 2004; Town et al. 2004); the functioning of its heart and liver is impaired (Wang et al. 2008); damage to its large intestine means it can no longer properly absorb some basic amino acids such as arginine (Wu et al. 2006); and its brainstem is poorly myelinated, affecting the animal's coordination, reflexes, and general ability to move in the world as an infant (Avant 2014). A new kind of animal appears to be emerging within concentrated animal feeding operations—one with new needs in terms of its dietary and care regimens. Yet despite the economic generation of animal disability (cf. Taylor 2017), large P/S/YS are being sustained as a norm.

As the depth of trauma to hogs comes to be acknowledged in pork industry literature, research monies are flowing to address runting. In spite of its obvious injuries, however, 30 P/S/Y continues unabated as an investment goal.

Researchers at the USMARC have moved from a singular focus on ovulation rates to trying to heal piglets. These scientists are now conducting experiments to select for larger uteruses, increase nutrient blood flow in utero, or for the use of drugs to supplement the neurochemical deficiencies of runted piglets (see, e.g., Berg 2009; Vallet et al. 2002, 2014). Others are trying to develop special markets and meat grades for runted hogs, creating a niche market of meat (Melgares 2016; chapter 10). Meanwhile, some aspects of runting may be invisibly and subtly affecting every single pig born to a sow with hyperprolific qualities, regardless of the baby animal's apparent litter size, weight, or external appearance. Given the increase in embryos generated by these sows, two seemingly identical litters of twelve pigs born could have been prenatally programmed differently by crowding and embryo death in early gestation (Foxcroft and Town 2004). Were these trends to continue in this direction, runting may become a basic condition of much of porcine life. As George Foxcroft, the former director of the Swine Research and Technology Center in Alberta, puts it, "We have a little pig that is severely compromised, and no amount of love, crossfostering, treatment, or feeding will make him a normal pig. He is not" (quoted in Miller 2007). I have never worked with a sow that was technically "hyperprolific." However, my period of time in Sow #6's farrowing rooms was spent working with a proto-generation of what are now called hyperprolific sows. Despite having cared for hundreds of animals, it is uncanny to think that many of the pigs with whom I worked closely may have been systematically runted.

On another level, the classic uncertainty in the very meaning of mass-production—whether it indicates producing lots of things in "mass" versus making identical things for the "masses" (Hounshell 1984)—is playing out in the sow's womb in ways that result in qualitative transformations to piglets' bodily form. Farms are producing a new type of meat hog characterized by a vital gap that requires specialized human labor to make these frail beings self-sufficient organisms. As Donna Jones (2011, 4) writes, "If biological life indeed consists in the sum of functions that resists death," then the American meat pig is a strange animal in that its quantitative maximization results in an animal that cannot resist death in life. In this chapter, my aim is to analyze how engineers' deep-seated attachment to animal proliferation refracts into the labor process, tracking this subjectivity alongside its relation to forms of craft and empathy that are emerging with *increased* industrialization.

The word "runt" is used colloquially as a relative term, denoting the smallest or weakest animal in a given litter. Runts are developmentally stunted beings, and their traumas are accentuated by malnourishment or injury by being at the bottom of a litter's social pecking order. To be clear, runting is a naturally occurring phenomenon in swine, due in part to the shape of the species' uterine horn. Prior to the emergence of sows with hyperprolific qualities, about two percent of pigs were born runted.[5] But what ultimately distinguishes the runt is not really its birthweight alone. It is, instead, the fact that it is an animal that is incapable of unassisted living. Thus, it is no surprise that saving the runt of the litter has long served as an icon of good agricultural husbandry in stories and fiction. However, what is striking is the way that industrial agriculture is reversing this mythical socionatural contract, whereby the farmer was able to secure a just and ethical livelihood in the taking of life by improving on what "nature" naturally makes. The runt is no longer a rare exception, a natural occurrence; nor can it be defined in relation to the rest of an otherwise normal litter. On some factory farms, it is possible that runting-like symptoms are affecting a large proportion of American hogs, debilitating the species as a whole in ways that render it dependent on the intimate *and* exploited care of workers.

THIRTY-FOUR WAYS TO DIE

On an American factory hog farm there are thirty-four officially codified ways that an animal can die. Companies' ideal manner is that a hog grows to be roughly 285 pounds within six months and is killed in the slaughterhouse by having its throat slit prior to disassembly by one thousand workers in forty-five minutes (chapter 8). A less desirable mode of killing is when farmworkers are forced to euthanize sick or injured breeding animals (or large grown meat hogs) by shooting them in the head with a bolt gun. A company form for recording mortality demarcates thirty-one other statistically significant types of death. They include bleeding, blind anus, chilling, clostridia, coccidiosis, congenital, deformed, E coli, greasy pig, injury/trauma, joint infection, laid on, low viability, meningitis, other, other disease, pneumonia, pseudorabies, rotavirus, runt, ruptures, savaged, scours, septicemia, shaker, spraddle leg, starvation, stepped on, strep suis, TGE, and umbilical infection.

Such bureaucratic lists speak to the biological fragility of confined pigs. They indicate that, as a Dover Foods veterinarian once put it, "These are not very hardy animals." The list of thirty-one types of death, however, is a reflection of more than just frailty. Its absences—the fact that there are *only* thirty-one ways that a piglet can die—suggest a shift in the state of animal death following the move to confinement. Pigs prematurely die when they are raised in pasture outdoors, and they die in more diverse ways. For example, the list does not contain a number 32, coyote, or a number 33, heat stroke. The condition of possibility for writing a list of (only) thirty-one deaths is radical in its projection that death can be perfectly scripted and anticipated.

That said, causes of death are often multiple, especially with complex categories such as "runt" (number 20) that encompass diverse traumas. They can be hard to narrow down with a glance at the piglet's body. In most cases I would appeal to the judgment of my more experienced coworkers, such as Blanca, Robin, or Rocio. I would pick a dead piglet out of a crate, exit into the hall, and hold it up by a hind leg, twirling it around to give them a three-dimensional view of the corpse. They would shrug their shoulders. *Doce? Doce*, or reason number 12, indicates "laid on." A sow crushing her young is the most common form of piglet death within factory farms. Definitively identifying a *doce* is easy when the piglet's corpse is dented with the pattern of the concrete slats on the floor. In most cases, however, the piglet escapes from under the sow and dies in the corner of the crate from internal injuries. Thus, *doce* was what Blanca and others taught me to mark when I was uncertain about how a piglet died. Mitigating *doces* in the confined spaces of pig production is itself a motivating rationale for the farrowing crate. The crate's metal bars curl under the sow's body and force her to slowly arch into a sitting position, instead of plopping her body down and crushing a piglet as it scuttles from one side of the crate to another.

During my time in farrowing, there was little pressure by management to investigate the root cause of piglet death. Never in my time in the barns did I learn how signs of disease outbreaks such as coccidiosis, septicemia, or TGE might be etched onto corpses. And I still do not know how to determine the difference between low viability as a singular category versus the other signs that indicate a piglet could not survive to slaughter. Multiple symptoms could be synonyms for low viability: savaged (a piglet that has been attacked by its litter mates), spraddle leg (one with weak muscles that cannot walk straight), or shaker (a condition of the nervous system that makes pigs twitch). The numbers are holdovers from when management was unsure of the leading causes of death. The practice was maintained in case they later wanted to run an experiment that appraised the ubiquity of a form, at which point they would teach employees the death event's signs.

However, I often found the fifteenth category—"other"—to be among the most perplexing. It is supposed to indicate a form of death that cannot be contained using the thirty other categories. A clear example of a number 15 is when a concrete grate collapsed in a farrowing crate during the evening. My coworker found a piglet drowned in the liquid effluent below. Yet number 15, "other," would appear frequently on spreadsheet columns, in multiple workers' handwriting, despite the fact that it is supposed to be a rare exception. It appeared to stem from some disagreements as to the logic of death's ultimate cause. Some people occasionally marked number 15, "other," when it was they who had euthanized the piglet by inserting it into one of the large plastic picnic coolers. This form of dying via carbon dioxide euthanasia is the thirty-fourth and final form of officially recognized death.

Repurposed blue-and-white Igloo coolers line the walls of every hallway outside farrowing rooms. They are connected to carbon dioxide tanks by a thin black rubber tube inserted into a hole on their side. The coolers are a recent invention, instituted in the mid-2000s so that workers would no longer directly experience killing by hand. Before the coolers, the sanctioned mode of euthanasia was "thumping." It involved bashing the weak piglet's head against the concrete floor or wall by swinging its hind legs with such a velocity that its neck snaps on impact. Workers lobbied against being forced to partake in such tactile euthanasia. Some of Dover's senior managers viewed the use of carbon dioxide coolers as a means of demasculinizing and democratizing pork industry labor. As Graham, the head of Dover Foods' Live Side put it, "Women are especially bothered by thumping, and we have to make sure that everyone can work here." Though framed in a language of accommodation to some primordial femininity, the blue coolers are better framed as a managerial means of explicitly attempting to transform the farrowing rooms into "feminized" spaces (cf. Salzinger 2004). The coolers mobilize the materiality of piglet euthanasia to *produce* particular kinds of nurturing femininities for industrial expansion.[6] In all of these senses, piglet death is wildly overdetermined in the farrowing barns. The death of piglets—though "bad" for the bottom line—is also standardized, delimited, and mobilized to produce ideal forms of workplace subjectivity. By the time I was working at Sow #6, thumping had become a distant memory that was unthinkable even in extreme circumstances. We once ran out of carbon dioxide in Sow #6 and would not get a delivery for another day. I asked my manager, Francisco, whether we could "thump" the suffering piglets. He looked at me with an aghast expression, sternly refusing.

The occurrence of number 15s indexes confusion over culpability for death. But there is a poetic twist in these accidents of interpretation. The occurrence of number 15, "other," on workplace forms was reflective of a crucial workplace sensibility. The overriding sentiment among some employees was that the cause of any given death was not the biological condition; nor was it tethered to the biological fragility of these confined animals. Instead, it was based on the worker's failure to "save" the individual piglet. Guided by the scenes of brutal violence in undercover exposé videos—alongside the fact that the labor process of the factory farm is premised on a desire for porcine uniformity—my assumption was that I would find a group of farmworkers who were unable to resist the infectiousness of porcine instrumentalization. I expected to meet people who—consciously or not—saw piglets as widgets, as disposable iterations of generalized industrial pigness. Instead, my coworkers exhibited sensitivity toward preserving every porcine being; some people would labor to the point of exhaustion to heal individual piglets, allowing them to be industrially slaughtered at six months. What, then, does it mean to "save" a pig born for slaughter?

THE STOCKPERSON

Long before my rubber-clad feet touched the concrete slats of corporate breeding barns, managers at all four companies hinted that there was something essential lacking in their employees' orientation with respect to the animal in confinement. Human resource managers claimed that their mission was to mold workers into a nebulous figure that they called the Stockperson. At Cardinal Packing, for example, a manager cut me off when I asked him what qualities make an ideal worker. "We don't want quote-unquote workers, as you put it," he scoffed. "We want stockpeople. . . . We've created a system [in the pork industry]. We should be creating a livelihood." As these managers first recounted this figure, it was someone who grasped the nature of the porcine species—abstracted from its animation in industrial confinement barns—in such purity that she or he could work without supervision. The task of management was to impart ways of thinking, seeing, and behaving around this "natural" pig, even though workers had not experienced the animal outside confinement. The Stockperson could be interpreted as a discourse on workers' essential shortcomings and, perhaps, as a rare type of self-critique of hog farm industrialization.

Or take the words of Craig, a twenty-nine-year-old former sow-farm worker turned traveling salesman. He was responsible for marketing mechanical devices such as gestation crates, feeders, and insemination back weights to companies such as Dover Foods. Complaining about animal rights groups that were lobbying to eradicate gestation crates, he declared angrily, "In the next ten years there will be a huge shift. We are at the end of an era. What's going to happen? Husbandry's gonna be real crucial, but no one has that. We're gonna need skilled workers. . . . We've made so much progress. . . . It feels to me like . . . like . . . I don't know, it's like we're almost traveling back in time." By "husbandry" Craig meant animal handling and other Stockperson skills that, he claimed, no one has in this gestation crate-driven era of production. He believed that this generation of workers needs to know very little about the animal and that experience of porcine nature is entirely mediated through the metal gestation crates and feeders he sells.

Yet I started to gain a more complicated sense of this figure of the Stockperson over time through hearing about its negation, as managers fretted that their employees lacked a proper orientation to porcine life. Or so I came to glean in the corporate office of a leading executive named John. Recently employed by Trenton Produce, John was legendary in agribusiness circles for turning around struggling animal production operations. True to form, he ticked through the things he noticed going wrong within Trenton's breeding barns when he had first arrived a year earlier: wasted water and feedstuff, high piglet mortality, and excessive antibiotic use were all contributing to the operation's failures. But the main problems were animal welfare violations that he felt were symptomatic of these barns' degraded company culture. "We have zero tolerance for that sort of thing," he stated. "I think we're a lot more effective at taking raw people and building them," referring to the bad habits he believed previous employees had formed over time. "When I first started to work here, I had to let about ten people go in a couple different instances where . . . they was . . . Well, maybe they seemed like not big things: the boys were drawing gang signs on the sides of pigs." "What?!" I asked, uncertain about how drawing symbols on pigs could constitute abuse. "So I'm going out there and seeing all of this," John explained as I imagined him walking past rows of sows in gestation crates that were tagged with livestock markers in the shape of, say, Cripps insignias, "and I'm, like, you know, 'You just defaced an animal that is a part of our livelihood.' [The worker's] reaction was, 'Well, it's just an animal. It doesn't care,' and I said to him, 'Well, you need to go and work someplace else.'"[7]

John seemed to suggest that a handful of workers across the breeding barns under his charge—which annually conceive about one million animals—did not have an adequate sense of the hog's ontology as an economic creature. As we have seen, hog-breeding protocol dictates that when you finish artificially inseminating a sow, you must draw your initials on its back so other workers know which pigs are finished for the day. In theory, this also potentially allows companies to collect data that can map an employee's insemination technique in terms of conception rates. As I think about it today, John's workers might have been flaunting this individualizing discipline by signing their collective "gang" affiliations on animals, or perhaps they were suggesting a sense of possession of the animal as a product of their labor. The gang signs minimally reflected a lack of respect for the biological autonomy and corporate ownership of the hog. When I recounted the story to Graham, Dover Foods' head of live production, he laughed but also agreed with John. "Yeah, I'd be pissed. Even if they're just screwing around, it's like spray-painting our corporate office," he said, suggesting that such behavior indicates a faulty mind-set toward industrial life. "These are meat animals, you know? They're not our employees' pets."

When I told other executives this story, they laughed at its absurd specificities but agreed that tagging pigs with gang signs indexed a dangerous sense of possession that they were struggling against in the barns. Byron Ross, one of the directors of Berkamp, admitted that, although he rarely set foot in the hog barns, he could still relate to John's frustration:

> We found that one of our biggest animal welfare problems was that some of our employees won't let the sick pigs die. . . . For a long time, at our nurseries, we had basically a female crew, and for whatever reason . . . , some of them just have this mentality of [the pigs being human] babies. They have some ownership in their minds; they're invested emotionally in those pigs. It can be pretty tough. It's almost like a doctor, you know? Where you have a patient that's gonna die on you. Well, you know, that's pretty hard to take. You gotta be clinically detached or whatever. At the same time, you don't want people so detached that they see [the piglet] as a piece of steel or a rock, that doesn't have any feelings, that doesn't feel pain.

They're invested emotionally in those pigs. Byron later recounted that, during his early farm tours of farrowing barns, he would catch workers hiding sick piglets in their coverall pockets in order, as he put it, "to give them a chance to live." He noted that he had barred both piglet "thumping" and, on his ranch, euthanizing calves with a blow to the head with a steel pipe. Thumping and steel-pipe beatings were appropriate to a family farm era of agriculture before industrialization, he explained: "Twenty years ago, it was

147

fine. Everybody grew up with it. It's in their brains. They're the same ones that had a pig named Porky or whatever and fed it for a hundred days; then they . . . cut its throat and hung it up on the deal. Well, the people who are working in those positions now are not those same people." Ross articulated a universal dilemma of animal farming, noting that one has to be "clinically detached" and kill to allow life to proliferate. But this is also a narrative that emerges from the post-confinement era. Now the people tasked with making life are (nonwhite, often female) wage laborers who do not necessarily have a background with animals. One of management's tasks, he suggested, is to balance affects of (implicitly "feminine") attachment and (implicitly "masculine") detachment in the barns. Byron described his clinical species detachment as ingrained from growing up with and euthanizing animals on a ranch. He claimed that some workers, however, failed to understand that the task was to optimize life and labor by euthanizing the weak piglets with ailments in favor of maintaining the viable strong ones. He suggested that the mass-production of life makes some workers sensitive to piglets and, in turn, makes them maximize life to the point at which the weakest pigs suffer. Rather than an ethic of "making live and letting die" (Foucault 1978), Byron suggested, an out-of-control attachment to piglets was driving a one-sided ethic of making live to the point where "saving" pigs was abusive.

What unites these managerial speculations is not a concern with the industrial conditions of animal existence but, instead, the fraught figure of the industrialized *human* at the heart of these Stockperson worries. John, Byron, and Craig brought together workers' failure to assume the figure of the Stockperson at the intersection of race, gender, and temporality. From collectivist Mexican gang signs to primordially emotionally nurturing women, from deskilled laborers who could not grasp the animal's nature to a workforce without the agrarian background necessary for proper relations to life and death, what was intriguing in their statements was how the very industrial universalization of the farming labor force contains within itself risks that could implode the entire project.[8] In prior eras of hog farming, they suggest, there was diversity in the vital manifestation of pigs that required "husbandry" and, allegedly, one type of (white, male) universal farmer. In factory farms, there (allegedly) is one universal type of pig and a plethora of people with incommensurable pasts such that management must cultivate a universal subjectivity.

It was Barry, the Dover Foods pod manager who started working in the pork industry after his family's ranch collapsed in the 1980s, who offered the most interesting interpretation of the Stockperson. As we drank beer together at a local bar after a few years' acquaintance, he reminisced about his legacy in the pork industry as a player who had imported manufacturing theory paradigms to hog farming. "So who's going to replace all you [pod managers] in the next few years?" I asked as I came to realize multiple eras were drawing to a close. "That's the million-dollar question," he replied. "That's what worries us the most." He continued:

> Me and all the other guys [the pod managers] started in this industry when the pigs were outside, when we had natural mating, you know? You had to know a lot more about the animal in those days. All these new guys and gals only know what pigs are like in the barns, and we don't know if we're always going to have pigs in crates and barns. People today have a lot of profound knowledge, but they don't know how to work outside the system.[9]

They don't know how to work outside the system. Barry's figure of the ideal Stockperson—embodied by his own generation as witnesses to industrial shifts—is more complicated than an agrarian in tune with the timeless nature of the porcine species. It is instead a figure who has witnessed multiple eras of pork production and, in turn, multiple modalities and expressions of the porcine species. By witnessing the reduction of expressions of porcine nature through farrowing crates, the Stockperson is a person who can still remember latent or vestigial manifestations of pigness. The Stockperson exists in the present day—attuned to current manifestations of the industrial pig—but is also capable of being out of time, drawing on different paradigms and embodied memories of animal life. In this sense, past expressions of pigness are still embedded in and haunt the industrial pig but are blocked from manifestation via confinement. If I understand this correctly, the American meat pig is not genetically predetermined, but its fuller expressions of life are temporarily suspended or at least minimized. The escape of this buried vitality—a return to multiple kinds of pig—threatens to destabilize the project, including the ability to draw from a large labor pool of people from diverse backgrounds to work in the barns.

Much like Craig, Barry was concerned about the banning of gestation crates and the consequences for his system amid the popularity of pasture-raised or heritage pigs. But his worries suggested to me something more general: how the industrialization of pork and the standardization of porcine knowledge around one kind of pig can also potentially lead to the broader project's unraveling. While this could certainly happen through the enactment of legislation banning gestation crates or even confinement barns (deindustrialization), it leads me to think about what happens when the genetic potency of the sows reaches the point that it manifests new animal kinds (hyperindustrialization).

AN EXTRAORDINARY C-SECTION

One chilly morning in December, after unloading my wheelbarrow full of piglet corpses into a dumpster for collection by Dover Foods' "dead haul truck"—which, in 2009, transported fifty-two million pounds of deceased bodies to rendering (see chapter 10)—I was scrawling my birth and mortality figures on a record form:

FARROWING INFORMATION

Sow ID #706055 18 Born Alive, 1 Stillborn, 0 Mummified, 54 Pounds, Assisted 2, Room 3, Stall 20

Sow ID #414114 12 Born Alive, 1 Stillborn, 2 Mummified, 36 Pounds, Assisted 3, Room 3, Stall 24

Sow ID #701604 14 Born Alive, 3 Stillborn, 0 Mummified, 42 Pounds, Assisted 5, Room 3, Stall 8

PIG DEATH INFORMATION

Sow ID #410041 1 Dead, Reason = 12 (Laid On), Room 17, Stall 15

Sow ID #071176 1 Dead, Reason = 20 (Runt), Room 17, Stall 8

Sow ID #706076 1 Dead, Reason = 12 (Laid On), Room 2, Stall 5

Sow ID #712333 1 Dead, Reason = 26 (Spraddle Leg), Room 3, Stall 11

I was startled by an excited voice from behind me: "How many times does a sow's heart beat a minute?" I looked up to see Robin, a worker in her late thirties. I shrugged, trying to concentrate on not making mistakes because my manager, Francisco, would insist that I fill out the form again if there was an error. "Sixty-eight," she answered.

Born in Chihuahua, Robin had spent her teens and early adulthood in Los Angeles. In the early 2000s, she packed up and moved to Dixon after what was supposed to be a weekend visit for the *quinceañera* (15th birthday) of a friend's daughter. She did not imagine herself as a countryside sort of person.

But she was taken with the idea of her children growing up in a small town with steady jobs. The only employers in the region paying a decent wage—at least, for an urban-born woman of color deemed "unskilled"—were the pork corporations. She laughed about how little she had known about pigs when she started: "All there is are dogs over there in the city." But nine years later, Robin had worked for multiple companies and was one of the most authoritative farmworkers I met.

Robin followed me as I walked to the storage closet to shove tools into my pockets. "How long is a sow's uterus?" she called out in a high-pitched, teasing voice. "Four feet," she answered as she followed behind me. She trailed me out the door to the hall. "How many pints of blood are in a sow?" she asked, keeping up the mock education. Before she could sing out another factoid, I turned to her, annoyed, as we approached a group of workers standing in a circle around Francisco. "Why are you telling me this?" I asked. She laughed loudly, causing the others to glance over, and said, "I dunno. Sows are cool." Robin nodded at the group. "Are you ready?" she asked. "Ready for what?" I replied. Her eyes grew wide, matching her energy from before: "We're going to save the piggies."

As I reached the group, Ruben, a solemn man who rarely spoke, reached out his arm without looking my way and handed me one of the metal wire hooks that we used to control the legs of the large animals. Felipe was flipping a thick pair of box cutters in his hands while staring at his feet. Ruben repetitively tested the tightening button of his leg hook, its wire loop expanding and compressing with an irritating scratching noise. Gonzalo held forward the black plastic case that contained the farm's bolt gun, as if he was making an offering to Francisco. Raul looked white as a ghost, his eyes wider and even more startled than they normally were. Although I had walked in at the tail end of Francisco's speech, it quickly became clear that this was a moment of some significance. "I like to let nature do her work," he said. "But this is when we have to take responsibility. You all have your roles. Concentrate. We only have thirty seconds, a minute."

Francisco and Miguel then went into the nearest farrowing room. They emerged with an agitated sow, bellowing and trying to dig her hind hooves into the concrete. Francisco was dragging her forward with a red-roped boar harness tied around her neck. Blanca, Rocio, Maria, and Robin were standing across from us, gathered around a wheelbarrow filled with a granular substance for drying wet piglets, a bright heating lamp suspended over it. Following Ruben's lead, the four of us tried to position our wire hooks under the sow's feet as she stomped around and her piercing shrieks echoed down the length of the hall. As her right hind hoof stepped into the loop of my hook, and her right rear side pinned my lower body tightly against the metal wall, I tightened the lasso around the midpoint of her knee, holding tightly while digging my own knees into her soft side to create distance. The problem became evident: a mass of pink flesh hung out of the sow's anus, drooping to the floor. "Prolapse," Francisco indicated, noticing my stare. "We have to give her a C-section or her pigs will die."

"Listos [Ready]?" yelled Francisco as Miguel pressed the plastic nozzle of the bolt gun to the sow's furiously twisting forehead, trying to keep the tip of the shaft flush against her skull. Felipe stood next to the sow's flank, his knees bent and his legs tensed like a sprinter awaiting the opening call to start a race. The four leg pincers pulled in opposite directions, and a loud pop came from Miguel's gun. The sow dropped and lurched to her right side, twisting the shaft of my wire hook as her leg shot into the air. For a second all was still. But as the bullet bounced around in her brain, involuntary spasms of her legs began thrusting her torso across the ground as we tried to splay out her legs and hold her powerful twitching body steady so Felipe could safely work with his bolt cutters around her belly. "Fifteen seconds!" shouted Francisco as Felipe appeared to be tearing through layers of flesh. "Thirty seconds! Hurry up!" Felipe must have lost his grip on the bolt cutters, which fell into the sow's belly; he started ripping layers with his hands to get at the womb. Pints of blood pooled out around his knees and rubber boots.

"One minute! Focus!" Felipe pulled out the first of the piglets, unmoving and covered in placenta. He passed it to the women, a gendered division of labor forming on the spot around death and life, killing and nurturing. "Too late—they're dead," rang out several times as piglets were passed from the puddle of red. "Give them air!" I glanced over at the women and saw them blowing into the piglets' tiny mouths, flexing the piglets' front and hind legs together to resuscitate them, their hands covered in the sow's blood. As the seventh piglet came out, and they continued this emergency oxygen delivery, Robin shouted, "It's alive!" as one of the piglets started moving in her hands. There were more cheers as piglets emerged with a sliver of life remaining, a sense of relief settling in the hallway.

This event was extraordinary—not exceptional, but, following Charles Perrow (1984) and Gabrielle Hecht (2012), it was superordinary, an intensification of the norm. The C-section was a window into normal trends that have been concretizing within industrial pigs, farm labor, and animal capital over the past two decades, as moratoria on the territorial spread of factory farms in the United States has confined them in place. The factory farm's mode of growth has shifted from geographic expansion to intensification of the productivity of animals' reproductive tracts. I see the C-section as fundamentally reflective of the shifting *terrain* of animal life that farmworkers must now navigate in these barns.

First, the C-section offers a clear breakdown of the transition in the sow as a gestator of fetuses in the breeding segment to a nurturer of pigs in the farrowing stage. Second, the C-section illustrates the surprising degree of pride, culpability, and identity derived from the process by some workers. Robin's sow factoids came to appear as a way for her to express that she had done this before; that she was an expert because, having witnessed such an unusual event as a C-section, she had seen the interior of a sow. A sort of craft pride emerged based on being able to work with *rare* manifestations of porcine life. Finally, breathing life into piglets is a vivid image of the ways that intimate labor is becoming necessary to maintain the factory farm. This reliance on human embodiment is not diminishing with industrialization but intensifying. In the fragility of these industrial piglets that required mouth-to-mouth resuscitation, and that were "saved" when they would have perished without assistance, we can see the outlines of a different logic of farmwork.

SPECIES LOVE

What I want to suggest is that Byron Ross's ideal of "clinical detachment" may be becoming an increasingly hard affect to maintain, given the state of the modern animal. It was Robin Garcia who helped me start to grasp the kinds of "surplus" affect, for lack of a better term, that are necessary to commune with these "surplus" pigs. She was a "Day One"—someone who helped sows with their litters while stabilizing the newborns. These delivery workers are tasked with, as Robin liked to put it, "saving" the weakest animals from euthanasia. Her interactions with pigs were focused on the most fragile specimens that modern agriculture can generate. And her job was a matter not just of ensuring the survival of weak pigs but also of making them uniform by day twenty-one when they are weaned to nursery barns. "Saving" industrial pigs from euthanasia is to transform them into uniform animals that can grow relatively unattended in nursery and finishing barns for the next five months.

With the exception of the slaughterhouse, this twenty-one-day window prior to weaning is the most labor-intensive site in (porcine) animal agribusiness.

This brief period is dedicated to preparing hogs to grow relatively unsupervised within nurseries, growing barns, or finishing barns. They will be, as this phase is called in the industry, "processed" during this period to prepare them for a life that will lead to a uniform death. The steps of processing include bottle feeding, segregating litters into batches for suckling at sows' teats, scores of injected vaccinations, castration of baby males with a scalpel to ensure their flesh does not develop a musty odor called "boar taint," slowly introducing solid feeds, and tail docking—cutting off the piglet's tail with a propane-heated knife. Hogs in tight proximity to one another will nip at one another's tails, and if they draw blood they may begin to fight. In extreme cases, they may eat one another. At day twenty-one, two or three farrowing rooms of animals—roughly six hundred to one thousand pigs—will be weaned and taken on a truck to nurseries and then to growing barns. Each growing barn holds about one thousand hogs, often with multiple barns at a site. Once they reach those "finisher" stages, labor becomes minimal. Traveling crews will visit each barn once a day to inspect the feeders, check the hogs for signs of illness, and deliver medicine if the barn is undergoing a disease event. On average, these hogs will grow to ideal slaughter weight within six months—a rapid pace of growth owing in part to uniform conditions, genetics, doses of antibiotics in feed, and a range of thirteen different feed mixtures tied to maximizing weight gain at a particular age. The weight that is considered optimal for slaughter changes alongside world grain and pork prices, as pigs convert feed into muscle more slowly as they age. In essence, the ideal killing time is right at the end of the animals' equivalent to human "teenage" years. In 2010, the ideal slaughter weight fluctuated, but it hovered around 285 pounds.

The most effort, however, is concentrated into the piglets' first moments on earth, and the "Day One" is one of the most important positions in a breeding farm. Robin had developed a unique ethical approach for making pigs flourish in confinement barns, one that transformed her into a knowledgeable collector of industry's atypical life-forms. She had become a skilled archivist of the rare bodies and oddities that perhaps can be witnessed only in a concentrated large-scale breeding site, where one gradually experiences the birth of hundreds of thousands of animals. Her means of communicating her skill at the position was based on the particular pigs she had encountered and tried to "save." When I asked Robin why she was more skilled than many of our coworkers, she replied, "What I know, what I've learned, what I've seen . . . a pig with two heads and a pig with two bodies. A pig with a trunk. A pig with no legs. Once you see it in real life, you're just like, 'Wow!' Probably it does happen with every type of animal . . . but you don't see animals like that on TV or anything. This place is crazy."

My days in the delivery stage often flew by in a blur of collecting cold bodies and euthanizing them in carbon dioxide chambers. But Byron's words would often replay in my mind as I watched Robin beam with pride as she went from room to room, carefully inspecting new litters, full of attention, impervious to our surroundings. Robin felt it was her moral duty to try to save every pig, even if the task was impossible. There were moments when I felt that the weight of the job might be taking its toll on her. One day after falling asleep and rolling her car while driving home from work exhausted, she reached into the slurry of urine and feces that pools under the sows to rescue two piglets that had fallen through the metal grates. She glanced at me with a look of joy and said, "Last night, someone [i.e., God] saved me. And I was able to save those two pigs."

Still, Robin taught me more than anyone else about what it means to be a farmworker who labors in constant proximity to agribusiness's waning yet abundant state of life. "The most important skill is learning to love the animal," she told me. "It is hard, but I have a lot of patience, and when you have patience, you learn to love them." For Robin, being a good farmworker was not just a matter of practice to master a set of tools and tasks. An ongoing ethical orientation to life was necessary to build real experience—marshaling constant attention, appreciating subtle diversities among animals, and resisting alienation from the porcine species. She criticized past coworkers who, she claimed, showed up just for a paycheck and labored according to the law of standard operating procedures: "They don't really observe what's going on in that crate." She saw this act of working to a model that everyone knows is an approximation of things—even if sanctioned by management—as abusive: "They'll just feed the animal, and they won't look if it's a skinny pig, or a lame pig, or if it's sick. There's so many ways you can look at a pig: the way she lays, the way she breathes, the color of her skin, her hair. Everything."

I have come to see Robin as something of a natural historian who was conducting taxonomical studies in a profoundly unnatural setting. Her aim was to know all the different types of pigs—and ailments—generated by modern genetics. Hers was not an irrational attachment to porcine life. It was a trained mode of attention necessary to sustain the animals she worked with in a context in which industrialization continuously re-creates what it means to be a pig. "Love" thus was not a matter of naïve affection for pigs, much less, as some might have it, a primordial femininity run amok, but an ethical *practice* of being open and attuned to new expressions of animal life.[10] Every one of Robin's active glances at piglets—from novel angles, tasks, situations, or positions—added to her knowledge of porcine possibility. She was building an archive of the industrial species as a whole—an ongoing catalog—in the specific ways it can manifest in this factory farm. In hindsight, she was a Stockperson who was adequate to the period of runted life: she was working to make herself into a prosthetic for pigs' development, someone with such knowledge of the specific ailments of sickly pigs that she could assist their injuries.

Or, to put things a bit differently, Robin strove to know everything she could about the 2010 version of the confined piglet that is one to twenty-one days old. She had never been inside the slaughterhouse to witness the death of the hogs she saved; encountered a grown hog at six months; or even seen swine standing outside. She did not purport to have knowledge of "the pig" as some kind of deductive, generic thing. Robin was seeking to build an inductive portrait of all possible ways that the porcine species can manifest at this specific age, in this specific barn. What always seemed crucial was how she refused to accept the idea that the factory farm has actually standardized porcine life. Some other people she worked with, she insisted, tended to go through the motions, which for Robin meant treating pigs as tokens of a generic type. Immersed in rooms with thousands of animals locked in repetitive crates, it was challenging, she suggested—a true skill—for workers to practice love and *see* all of the unique animals still in front of them. Her degree of specialization at one part of the lifecycle, combined with her ongoing practice of "love," leads to a striking conclusion: Robin may have deeper knowledge of confined runts than most any other person on earth. While animal scientists might have an intense understanding of the musculoskeletal physiology of "the pig" as a generic organism, Robin has cared for more than 400,000 unique tiny piglets and become attuned to all their earthly manifestations and differences.

It feels too dramatic to frame Robin's everyday acts of attention and care as a matter of active resistance to the factory farm, but she never struck me as a fully willing participant. It seemed more like she was trying to preserve a sense of ethics for herself in spite of working to forcefully maximize life; her practice of love was an attempt to directly commune with the animals in her care *in spite* of the conditions of their existence. But what remains troubling is how the factory farm seems now to require this kind of active engagement from its workers. The industrial pig, especially in the looming hyperprolific era, is a fragile creature that ontologically depends on this kind of deeply attentive "love."

In her analysis of Italian family silk firms, Sylvia Yanagisako (2002) reinterprets the notion of "forces of production"—which usually refer to technologies external to people, such as machines—as a matter of human capacities. Her analysis of Italian bourgeois desires in silk manufacturing firms, which are equally about reproducing family as they are about producing capital, tracks how sentiments—"affective ideas and ideas with affect"—"incite, enable, constrain, and shape production" (Yanagisako 2002, 10–11). What I am suggesting here is that industrial expansion of sow reproduction requires new forms of worker-piglet relationality, sentiment, and sympathy to mute its contradictions. This is where Robin's practice is tense: these sentiments are at once an ethical means to commune with animals in spite of all of this violence, yet they are enlisted to sustain genetic violence.

LIFE FORCE AND LIFE-FORMS

From the moment I started working in the farrowing barns, the delivery process was charged with a frenetic energy relative to other stages of "live production," such as artificial insemination and vaccination. Unpredictable in its exact timing despite our efforts to routinize it using induction drugs, the birthing pace could shift in minutes from a break sitting around the workshop to racing through the cavernous halls after someone announced that another room of sows was farrowing. This tempo reached a fever pitch on the Monday that initiated my second week of work in this department of Sow #6. After showering in, I waited for Francisco to return from the breeding department to assign me a task. He had suggested that I would be power washing emptied farrowing rooms to get more familiarity with sanitation and disease. Blanca was standing at the workbench looking aghast while staring at a piece of paper on a clipboard and shaking her head. "This is impossible. This is impossible," she muttered. A pause. "OK . . . OK . . . Let's go!" she declared in an irritated tone that set the others standing near her scuttling toward farrowing rooms. She turned to me, knowing that I was tired of feeding runts, and said, "Sorry, Alex, but you have to do the nursing this week."

After collecting my blue bottles of milk for the first run, I encountered Rocio at the edge of the farrowing room's northern hallway. "Where are the runts?" I asked. She let out a deep bellow, waving her hand toward the ten north rooms. "They're all runts!" For the next few days I was hand-nursing at least half of the pigs in many litters, rarely taking a break. Confused, I sat in silence on the edge of a crate feeding piglets as I watched my more experienced coworkers frantically enter and leave the room with wheelbarrows of newborn piglets under heat lamps, trying to find them places where there were open teats. A new set of techniques for "saving" piglets unfolded before my eyes. Rocio's wheelbarrow of pigs overflowed into her pockets as she argued with others about which litter might contain room in the social pecking hierarchy for a runt to survive. Blanca was using milk crates to enact segregated feeding times on every litter, appraising which animals were strongest when, to me, they all looked weak and emaciated. Robin constructed elaborate body casts out of duct tape in an effort to help the piglets stand and develop their muscles. Her eyes were searching their unusual bodies to find the weak points and contours.

As the workweek neared its end and the pace started to return to normal, a fuller picture emerged from talking to Blanca, Robin, and Francisco. We had experienced a temporary crisis in the overproduction of life, a random fluctuation in high litter numbers across the whole system that resulted in part from two potent lines of sows crossing in their farrowing cycles. Francisco was at the tail end of phasing out a line of pigs called MDM707S: "These sows weren't very good pigs. They make lots and lots of piglets . . . sometimes eighteen, twenty piglets in a litter. But they aren't good mothers, so it doesn't matter how many piglets they make." The MDM707S appeared to be something of an early proto-hyperprolific sow, but they were incapable of transitioning seamlessly from breeding to farrowing. Many of their teats stopped working after a couple parities (pregnancies), meaning that they might give birth to eighteen animals but could raise only nine. In addition, the new line of animals in Sow #6—DB241S, a more well-rounded sow—were reaching their second and third parities when they tend to have the large litters. The result was twofold: there were not enough teats available for the piglets, and the litters across the barn were so large that many piglets were emerging with what, in retrospect, I now understand to be engineered runting.

Francisco reflected on what had occurred earlier, perhaps because it offered a premonition of how he might have to begin to adjust his own breeding strategies in coming years. "When you see a pig with a small litter . . . ten or twelve pigs . . . they are big and strong," he said, pointing to a crate full of baby piglets with well-defined shapes and muscles. "Thirteen, fourteen pigs . . . there's a runt or two that maybe we can save. Then we get an extra pig, and that's a good thing." As we approached a farrowing crate where all of the tiny piglets were sleeping on a plastic heating pad, their backs carrying the bright blue crayon slashes I had drawn to mark them as animals that required bottled milk, he grabbed the ID card off the wall and looked at the numbers: "This sow, she had eighteen piglets and, look, they're all small and tiny. These litters are too much. . . . They don't have any energy, you know, any life."

The outlines of managing life in the abstract emerge here at the intersection of modern sow genetics, farm labor, and (bio)capitalist strategies of profit. Sow vitality is figured as something of a zero-sum game, which challenges some earlier managers' distinctions between optimizing and maximizing animal life. At the same time, Berkamp Meats has an agreement with Dover Foods' slaughterhouse to supply 300,000 pigs each year—no more or fewer. Increasing this contracted number of pigs would necessitate building additional feeding and finishing barns for the growing animals, which was not an option.[11]

For years companies such as Berkamp have increased their profit margins by making more pigs using fewer sows. Sow #6 is built as a 2,500-head sow farm, but at that moment it held 2,307 animals because, as a result of "progress" in genetics, artificial insemination, knowledge of diet, and skills for "saving" weak piglets, the sows were reproducing about two more pigs per litter than they did in 1995. Depending on the market cost of feed and drugs, it takes $2–$4 to house a sow for a day. Decreasing two hundred animals from each of the six sow farms can save the company about $1.3 million per year. Despite Byron's emphasis on optimizing life, this kind of contract model is structurally premised on maximizing life by expending labor power on "saving" pigs that might otherwise perish.

At Dover Foods, which owns everything from farms to the slaughterhouse, the vital strategy is structurally different. They have no upper threshold in the number of pigs that they produce per year and would likely be happy if their 180,000 sows created seven million hardy and robust piglets in a year instead of five million. They would use grandfathered building permits to construct new finishing barns—as when they recently built fifty new ones—rather than decrease the size of their sow inventory. However, their strategy is based on minimizing labor expenditures, with only three people working on a 2,500-head sow farm (versus ten at Berkamp). As a result, they are capable of optimizing life by killing or selling nonuniform piglets (see chapter 10). Different (bio)capitalist strategies based on the contingent facets of vertical integration, slaughterhouse ownership, contract production, building permits, and ideologies of efficiency result in the manifestation of distinct porcine bodies.

We might note, then, that this is a particular type of biocapital that differs in substance from theories articulated from the life sciences' perspective (see Helmreich 2008). Biocapital is not, here, premised on converting biological materiality into information for the purposes of patenting (Sunder Rajan 2006). Nor does it operate at the level of the molecular (Rose 2007). Instead, biocapital is here a molar, material, and deeply tangible manifestation in the physical form of piglet bodies.

In Francisco's theory of industrial sow vitality, he strives to hold the line at an upper threshold before the point where runting is universal. His reading of litter sizes suggests a conflict in the factory farm between managing two forms of "life" that usually appear seamed yet become distinguishable within piglets once litters reach a certain size. We might dub this distinction as one of "life-forms" versus "life force."[12] In his description of intrauterine growth retardation there is a finite amount of animating vitality within a single sow. This vitality is static over time, while genetic "progress" in new models of sows by companies such as DanBred and the Pig Improvement Company results in more life-forms—more bodily forms—sharing this finite pool of animating matter in the womb. Industrial intensification at this stage of the factory farm is becoming about creating surplus life-forms using the same amount of life force. Biocapital creates *forms* even when it cannot fundamentally affect the "life force" in the porcine species. Once the factory farm reaches a level of proliferation, then, normally seamed types of living matter become separated and analytically distinct as capital begins to dissolve the piglet's integrity.

This is a working and workplace definition, a practical off-the-cuff theory. But the elegance of Francisco's formulation emerges from the way that the runt is characterized by an essential gap, a lack of vitality that must be in-filled with specialized feeds, extra drugs, and a knowledgeable labor force attuned to its particularities. Factory farm biocapital shifts this missing vitality—"life force"—onto human laborers. Agriculturally farmed pigs, whether outdoors or indoors, have always required human inputs. They need to be fed, given water, or treated when they are sick. But the runt is a form of death in life that is not self-sufficient at even the biological-organismic level of forming its own muscle fibers. It requires human workers and working actions to become prostheses to its body. The skilled work of Robin and other workers kept the majority of the piglets alive and routinized their bodies during that week of fluctuation, but this should not be read as a heartwarming story. In the American context, this should also be seen as a racialized capitalism that has manifested within the genetics, muscle fibers, and brainstem myelination of American hogs' bodies. It is the explicit creation of an animal designed to absorb the energy of workers. The model of this pig is really a reflection of the unequal and racialized state of labor and the *human* body. Systemic runting makes sense only once conditions of migration, hiring, and valuation lead to abundant and cheap labor. Engineering a pig that depends on exploited workers' prosthetic "love," in turn, might be better glossed as a matter of interspecies violence, a biological and emotional assault.

THE OVERWORKING OF PIGS

This chapter has touched on some of the ways that agricultural engineering is systematically debilitating the porcine species through single-trait selection for ovulation, making sows proliferate through massive and frail litters. Moreover, I have argued that this ongoing process of runting is being sustained by postmodern Stockpeople whose labor is becoming a prosthetic to discrete physiological elements of pigs, such as decreased density of muscle fiber. What it means to labor in these places—in terms of mental well-being, work's value, and personal ethics—is changing alongside the shifting state of American industrial animal nature. I do not ultimately know why Robin tried so hard to "save" all of those pigs that were born to die. It could be a result of anything from religious faith to simple pride in work. Minimally, it does seem that workers with similar forms of engagement with the porcine species are something that helps sustain contemporary sow genetics. Perhaps most important, however, is that this case should make us rethink what the industrialization of pigs actually entails. Unlike modernist scenes of a dominated nature, the runting of life suggests a matter of exerting incredible amounts of social knowledge and capital—in the forms of breeding and genetics—to make hogs and humans codependent at a fine physiological level, embedding work into the development of even things such as musculoskeletal structure. From farrowing, making the sow akin to an industrial worker—in this case, as one specialized in ovulation alone—also requires human workers to take on many other forms of action that sows used to do on their own, such as forming piglets' muscle fibers.

The critique of agribusiness here is primarily founded not on problems of human-hog detachment but, instead, on excessive, mutually dominating industrial proximity.[13] Standardized life is premised on the cultivation of a historically specific form of capitalist intimacy between species. To be clear, this is not a heartwarming matter of intimacy and care with some intact and natural animal called "the pig." It is not a face-to-face relation so much as it is one engaged with muscles, instincts, or hormones. This is a kind of vertically integrated intimacy whereby each person has one intense and exceedingly close form of relation to a facet of the species, while the broader industrial pig as a whole pools together, and is composed of, all of these intimate knowledges and practices. Dover Foods and others are creating a division of human labor around, and embedding workers within, facets of hog biology; as a consequence, they have reorganized human class, gender, and race relations through these now-discrete biologies. This industrial form of intimacy is a relationship whereby workers accrue radical familiarity with one (and often only one) embodied dimension of the hog as they become embodied prosthetics for porcine biologies. The industrial pig lives in workers' behavior as much as it does in porcine nature.[14]

At the same time, I think it would be an injustice to people like Robin to leave things there. What does it matter that the factory farm—as site of standardized exploitation—is also generating (and relying upon) quite radical forms of interspecies knowledge and relationships? How might we write about industrial agriculture that takes seriously and makes politically consequential the historically unique expertise of factory farm workers—rather than dwelling in their bodily or mental suffering, or lamenting their alleged deskilling and society's attendant loss of agrarian knowledge? These are not easy questions to answer, in part because the way that we talk, in mass media and scholarship, about the "deskilled" logic of farmwork makes skilled people such as Robin subaltern: mute and inarticulate within the very logics of the system; they seem to be necessitated by hog genetics, yet ignored and unable to be acknowledged within ideas that these kinds of places are entry-level, fully engineered sites that require only raw "manual" labor.[15] What this case suggests is that the well-being of both individual hogs and human workers is inseparable from the broader engineered state of life into which they are born and their labor unfolds—and that it is workers' *knowledge* of pigs that keeps these operations running. At a moment in which definitions of what constitutes animal welfare and the ethical treatment of farm animals tends to be decided by scientists at universities, what seems clear, at a minimum, is that workers—those who know the conditions of modern hogs most intimately—should have an intellectual say in what constitutes "humane" agriculture in the first place.

But, more expansively, I once met a farmer from Iowa who runs what is one of the most important pasture-based hog farms in the United States. It is not a "traditional" farm but one that is trying to develop new visions and practices of an animal-centered forms of agriculture. At the conference where we met I was presenting a version of this chapter. When I explained my topic he let me know something I find startling: his most crucial employees, those who run the farm on a day-to-day basis, are all migrant workers who left factory farms because they could not tolerate it any longer. They are more capable of working with pastured hogs than anyone else he has met. Perhaps the deep intimacy of labor on factory farms—and how creating standardized life-forms requires focused attention and labor directed towards porcine difference and particularity—has enabled a method for knowing and relating to hogs that is transferrable to other contexts. What if alternative agricultural visions started at these kinds of capitalist intimacies and the ways they concentrate historically unique commons of animal expertise in the hands of workers like Maria, Raul, and especially Robin? Some of the most influential practices in American alternative agricultures have been imagined and articulated through the productive negation of agribusiness. Local pastured pork is, in part, sensible as a refusal of the unendingly long food chains of factory farms; the recent attraction of heritage-breed animal rearing is partially a critical response to the low-fat, fast-growing bodies of industrial hogs (see Weiss 2016). It strikes me not only that factory farm workers know these agribusinesses best, but also that they are an untapped source of *intellectual* knowledge for understanding and building the kinds of different agricultures that might actually be able to make a difference.

PART IV
CARCASS

7.2 **PLANT**
Hundreds of workers make single slices on the pig's body, taking it from a full carcass to small portions in forty-five minutes.

7.1 **STOCKYARD** (overleaf)
Thousands of hogs rest after transport at the packing-house. Those in the right back file are being led to slaughter.

SEVEN MISS WICKED

THE FIRST TIME I encountered Charles King was during a slaughterhouse tour as our group paused to watch the mesmerizing repetition of the kill floor. I vaguely remember Charles standing on the line—like others, his frock was splotched in blood—with a mocking grin on his face. He was tauntingly laughing at our group's palpable shock at the sight of hogs being killed every few seconds. The scene, in spite of the whirring saws, blood cascading out of hanging hogs' necks, and bundles of organs being pulled from split-open bodies, had an air of rhythmic calm.

We got to know each other better a couple of years later. I was living for the summer in a homeless shelter where I had previously volunteered. The shelter was intended for new migrants to the region who were awaiting their first paycheck from the slaughterhouse so they could put down a deposit on a rental apartment. The place reverberated with the desperation and hope for a new beginning that underpins a lot of slaughterhouse labor. Charles liked to visit the shelter as a volunteer. He wanted to give something back to the place after it had got him on his feet when he first arrived in town. His visits were becoming more frequent during that summer, as he was on medical leave from the slaughterhouse following his second back surgery. He was walking around with a white neck brace that made his thin, six-foot-five-inch frame seem even taller. After learning that I was writing a book, he lent me his memoir in progress, scribbled over the years by hand in three different colors of ink on ruled paper. He started writing it after spending a few years in jail on drug charges. The memoir was originally a means for him to move on. He was now finishing it to use as an aid to counsel addicts who passed through the shelter. He saw the memoir as a first step toward opening himself up to others who were also working through their regrets.

"Miss Wicked's pearly white teeth are biting into his soul." In beautiful, searching prose the memoir describes the irresistible urges and forces that compel him to leave his family's home, and drive to a dilapidated house in a run-down section of an impoverished midwestern city where he grew up and had built a thriving construction business. Miss Wicked, a woman—perhaps his dealer—appears in the house as a feminized version of drugs incarnate, always waiting for him. "You know, I never really say 'cocaine,'" he would explain to me one afternoon after I had read the draft. "I try to portray it is as a vampire. . . . To me, that's what it's like, once it bites in. It just drains you. It doesn't stop."

The slaughterhouse is a challenging thing to represent as a "thing." Among the most radically divided forms of labor in human history, the line contains so many distinct positions from which to see, touch, and experience Dover

7.3 BIBLE
This recently evacuated room is at the local homeless shelter.

Foods' "biological system" of mass killing. As Timothy Pachirat (2011, 47) puts it in his ethnography of mass death in a beef plant in Omaha, "There are 121 job functions, 121 perspectives, 121 experiences of industrialized killing." I never did interview a manager who was capable of guiding me step by step through its slices. One senior contact in human resources was adamant that there was no one who could guide me through the kill from start to end, coordinated as they all were by conveyor belts that fragment labor processes down to a motion. A few people spoke with a tone of sublime awe about the two places where one can sense the scale of death in a glance: the "dead room," where thousands of euthanized piglets are ground up for rendering, and the basement chamber under the kill floor. A man is said to spend all day in that chamber watching for errant bits of flesh that could clog the drains that transport blood.

The work of slaughter begins as trucks back into long concrete loading chutes and unload sets of sixty hogs. These hogs are quickly tattooed on their

170

7.4 HOME
A standard
home of the
kind funded
through slaugh-
terhouse labor.

back with an identifying number, and they walk down a dark concrete path with high walls until they arrive for sorting in the stockyards (see figure 7.1). Pigs rest in the low-lit stockyards for an hour or so, cooled by mist-making machines, to calm down after the voyage. The high walls of the concrete pens are designed to make them feel as if they are in a comfortable, secure space. If the hogs are agitated prior to when they are killed, the pH levels of their meat change.

Groups of six hogs walk up a wide metal ramp and into a series of large hydraulic carbon dioxide chambers that render the animals unconscious within a minute. As the hogs' limp bodies are ejected on the other side of the chamber, their legs are affixed to moving chains, and their bodies are hoisted up into the air, the head facing the ground. One person cuts the hogs' carotid arteries, and their still-beating hearts propel the blood out of their bodies. The bleeding carcass moves on an automated chain to the rest of the stations, where people gradually remove the head, split the carcass, and eviscerate the animal. From there it passes through fiery incinerators that singe off the hair into a chilling room to get the carcass down to a temperature just above freezing (see figure 9.1). The carcass will pass onto the refrigerated cut floor, where it is broken down into hundreds of vacuum-packed pieces (see figure 7.2). Pieces of muscle and organ are packaged into fifty-pound cardboard boxes and loaded into trucks that are bound for other parts of the United States, Mexico, and ports in California. From there they are loaded onto refrigerated ocean liners to be shipped to about twenty other countries. The lower-grade muscle cuts for Russia and organs for the Philippines are likely frozen. The high-grade loins and shoulders bound for Japan will likely be kept fresh and must be consumed within forty-five days of the moment of slaughter (see also Curliss 2014). The primary thing—other than the type of cut and the right texture of fattiness for a particular flavor—that differentiates high-grade Japan-bound pork is its longevity and ability to retain a deep color and water during travel. This is logistical flesh, sorted based on the distances it can travel (cf. Cowen 2014).

Most people could only narrate their knowledge of a single motion—the height of a hook, the cold of a hoof, or the skin-denting weight of a box's corner. In the next chapter, I will argue that every worker comes to embody this slaughterhouse, yet it leaves physical traces on their bodies that are so fine that each person's body becomes just a tiny bit different. This part moves from the overwork of porcine bodies to that of human biology; it traces the surprising overlaps and entanglements between the state of American (porcine) animality and the bodies of human workers. However, if there was one person I encountered whose experiences and physical state fully represented the contemporary industrial slaughterhouse as a broader late industrial institution, beyond the fine-grained muscular traces from a single-motion slice of a knife, it was most certainly Charles King.

Charles taught me a lot about the physical and psychological rigors of the modern slaughterhouse. But it was his arrival story that was most troubling. Dover Foods started operating in the manner it was originally designed only in the aftermath of the U.S. recession of 2008. Until the late 2000s, the slaughterhouse had struggled to run at its full estimated capacity. It was hard to find enough human bodies to kill sixteen thousand hogs per day, let alone the 2,500-odd workers required to increase the line's output to a full twenty thousand. This led, as I heard a human resources manager euphemistically put it, to a series of "creative efforts" at recruitment. After his release from prison, Charles returned to menial construction jobs but felt the need to escape from

7.5 **SHELTER** A woman walks up the stairs to her room at the shelter, where new migrants stay before they receive their first paycheck at the slaughterhouse.

the lure of his familiar urban haunts. He heard of an obscure company called Second Chance Solutions that took recently released ex-convicts and transported them to a small town named Dixon, to work, as he was told, in "pig factories." Charles was promised a month in a hotel, meals, bus passes, the first month's rent on an apartment, and a rental deposit. He later learned that Dover Foods was paying this outfit $1,000 per head for each ex-convict who would work on the kill floor. Charles was dropped off at the shelter, told to walk two miles to a restaurant where the job placement company held an account, and show up at the slaughterhouse the next day. He never did receive the deposit or that first month's rent.

After a couple months of work, on the final day of his probationary period—when he could still be terminated without justification—he was called into a human resources office. The official told him that he was fired even though he had been receiving praise from his supervisors. After some random break-ins

7.6 **CAFÉ** Dozens of popular new businesses, including this café, have been funded through slaughterhouse labor.

across town, the Dixon police found out that the company was recruiting ex-convicts to staff the slaughterhouse; Charles was told by the human resources officer that the police were threatening to run the ex-convicts out of town unless the corporation terminated them. Once the dust settled, a human resources supervisor asked Charles to return as a full-time worker.

"My life has been one big long adventure. I drifted to the bad side early," he said, "so I did a lot of bad things that I regret doing now. Lot of those things became a habit. I had a lot of addictions. You can call them habits. I'd say habits and addictions are about the same things." His memoir begins with Miss Wicked's vampirism, but it does not stay there for long. It leaps across time to chart his histories of repetition, compulsion, and dependency. His book moves to the first habit he remembers: the childhood joy of his grandmother's pancakes. It then traces a series of impossible wishes and desires built around a chapter on attempts to fly as a young boy, which left him with a broken arm.

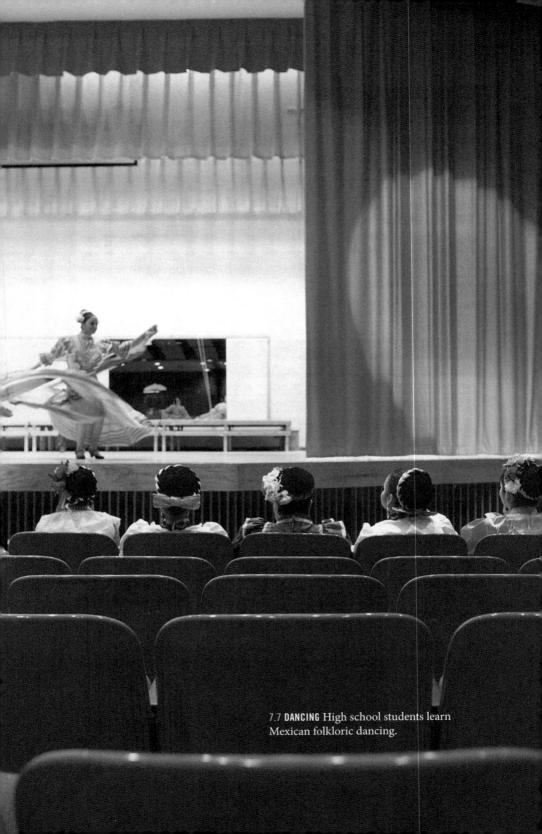

7.7 **DANCING** High school students learn Mexican folkloric dancing.

Before I read his memoir in progress, Charles and I had sat on the shelter's porch together late at night discussing his years on the kill floor. His stories always ended with almost comical bouts of rage, recounting how he would get angry for no reason, storm off the kill floor, and ask to be fired. He had gained grudging respect over the years through this steadfast will, by mouthing off to belligerent supervisors while ignoring the body parts passing by on the line until they begged him to return to work. The kill floor sounded like a constant provocation, and the only respite seemed to be his ability to dominate superiors. "Worst job I've done is fecal monitoring," he told me. "It's the easiest job there, but that's what made it so hard. What you do, you're standing on a grid, and these USDA people are standing behind you. And they rip the guts out and you have to look for any contamination. Shit, abscess, hair. . . . If you don't mark it, you got the USDA breathing down you. . . . God, I hated that job. They will stop [the line] for a hair." He stuck with the kill floor for a few years, gradually working almost "everything" on the kill floor section—"pulling guts," "breast saw," "cleaning heads," "trimming heads," "dropping heads," "hanging heads," "rolling hogs," "hanging hogs," and "auditing"—except slitting the hogs' carotid arteries ten thousand times a day.

7.8 **HAM LINE** Full carcasses (left background) are sawn in half; the hoof is sliced off; the bones are ground down; and the legs are cut into hams.

The only job he "loved" on the kill floor was "hanging heads," which was robotically ingrained into his body. "I can feel where that hook is going to be," he told me. "I don't even need to look. I can keep moving, keeping my rhythm." The trouble was that hanging heads was a hard job because of their weight. Hanging heads could have been the culprit responsible for three surgeries—two to his back and one to his knee. Regardless, he estimated that he cost Dover Foods' insurance plan $400,000 in surgeries, and these benefits—which he perhaps needed *because* of the job—were what kept him on the line.

I once asked Charles whether his bouts of anger might stem from the feeling of dependency starting to form on the kill floor—of doing the same thing every few seconds, of the machine acting as a compulsion on the body. His memoir's narration of Miss Wicked sinking her teeth into his body, of an external force directing him to drive toward her house, sounded so similar to how he discussed the feel of kill floor labor. There seemed to be a parallel to the pleasurable and painful rhythm of hanging heads—of being in sync with the machine—so that he did not even need to use his eyes. It mimicked the words he used to describe things as habits. "I hadn't thought of it like that," he said and paused. "But, yeah, I can't be controlled. When I walk off the line, I say, 'Fuck it. I don't want this job.' That was my attitude. You ask me why? You can't ask me why. Sometimes I did it because I was in a bad mood. I'm like, I'm going home." Shortly after that conversation, he finally did go home, quitting the plant and moving back to the city where he was born. It was probably the right time to leave. The year was 2011—one of the first times the slaughterhouse was running at capacity—as the loss of blue-collar employment in the United States drove thousands of desperate people into midwestern meatpacking towns in search of work. Dover Foods would no longer need "creative" recruiting. The plant had enough human bodies to operate at its full speed of almost twenty thousand hog bodies per day. But Charles's neck brace was a potent sign of how human labor was emerging as value in a different kind of way. That neck brace, and other kinds of injuries, was becoming a pivotal part of American animality.

EIGHT **BIOLOGICAL SYSTEM**
Breaking In at the End of Industrial Time

VERTICALLY INTEGRATING TENDONS

A few weeks after I first moved to Dixon, the town was awash with gossip about an event that had occurred in the slaughterhouse. I made no effort to confirm the details. It felt wrong to turn this incident into a piece of anthropological research, although it was impossible to avoid all of the chatter as people tried to puzzle out the meaning of the act. The rumor was that a young man who had recently moved to town had committed suicide in the slaughterhouse using a bolt gun. We used bolt guns to euthanize large breeding animals on farms; that is not the usual way industrial pigs are slaughtered. Occasionally, hogs are injured in the truck on the way to the packinghouse and cannot walk. These nonambulatory hogs are shot in the head in the stockyards (figure 7.1) and then rendered for pet food and biodiesel. The man must have got hold of the stockyard's bolt gun.

An elderly woman at a truck stop diner mentioned the incident first. Her rhetorical question was the same one that everyone else in town was asking: "Why would he do that . . . like that?" Many seemed to believe the act must carry some kind of profound statement—that it was performative, a symbolic gesture—rather than a matter of opportunity in terms of a suicidal man suddenly finding himself with the means in hand. An inebriated former slaughterhouse worker at a bar, a few nights later, recounted details of how he was abused by superiors and then fired. He saw the suicide as a fitting tribute to the spirit of packinghouse work. "They treat people like they're pigs," he bellowed to everyone within earshot. This is a well-used phrase in meatpacking communities, an expression that seems to just roll off the tongue. Many slaughterhouse stories contain some variation of this phrase (see, e.g., LeDuff 2000). It indicates that people working in slaughterhouses are used up like disposable animal bodies. The phrase's charge is that slaughterhouse operators do not care about workers' well-being; that they do not afford them special dignity as human beings.

This chapter argues that there is some truth to this charge, though it is complicated: workers in vertically integrated systems are not disposable, but they are treated in ways that parallel those of *industrial* pigs. In mid-2016, the social justice organization Oxfam America briefly made waves with its disturbing investigation into labor conditions in some of the largest American chicken plants. The report that, perhaps surprisingly, received the most media attention was titled *No Relief: Denial of Bathroom Breaks in the Poultry Industry* (2016). Oxfam investigators interviewed slaughterhouse workers who alleged that they were rarely allowed to step off the cut floor to use the bathroom (see also Ribas 2016). Workers were being humiliated on the line. They were forced to choose between urinating on themselves, not drinking liquids, or wearing diapers to work. The report offered a jarring image of industrial modernity in that key factors in the cheap price of chicken nuggets are diapers and urinary tract infections. The report and subsequent media commentaries pushed the poultry industry to adopt and follow its own "best practices" of employing additional employees to step onto the disassembly line as floaters and provide others with a few minutes' break. This is an important intervention given the acute and immediate needs of laborers in slaughterhouses. But there is also the issue of requiring floaters in the first place, for what is remarkable in this case is that so-called efficiency in meat systems is so out of control that corporations must now solicit an official bathroom reliever position. The human bladder is a problem of production.

This chapter is about the evolving place of the human body within modern meat; it explores a series of jarring ways that human workers' and industrial "meat" hogs' corporeal forms are entangled on the disassembly line. It examines the vertical integration of human physiologies—the uncanny joint production of human and hog muscles—at a moment in which two hundred years of industrial refinement in slaughter has resulted in a system that is operating at the very limits of the working body. Meatpacking historically has often acted as a preview site of forms of industrialism to come. Henry Ford (1923), for instance, claimed to take the idea of the assembly line from the Chicago packers' disassembly line. What I want to suggest is that this may still be the case. The slaughterhouse continues to forecast the state of global industrialism, along with the changing value of capitalist labor.

Every year or so, Dover Foods tends to add another venture that deepens its capitalization on the porcine species. Sometimes this is an extension of the existing system's scale. In the early 2010s, for instance, it built an additional fifty finishing barns for meat hogs to accommodate growing average litter sizes. Too many pigs were moving through the networks of barns, and the Live Side found itself using what it calls a "push system." Hogs were being slaughtered too early, under their most profitable weight. Other, more geographic modes of expansion include constructing new bacon, ham deboning, and processing plants in strategic locations across the United States and Central America, where labor costs are much lower. A third, more intriguing form is when Dover Foods tries to capitalize on qualitatively different phases of the pig's death by rendering blood plasma or manufacturing biodiesel using hog fat. The factory farm is still a project in formation. Dover Foods is searching for ways to increase the scope of its vertical integration of American animality and extract hidden forms of "new money" from within the porcine body.

During my first year of research, I expected to see the construction of a building or machine that would remake a porcine muscle or gland. Perhaps it would be some kind of biomedical harvesting process of heart valves for implantation into human beings (see Sharp 2013). Instead, Dover Foods announced that it was going to construct a health clinic for employees. During his speech at the public grand opening, Dover's chief executive framed this operation as an altruistic gift to the community. It was sorely needed. Most people believed it would benefit everyone in Dixon. It was a place where employees on both the Live Side and the Plant Side could seek medical care for themselves and their families. It would decrease the long waits at the struggling, overcrowded local hospital. The clinic would relieve pressure on the community's few existing doctors, especially at a moment—in the aftermath of the U.S. recession—when the town was growing in population. It was, as someone said, "a win-win solution." As an executive later recounted to me, "It is great when our needs and those of the community overlap and we get these opportunities."

I was perplexed about why workers' health was a key site of industrial expansion. I initially wrote it off without too much thought, plugging it into my usual habits of interpretation. I assumed that this could be figured as a typical industrial story of maintaining a reserve of willing and able bodies for providing labor power to the slaughterhouse (see Marx 1992; Sunder Rajan 2007). The health clinic functions as a place where employees can be treated for illnesses such as a fever or strep throat. In terms of the corporation's bottom line, this could theoretically lead to fewer sick days by having workers and their families promptly treated. A bit more nefariously, I figured it would also function as a place where an employee could receive rapid treatment for an injury that she suffered on the packing line's cut floor. Perhaps this would reduce an injury's severity, decreasing the number of days off and the size of a compensation claim to be paid by the corporation's insurance. It felt perfectly sensible, though certainly no less disturbing, to think that a slaughterhouse merits its own hospital. And to be certain, the health clinic does provide these kinds of services in managing workers' bodies. From the community's perspective, it keeps people healthy. From the corporation's view, one could say that it maintains workers in a remote town.

But the situation is more complicated than this. The health clinic was operating in such a way that the "new money" that the company aimed to unlock within the industrial pig was actually residing in its human employees' muscles and tendons. As I would learn while talking to managers and reading newspapers, the clinic's third purpose was to evaluate human bodies—and the differences across a single body—for their suitability for work on parts of the disassembly line. Upon being hired, a person undergoes a series of tests far more extensive than the standard physical and X-rays that I underwent at the doctor's office before beginning work at Berkamp Meats. For instance, potential workers at this clinic are asked to engage in various forms of repetitive motion or to lift a progressively heavier series of weights from distinct angles and postures. Perhaps their range of motion for reaching is evaluated, or the strength of their pinch grip is being appraised. Each muscle group is separately evaluated, and the strongest segment of a person is matched to a cut floor motion. Thus, the corporation can gauge distinctions in the physical fitness of each body, assigning a given individual to the spot on the disassembly line that is most suited to their musculoskeletal state. In simple terms, this is done to decrease the probability that a person will be injured and file a compensation claim. More elaborately, it suggests how workers' bodies are becoming pools of potential value—and not simply in the standard terms of labor power, but as *differential biologies*—once the increasingly fast-moving disassembly line of cheap pork itself becomes a liability to corporate profits. Disassembling industrial hog muscles is becoming more profitable by parsing differences in workers' bodies.

Let me be clear that the point of this chapter is not to offer a superficial critique of the health clinic or even of corporate efforts to profit by reducing injuries. It is clearly desirable to invest resources in limiting injuries on the line, regardless of the impetus.[1] Within the arena of U.S. meatpacking, ethnographers have found that many people truly are treated like disposable biologies and surplus lives to lower the price of meat (see Ribas 2016; Stuesse 2016). When a broader industry is quite literally premised on draining the "vital energies" of workers (see Vora 2015), even small efforts to maintain workers' bodies can feel progressive.[2] But I do want to reflect on what this health clinic suggests about the biology of labor in late industrialism. Workers in the slaughterhouse are not disposable; the management of their muscles has become a site of investment in a vertically integrated system. Workers are treated not like generic "animals" but instead as akin to one way I have been describing *industrial* pigs: as distinct and segmentable physiologies. What we are seeing here is how slaughterhouses are pushing outside of a standard labor theory of value whereby the cost of pig meat ultimately boils down to the amount of average social labor time exerted in its generation. Instead—or, at least, in addition—it marks a situation where decades of effort to wring more value from porcine bodies are now doubling back to remake how the human body is marshaled as an industrial site of "new money."

What is the changing relation between pig bodies and human muscle? How did working human muscles become entangled with the state of porcine muscles? This situation suggests how the industrial pig is paradoxically at its most vital—in terms of resisting human agency and will (cf. Bennett 2010)—only at its moment of death. This chapter develops by situating some slaughterhouse managers' claims that they have reached the maximum point of efficiency at which they are pushing the human body to its limits using machines, and are now dependent on additional pig standardization from the Live Side to continue increasing automation and output. It elaborates the notion that factory farming is a dualistic "Biological System" in which both vitality and capital determine managerial actions. Meanwhile, it juxtaposes these managerial words to workers' counterdiscourse of "breaking in" to describe an industrial system that transforms their bodies, muscle tissues, and hands via repetitive motion. The not-yet-perfect standardization of the pig results in managers' feeling forced to increase the speed of the disassembly line in a way that pushes the limits of human biology; by doing so, the machine begins to destandardize human bodies.

THUMBNAILS

[Upton] Sinclair's overdrawn prose notwithstanding, he effectively
captured the endemic character of workplace dangers in the modern
meatpacking industry. . . . [M]eatpacking's greatest danger was the way
it progressively wore down the human body. Cold attacked lungs, salty
brine solutions wore down flesh, and knives cut hands and limbs. . . .
Yet the real dangers lay in the smaller incremental injuries. . . . [In a 1943
study, o]ne operative cutting up hogs had twenty-two knife wounds in
one year; three with equivalent jobs in beef processing experienced a
total of sixty-seven injuries, of which fifty-three were by cuts and lacera-
tions. *The job of these workers could be read in their hands!*
—ROGER HOROWITZ, *"THAT WAS A DIRTY JOB!"* (2008) (EMPHASIS ADDED)

One evening I was eating dinner at the home of a meatpacking worker named
Sergio Chavez. We were discussing how he was recruited via relatives from
Chihuahua to Dixon to work in the pork industry. Sergio's story was not premised on coming to town in desperate search of income; his is not the meatpacking tale of crossing the border for backbreaking labor as a matter of last
resort (cf. Schlosser 2001; Stull and Broadway 2013). He was the scion of a
family of businesspeople. The modest yet beautiful home where we were eating, in one of the affluent parts of Dixon where company managers live, could
not have been the product of laboring on the cut floor alone.[3] Sergio vaguely
explained that his youthful leisure and partying had spiraled out of control to
the point at which he risked falling into danger in a northern Mexico on the
verge of drug wars. His decision to leave was affirmed by the number of his
childhood friends who had become victims of violence between the Mexican
government and the drug cartels, or of kidnappings for ransom. He seemed to
be suggesting that his move across the U.S.-Mexico border in the 2000s was a
self-imposed journey of moral rehabilitation to escape his youth. He claimed
there was little worth remembering from his arrival except that it was snow-
ing, he was living in a trailer, the place was barren, and he had work on sow
farms. "I came here to work," he explained, using a phrase echoed in my conversations with laborers and even management. "This is only a place to work."

Within a few years of joining relatives in Dixon, however, Chavez was mar-
ried and discovered a newfound communitarian purpose in church, although
he still described the town's overriding value using a motif of ascetic labor. He
acquired a job in the slaughterhouse on the evening B-shift, from 3 p.m. until
as late as 3 a.m., so he could spend the mornings with his young children. He

cycled through various positions for the first two years. He said, "The first sixty days were always a struggle. Every second was a fight. Every day was a rematch." Moving boxes of vacuum-packed meat across conveyor belts in shipping tore apart his upper back. The knife work of making one little slice across flesh five thousand times a day strained his hand muscles to the point where he once struggled to pick up a lime at Wal-Mart after work. Working on the kill floor amid all the hot bodies was like being in a sauna; slicing parts of the loins on the refrigerated cut floor was an exercise in enduring bone-numbing cold. His invocation of the slaughterhouse's inescapably intemperate environments reminded me of one man in his fifties, a maintenance tech for the disassembly line's conveyor belts. He moved on high overhead rafters across all work areas and said to me (in a proud register) that his job tested his mettle by making him sick. "We see all the seasons in a day," he declared. "Every hour I go from twenty-five degrees to one hundred degrees." Just as Sergio's body would adjust to the line's minute motions at a location, management would institute some change—in one example, moving the official fifteen-minute break back a half-hour—that would disrupt his painfully ingrained bodily rhythm.

Yet Sergio now spoke with masculine pride about this period of (self-)flagellation once his muscles and mentality had molded to the repetitive pain of the disassembly line. Each day he made the same motion of scraping blood and shit from ten thousand pigs' intestines, cleaning them out before passing them down the line for the next step in their treatment. Over the time prior to when we spoke he must have run the tips of his thumbs over the surface of at least a million intestines. He flipped over his hands on the table and nodded, grinning proudly, at the history of hard labor and sacrifice scarred into his thumbs. Repetitive motion was permanently etched into his thumbnails. The white of his thumbnails—the edge parts that usually begin at the tips of the fingers—went down to his cuticles. Over the years of scraping these hog intestines, his fingernails' shells had delaminated from the raw flesh that they were supposed to be protecting.

Upon seeing this proud gesture, one of Sergio's urbane younger friends chimed in across the table that he, too, wanted to try working at the slaughterhouse. "Why?" asked Sergio, in a flabbergasted tone. "I have to try it," insisted the man, nodding, as if he was convincing himself of his genuine desire. "So many people talk about it. I don't care if it's hard. I want to feel it." The slaughterhouse, for this physically fit friend, not unlike Sergio, was more than just a dependable blue-collar income. It was a test of character. As I understood this man's yearning to suffer, those sixty days—what others label the breaking-in period—were the basis for an embodied material experience that would help him share sensate bonds, and become part of a "sensory public," with Dixon's laboring populations.[4] In those fingernails and the histories of motion they indexed, this friend might have seen complicated forms of masculine mastery and will: over the grinding pace of slaughter that made many people quit,[5] over the embodied sacrifices to support a family, and over being defined by one's past and current station in life. For my part, I have never gotten past how his fingernails hinted at the ways that the disassembly line—a 200-year old capitalist technology that has only intensified in speed over the years—was now moving so quickly that it was pushing beyond the limits of the human body.

In terms of injury rates, the slaughterhouse has historically been one of the most dangerous places to work in the United States (Horowitz 2008; Human Rights Watch 2005). Most exposés of meatpacking feature the story of someone who has lost a limb or who has such severe carpal tunnel syndrome that she may never work again. Ethnographic accounts from chicken and beef plants illustrate a picture of ergonomics and safety training as a bureaucratic chore during orientation week videos that tends to get ignored in practice (see, e.g., Pachirat 2011, 104–5; Striffler 2005, 129–33). Rare stories of someone's hand being ripped off by a machine would trickle out of the slaughterhouse. But these shocking examples are almost red herrings. Dover Foods is not teeming with amputations and death. As others have noted, the modern slaughterhouse is a story of mundane nicks, strains, and pulls that build over time until the person gives up and finds a different job (Horowitz 2008; Striffler 2005; Stull and Broadway 2013; Stull et al. 1995). A friend, an ex-"nurse" in the slaughterhouse who thought this position might help him train to become a real nurse, described to me a workplace lexicon of classifying the escalating severity of routine and minor violence in terms of the "flesh pokes," "slashes," "gashes," and "tendon cuts." His job was not to mend these wounds, "because there's only so much you can do in a place like that." Instead, his task was to sort cases and "paperwork" as he decided whether an injury could be fixed with Band-Aids and ointment, or if it would require a visit to the county emergency room (and hence carry with it the threat of a workplace compensation settlement).

In Sergio's fingernails, however, there are hints of another form of violence that is not an accidental injury caused by an exception, however systematic "accidents" may be when thousands of people work with sharp knives. This is a consequence of the line running normally. His fingernails point toward an embodied history of labor extraction etched into the surfaces, musculature, gait, posture, and movements of Dixon's population. They point to a population that has been biophysically molded by industrialization; this is a situation where the manipulation of porcine carcasses transforms the human body, and, in turn, gives a cross-species meaning to managers' discourse that they manage a Biological System in the slaughterhouse. Though it is less viscerally shocking than the sight of missing limbs or stories of repeat back surgeries—and Sergio's and others' deep masculine pride in their jobs makes it more morally ambiguous—I am haunted by impressions across interviews that no one knew how to control the packing plant, that this biological machine had become almost agentive and lively. If, as the labor historian Roger Horowitz (2008, 14) writes, the "job of these [packing] workers could be read in their hands," then what can Sergio's thumbnails tell us about the factory farm at the stage of the slaughterhouse? This is not meant as a story of exceptionalism, but rather of intensity—work, like sports, always shapes bodies. Live Side managers frequently had damaged knees from walking on concrete in rubber boots for many decades; wrist and back strains are common among office workers and book writers toiling on keyboards (see Jain 2006). What is striking about Sergio's fingernails, however, is the localized nature of the repetition that suggests how the slaughterhouse has refined its process to such an extent that it affects the most precise of muscle and tendon groups. Moreover, these motions are so precisely spread across populations that each worker's body becomes slightly different.

BREAKING IN

It is hard to remember the first time that I heard someone use the term "breaking in" (or, alternatively, "break-in") to describe the agonizing process of molding the human body to the disassembly line's machine-driven repetition. Every employee I met had a breaking-in story. Preparing new hires for this shock of pain—and emphasizing that it is a temporary ache—was part of the plant's orientation training and the origin of the term. The Human Resources department was trying to decrease the number of workers who show up for one week and never return. It was not unusual to hear rumors that the plant was hiring fifty new employees in a week during the peak of the recession. The U.S. Department of Labor's Occupational Safety and Health Administration (Occupational Safety and Health Administration 1993, 5), as part of its nonenforceable "voluntary ergonomics guidelines," developed in conjunction with the industry trade group the American Meat Institute, defines "break-in" as an initial period of decreased workload to "condition [employees'] muscle-tendon groups prior to working at full capacity." While some people recounted having a lighter workload on the line when they first started, breaking in was always narrated as a period of suffering and a process of learning how to reinhabit one's body once it is suffused with aches and pain.

Breaking in is an experience that can unite slaughterhouse workers from across the country. When I lived in a homeless shelter for new migrants, I met a man from Minnesota who had grown up working in slaughterhouses and developed his own breaking in remedies. Flexing stress balls after work, dipping swollen hands in ice baths, constant movement to keep from seizing up: these were home remedies that he taught new residents for overcoming the traumas of the line. Evenings in this shelter were often surreal, with people in too much pain to talk as they sat on couches and kept squeezing stress balls. Some managers—most of whom grew up in packing towns, took a job immediately after high school, and rose internally through the ranks—would proudly recount their own teenage experiences of fingers, hands, and arms shooting with sharp pain as if it was yesterday. Even the plant's senior vice president acknowledged the physical challenge of finding, shaping, and maintaining adequate bodies. "You're learning to become an athlete when you're not [an athlete]," he said, suggesting how hard modern packing was to maintain in the face of a postindustrial North American populace without the required physical specialization to thrive in this kind of extreme environment.

I once saw a tough Eritrean refugee curled up on the couch and fighting back tears as another man pried open and flexed his hands to keep them from seizing. As I overheard one new hire warn another about the temporary pain in the hands, "I can't take a shower; you can't even move a finger." Another woman, a roaming Christian mystic, had stayed in this shelter as she passed through town. These sorts of haunting sights of strained bodies, of people being treated, as she put it, "like the slaves of Judah," made her decide to stay in town and begin a mission after she saw a vision of "The Beast" (Satan) while driving her truck past the plant on her way out of town.

Alicia, a strong thirty-year-old who was originally from Chicago, began six long slaughterhouse years with the job of using enormous scissors to cut out part of the pig's stomach for tripe (or "paunch," as she put it) on the humid kill floor, or "hot side." She narrated breaking in as a deeply internal pain, as if she was being gradually torn apart:

> In the orientation classes, they have that break-in pain they tell you about. And you feel it. It's all in your body because you've never worked like that before. You're constantly moving, you're standing there on concrete.... It feels like you're flammable or something. Your bones really hurt. Your hands hurt. Your back hurts. Like sometimes I would get off a shift, because I worked on the kill floor for ten hours a night, and I couldn't sit down. I couldn't lie down in bed because my body was so sore. My back. I had to sit down on the couch for an hour before I could even lie down. It's just some kind of pain that you get that your body hasn't sensed before. It's this pain that your muscles are working more than ever, just something that you've never felt before. That's what they always say in the orientation classes.

Alicia described breaking in as a 24/7 pain that followed her home as her body was re-made. Her suffering occurs most descriptively not as she wields scissors on the kill floor but as she sits alone at home. As one of the anthropologist Steve Striffler's (2005, 129) coworkers on a chicken line described the consuming and almost addictive quality of the slaughterhouse, "As soon as I start hanging chickens I feel fine. It's like that is all my muscles know how to do. I am in constant pain when I am not at work." This is a radically "manual" labor in the sense that it forces all "mental" attention to the body and its senses; it is a novel form of embodiment for Alicia, "just something that you've never felt before." She described herself as doubly isolated by the disassembly line: unable to think of anything except her body's movements at work and unable to have a social life outside of work due to the pain's constancy. For Striffler (2005, 134), this "oppressive routine" left him so exhausted during two summers of undercover research he could not even take a break to get a haircut or otherwise "establish a viable routine beyond the factory gate."

The second step of some breaking-in narratives is the bodily release from the line's grasp and the overwhelming sociality that suddenly emerges. The slaughterhouse's senior vice president himself was not atypical when he claimed that, during his teenage years on the kill floor, the "work was always very hard, but you learned to also laugh. You are constantly talking with people for eight, nine, ten hours." Indeed, despite Alicia's recollections of breaking in, the majority of our two-hour interview concerned the pleasures of social life once she got "used to it. You learn to talk, work, talk." Describing the slaughterhouse as something between "a city that never sleeps" and a "high school," she asserted, "I had a community. I really liked it." Although she quit once her thirty-year old body could not keep up with the line—which also increased from sixteen thousand to nineteen thousand pigs per day while she was there—Alicia maintained her contacts to learn about the rumors and relationships forming on the cut floor. Once one gets past the sixty or so days of breaking in, a social world opens up in a way that many who spoke English or Spanish described as an almost joyful feeling of release prior to the onset of ensuing monotony.

For others, though they also described the release from the grip of pain as an initial period of liberation, this post-breaking-in sociality and boredom management could come to dominate the experience. Many women complained about sexual harassment. A Karen Burmese migrant whose job was to separate the semi-frozen trotter, or "wrist," of the pig and hang it on a hook spoke about the initial pain in his own wrists that blocked him from even noticing how many trotters he was handling. As the breaking-in pain receded and his feeble English and Spanish left him too shy to talk, he noticed that co-workers were entertaining themselves by taunting him as a "Chinese": "They call[ed] me *marrano* [pig/boar]." The only way to avoid racial harassment was to joke and appear to enjoy the labor process, he said: "To be like them . . . you have to pretend to be happy and talk about how it is good money." This forced display of carefree emotion was necessary to make the job livable, but it also entailed a burden of having to perform socially on the line.

Theorizing the body politics of Fordist labor process in the 1920s— especially in terms of whether the (dis)assembly line could be redeemed for building a socialist future—the Italian Marxist Antonio Gramsci (1971, 295) analyzed proto-forms of breaking in. He was curious about whether industrial work could become ingrained in the body so that it is as natural as writing with a pen. For Gramsci, however, the problem of Fordist production was the mental remainder: it was inhumane to make someone repeat the same task for hours on end without a higher social purpose beyond surplus value (see also Bell 1947; Buck-Morss 1992). It is a remarkable and disturbing reflection on the state of society and social consciousness that today, to prompt any kind of public concern about slaughter work, social justice advocates need to investigate whether people are urinating on themselves. Even Henry Ford (1923) felt obliged to respond to this kind of charge of mental abuse in a chapter titled "The Terror of the Machine," arguing that, "to a certain kind of mind," repetition is pleasurable (see Peña 1997). Such austere anthropologies—almost one hundred years later—still rationalize the work of (dis)assembly. Slaughter managers tended to deflect my criticisms and stories of industrial violence using similar neo-Fordist notions that the full scope of human desires could find a place on the line. The ensuing examples, however, revealed a rather paltry set of human natures that can be accommodated by industrial killing. One told me, "The type of person who works on the cut floor is the type who is content with doing the same thing over and over," while "the type of person who does material handling is the type who likes to move." The ideology of labor proposed here is that the workforce is one of simple minds and highly complex bodies.

But what Sergio Chavez's fingernails illustrate, at least as I see it in retrospect, is the impossibility of bodies' ever "fully" adjusting to the pace of this killing machine. The third step of breaking in, that which arises from a molded body, seemed to stand outside standard genres of narration that I heard recounted. After meeting Sergio, I asked others how the disassembly line was changing their bodies now that it moved at a rate of one hog every three seconds. Some men enthusiastically lifted up their T-shirts to reveal subtly different patterns of muscular development etched across their backs, while others showed how one of their wrists, arms, or fingers differed from others' in size or shape. In Sergio's grin I sensed a record of sacrifice for a better life—not just for monetary income but in terms of an honest way to make a living. For others, this third step was attached to a sense of fear. Some fretted about the possibility of chronic repetitive motion disorders. These people asked to switch positions on the line, even if it meant repeating breaking in. One woman, long after she stopped working at the plant, told me that the cold of the cut floor made her fearful of premature aging—that the years on the line had subtracted from her able-bodied life: "You can get arthritis early in life. I don't think I have it, but I don't know. My grandmother has it, so I was worried. My hands were always hurting . . . even after I quit." In patchy English, a skinny man from Burma seemed to suggest that the third step marked a race to either overcome or get off the line. "We're too weak to do the job," he said. "We need to build." I was not sure whether "building" meant that he must become stronger to resist permanent injury or, as he was doing at that moment, learn English to get his general equivalency diploma and leave town for other work. Minimally, this third stage of breaking in indicates a form of industrial capital that both gets inside the body's fibers and gradually manifests in a series of unendingly permanent transformations.

TWO CENTURIES OF DEAD LABOR

"Since the opening of the nineteenth century," writes the slaughterhouse historian Paula Young Lee (2008, 239), "the guiding imperative behind the slaughterhouse's creation was the extraction of animal slaughter from quotidian experience." It was a matter of controlling the public image of death (see also Pachirat 2011). In popular narratives, perhaps because of the invisibility of animal death, "the slaughterhouse system was completely 'modern,' a gigantic machine without narrative or history, perpetually regurgitating a product issued inside a moral vacuum" (Lee 2008, 3). Horowitz (2008, 13) notes that "our cultural sensibilities are shocked by the very presence of an industry given over to death," and it can become easy to neglect how mass-killing is changing. Too often, journalists' reports on the slaughterhouse presume that the violence—toward pigs and people—has gone unchanged since the publication in 1906 of *The Jungle*, Upton Sinclair's vividly brutal pre–New Deal exposé.[6] On the one hand, this is worth critically problematizing: the form of killing animals is changing in history with technology and capital, bringing with it accompanying forms of impact on workers' bodies. On the other, tracing technological innovation and mutability risks underplaying the sheer degree of industrial intensity compounded into the slaughter machine over the past two centuries. This is two hundred years of industrial refinement bearing down on fingertips and wrist tendons.

At the heart of the capitalist mass-production of death is a simple paradox: the fixity of the biological form of the hog—its legs, spine, and ribs always in the same rough relation to each other—enables extremely precise divisions of human labor around the carcass. Yet, subtle variations within these body parts—the fact that the pig is not "fully" standardized at the level of weight, tendons, muscle distribution, or gland locations—blocks automation and the replacement of human labor with machines. The perfectly standardized pig is very far from a reality. The slaughterhouse requires upward of one thousand workers per shift to trim the meat until it manifests the appearance of uniform pork.

In this sense, the scale and speed of the slaughter has increased in intensity over the twentieth century while the cut floor remains utterly dependent on human bodies, retinal perception, and on-the-fly judgment. Dover Foods' slaughterhouse was built with laser-sighted cut-assistance systems, machines that marble fat from the shoulders into tenderloins, and automated truck-loading devices. But the primary tools of the job remain—not entirely unlike those of earlier, nineteenth-century Porkopolises—a motor-driven chain, conveyor belts, knives, and human hands and eyes that can adjust as they address subtle carcass differences.[7] While human judgment cannot be obviated entirely, relatively more uniform hog carcasses can simplify this work and allow increases in line speeds once there is greater predictability to the body parts moving down the line. A key point to underline here is that the pig's body is itself being shaped for increased rates of labor exploitation. The hog that enters the integrated slaughterhouse is not a "raw material," but a being whose very body and carnal composition operates as a kind of biological technology for the extraction of value from human workers.

The origin of Dover Foods' slaughterhouse is not, however, *The Jungle*. Instead, it dates to 1967 and Iowa Beef Packers (IBP). Seeking to reduce well-paid line butchery to break the hold of unions and thus lower wages, IBP invented a new category: "boxed beef" (Broadway 1995; Horowitz 2006; Stull and Broadway 2013). As the company's founder said to *Newsweek*, "We've tried to take the skill out of every step" to produce cheap and uniform labor (quoted in Broadway 1995, 19). Rather than shipping entire sides of beef to regional butchers, who would then break down the carcasses into primal cuts such as tenderloins, IBP began dividing labor in the slaughterhouse around minute portions of the animal and vacuum-packing the pieces for direct sale at grocery stores. After a series of failed worker strikes around older plants that tried to match IBP's competitive advantage—most famously, the Hormel strike in Minnesota (Rachleff 1993)—the result was a dismantling of union bargaining power, wages, and safety provisions across the United States. In 1982, IBP entered pork processing in Iowa using the same system (Broadway 1995). Dover Foods' slaughterhouse, which breaks almost twenty thousand pigs down into as many as 1,100 product codes using upward of two thousand workers each day, is one of the many inheritors of IBP's dubious legacy.

As noted, the slaughterhouse has always been one of the most dangerous American spaces of labor. But as Horowitz (2008, 13) writes, "The kinds of dangers have changed, as have the location of the injuries that scar packinghouse workers for the rest of their lives." In 1943, a study commissioned by the U.S. Department of Labor found that accidents that cause absence from work in the slaughterhouse were double the national average for manufacturing (Horowitz 2008, 14). These were often injuries that maimed the worker in one fell swoop: amputating fingers on power saws or mangling arms in grinders. Unionization from 1943 until the 1970s changed this by enforcing safety protections on machines and giving workers sick leave with pay to ensure that minor injuries would not become more serious. In seven years "the injury rate fell to 15.1 percent, one-third the 1943 level" (Horowitz 2008, 16). However, as packing companies such as IBP responded to workplace organizing, they found ways to deskill butchers; they used conveyor belts to coordinate across sections of the plant; and they broke down the tasks of killing and cutting animals to finer motions. By 1970, the slaughterhouse's injury rate was again at the 1943 level of almost 47 percent and was three times greater than the manufacturing average (Horowitz 2008, 16). These were new forms of injury, however, in that the accidents were less severe—requiring fewer sick days per incident—as cumulative strains and cuts replaced maiming.

Horowitz (2008, 18) notes that in the 1980s there was an "appalling collapse in working conditions . . . as meatpacking employment changed from a middle-class, blue-collar job to an employment of last resort." In 1979, meatpacking wages were 15 percent above the national average; by 1990, they had dropped down to 20 percent below wages in other manufacturing industries. In 1970, the Bureau of Labor Statistics began tracking repetitive motion disorders under the category of "industrial illness," and these incidences grew 442 percent between 1981 and 1991 (Horowitz 2008, 18). As health insurers pressured meat corporations to limit their worker's compensation claims, injuries causing lost days dropped 50 percent from 1991 to 2001. Packinghouses had begun to use the radical division of labor designed into their factories to reassign workers so they would not miss work because of strains. By 2001, the slaughterhouse was the leader in repetitive motion disorders, with 11,700 cases in a national workforce of 147,000, or *thirty times higher* than the industrial average. Yet its compensation claims still dropped significantly. In 2002, the Bureau of Labor Statistics, via bureaucratic magic, made the slaughterhouse "safer" by changing reporting rules in ways that made the category of "repeated trauma" disappear. Slaughterhouses no longer needed to report injuries as long as the resulting absence was restricted to the day the injury occurred; the nature of what constitutes "restricted work activity" changed, and relapses of previous injuries would not count as new cases for reporting (Horowitz 2008, 22–23). The reported injury rate fell by half between 2001 and 2003 when these rules went into effect (Horowitz 2008, 23). While reported cases and workdays off have decreased at a slower rate since then, the forms of reporting for modern injuries makes these statistics suspicious.

The point of Horowitz's analysis is that the form of violence in the slaughterhouse is changing from accidental amputations to chronic forms of muscle and nerve damage; it is shifting from sudden external trauma to slow internal bodily transformation. The modern slaughterhouse is one of the world's original industrial forms (see Hounshell 1984). It may now also be the among the most precisely divided systems of labor, with hundreds of unique working motions divided around the finite body parts of a pig. The laboring movements of humans' muscles are being as finely physiologically divided as the finely sliced hog.

BIOLOGICAL SYSTEM

The term "Biological System" was one invoked by managers across almost all sites at Dover Foods that involve pigs—from artificial insemination planning to truck washes where two people power wash bacteria from the crevices of metal screws. Regardless, I was always perplexed by the tone of insistence with which slaughterhouse managers used the phrase in Continuous Quality Improvement (CQI) classes. I initially understood the phrase in ways that resonate with theories from agrarian studies and geography: it was an expression of impediment or recalcitrance to human will and total industrialization; that there is an inherent unpredictability to engineering biology relative to, say, metal (cf. Goodman et al. 1987; Goodman and Watts 1997). When a feed mill operator in these classes would ask why the rendering department could not predict how ground piglets would clog pipes, a manager would shrug and say, "Well, it's a Biological System." When I overheard Dover Foods' chief executive ask managers on the Live Side whether they could reproduce the oddly low piglet mortality rates of 2010 in a Biological System into the far future, the term made sense. But as one of the *Ur*-forms of the industrial, the slaughterhouse might appear to be just a "system" filled with automated machines. The animal at this point—as dead, inert body parts—would seem to be least vital in terms of resisting the will of capital and human agency.

Yet manager after manager would point to surprising forms of variability in the dead carcass as a problem. The first was seasonality. Mosquito bites on pig carcasses during the summer could account for as much as a 3 percent decrease in carcass yields, while litter sizes and hog weights also shifted with the season. The second form of biological variation that slaughterhouse managers invoked was accidental short-term variation that, some argued, should be controllable. One barn's pen structure, workers' habits, and pig genetics can lead to additional abscesses or bruising on the carcass, which can change flesh yields. Alternatively, the company is always developing new processes to derive more value out of the pig parts. This means that rendering—the department that boils diseased pigs, floor trimmings, and excess offal for proteins, fats, and collagens (see Shukin 2009)—is constantly dealing with shifting quantities, ratios, and forms of biological materials. This variation can cause breakdowns to the boilers and pipes. Most fundamental, however, is long-term variation: the fact that the pig is not yet standardized enough to replace human laborers with automated machines. While the labor process employs conveyor belts to bring a new piece of the hog's carcass to a line worker every few seconds, most of the company's attempts to use laser-guided cut systems or meat separators were abandoned years ago. As the senior vice president at the plant stated, "I'm not one to believe that you'll ever have a machine that can separate muscles" because of their variation. When the task is to cut meat apart at the minute scale of hundreds of different pieces, the complexities in tendon, muscle, and bone placement will overwhelm any machine. Moreover, at the broad scale of nineteen thousand animals per day, even a set of two hundred carcasses that weigh ten pounds less than others require human workers' manually cutting to adjust to their specificities.

As I noted in chapter 4, CQI classes were records of an internal struggle within the company. They were an attempt by the Live Side to force the Plant Side to reimagine what is possible within the slaughterhouse. For Live Side managers, the Plant Side was so caught up in its fragmented process— its throughput system measured by the minute—that they were not leaving room to search for a "paradigm shift," perhaps one on the order of the IBP model of the 1970s. "Biological System," as I heard its early enunciations by slaughterhouse managers, illustrated this quite neatly: to invoke it was always a defensive move designed to resist statistical measurement and sampling in ways that could illustrate gaps in the system, preferring exhaustive visual and timed appraisals. In a simple sense, the problem is that the product is ingestible meat intended for human consumption. One disagreement between the CQI guru, Doc Goodman, and managers concerned how they should achieve quality control. Goodman believed that sampling carcasses was a more effective means of ensuring quality than trying to inspect every hog body (which, as he described it, was akin to wasting one's time "counting dead fish" floating by in a river rather than finding out what killed the fish in the first place). The Doc offered case studies showing how sampling, say, a certain percentage of a product was a more effective means of ensuring consistency in output than counting (and inevitably missing) every single carcass. The Plant Side resisted, arguing that if one pathogenically tainted carcass out of 100,000 escaped from the slaughterhouse, the damage to the company's reputation would be irreparable.

Dover Foods, as I noted, used manufacturing theory across its managerial divisions for three reasons. The training was designed to provide a shared statistical language for managers to communicate across production phases that are materially distinct. These specific lessons in Japanese manufacturing theory were also a way to convey industrial control over the animal using the same terms favored by many of the company's investors and wholesalers in East Asia. Finally, CQI sessions could be grasped as a series of consciousness-raising exercises to militate against debilitating notions that the biological was a blockade to human will. As one manager who subscribed to Doc Goodman's maxims insisted, "Variation is fine so long as it's predictable." One of the basic tasks of the class was how to teach managers how to measure the range of variation in fluctuations of a Biological System for the purpose of identifying the most variegated links in the system from life to death.

The point of CQI is precisely that *all* forms of production are subject to "natural variation"—the crucial term in the philosophy. This is true whether one deals with a live pig, a human being's actions, an industrial disease, a tire, or a sheet of metal. This philosophy is comparable to a working, capitalist version of so-called new materialism. In her book *Vibrant Matter* (2010), Jane Bennett attempts to develop a vitality that is common to all "inanimate" things, from pencils to human flesh. As actants with a certain contingent agency in an assemblage that cannot be identified beforehand, her claim is that all things have a vital capacity "not only to impede or block the will and designs of humans but also to act as quasi agents or forces with trajectories, propensities, or tendencies of their own" (Bennett 2010, viii). The notion of "a life" (as opposed to "Life" in the abstract) is one that exceeds unified characterization, and "the aim is to articulate the elusive idea of a materiality that is itself heterogeneous, itself a differential of intensities, itself a life" (Bennett 2010, 57). We might say that vibrant matter is a proposition of radical ontological resistance to archetypal industrial standardization as an idea(l) and as an orientation—perhaps even resistance to the unity of form itself. Bennett argues that in "vital materialism there is no point of pure stillness, no indivisible atom that is not itself aquiver with virtual force" (Bennett 2010, 57). Even metal has a vitality, "a (impersonal) life" (Bennett 2010, 59), in that a hunk of metal is never composed of indistinguishable metal despite its appearance to the untrained human eye. Metal contains a "variegated topography" of imperfections and gaps at the "interfaces of grains" (Bennett 2010, 59), something of which all actual metal workers are cognizant.

In a sense, Continuous Quality Improvement is designed to attune managers and industrial architects to the ontological notion that everything has its own shimmering singular vitality—"a life" or "natural variation"—whether it is a piglet, a knife, or a pork chop. But the similarities between the two end there. Vital materialism pushes beyond viewing the material world as "a passive environment or perhaps a recalcitrant context for human action" (Bennett 2010, 111). It strives to engage the irreducible multiplicities of a material world for the purpose, in part, of imagining new modes of political engagement with nonhuman artifacts, beings, and infrastructures that does not simply boil down to human will. It enables an orientation that human life—for better and for worse—is tied up with environmental forces whether one is on an urban street corner or hiking through a nature preserve (see also Chen 2012; Murphy 2017). Continuous quality improvement aims to measure vital materiality on a quantitative plane to make the objects and subjects of production relatively *less vital* (or, what is the same, predictably vital). The "continuous" element of cQI accepts the ontological principle that standardized vitality is never total. The material world will always exceed engineering. In this sense, under the dictates of cQI, the pig cannot be a "machine" in the popular understanding of that term. This is so not because of ontological difference among lively life, dead biology, and metallic motors but because no machine is a perfectly standardized "machine." At the same moment, cQI's ambition is to make bioindustrialization more like our images of the standardized factory and perhaps, due to its reflexivity, more factory-like than any hitherto existing factory. Dover Foods is a practical project designed not only to standardize the vital—to mold the diversity of pig forms into something closer to a single "pig" for the purposes of extracting additional capitalist value out of these creatures and those who slaughter them—but also to vitalize the standard by rethinking the "factory" as a socioeconomic project.

As the cQI course progressed over the next eight months, it became clear that I was misunderstanding the meaning of "Biological System" as an abstraction for the factory farm. Under vertical integration, the shimmering "biological" can be interpreted as a potential source of innovation, and the deadening machinic "system" is the blockade to improvement (see Beldo 2017). As the plant's vice president put it, owning and controlling the pigs through "vertical integration ensures that we get a higher quality raw material coming in." But such dependence on the pig illustrates why the Live Side was intellectually dominant within the company, since the known paths of industrial intensification were through the animal's body.

Variation in the vitality of animal carcasses could be seen as open-ended sources of industrializing possibility, albeit ones that were mostly outside the Plant Side's control. By contrast, all of the managers with whom I spoke discussed the extreme pressures they felt to keep the line moving. They presented themselves as controlled by the machine and narrated how one breakdown in the process of one thousand people cutting animals would reverberate across the whole of the disassembly line. They could cite—with values for any day—how much money the packing plant would lose in a minute when a piece of the line broke down. The figure often started at $1,000. Line maintenance workers, whom kill and cut workers often claimed had an easier job, discussed constant mental stress that made them want to quit their positions. Whenever the line's conveyor belts broke down, managers screamed out figures for how much the stoppage was costing the company as maintenance crews tried to replace parts or fuses. As one shipping manager put it, "We don't have a chain pushing us, but we have a clock. Every minute of the clock, you're losing twenty boxes [of meat]." A delay in the loading of boxes onto trucks destined for the port of Oakland, en route to an eighteen-day journey to Japan, would cascade back onto the cut floor once the refrigerators with reserve space were stuffed full.

The problem that became clear in talking to plant managers was their inability to imagine both the killing machine and the human body as subject to higher speeds. They felt that—in my words—they had reached *the end of industrial time* after two hundred years of refinement, when (dis)assembly is so perfectly worked out that it operates at the very limits of the inescapable human form. It was in talking to shipping managers—who deal with cardboard boxes and thus are least tethered to animal biology—that I realized it was partly the (machinic) system in Biological System that is a roadblock to realizing capitalist "growth" in this plant. "Those conveyors are currently maxed out," explained one shipping manager. "We've run lots of tests. There's only one speed." That is, through years of time-motion studies that shave minutes off the line's speed, and of decades of seeking to fragment processes even further to kill more hogs, the manager claimed he had identified the maximum speed for the average person to sort boxes and move them from conveyer to conveyer without threatening a spiral of acute injuries.[8] Employees must scan, sort, and move boxes across conveyors that automatically load the boxes into trucks in batches graded by hog piece for a specific market. "There's a psychology to moving boxes," he explained after I told him stories I had heard about the pain-laden first two stages of breaking in from the perspective of lifting fifty-pound boxes all day, "and people need to get past that." But he went on to state that "the maximum is ten boxes a minute" and said that the human body simply cannot go faster than that point on a consistent basis.[9] This is a startling sense of the biological in Biological System not only because this man cannot see the possibility of industrial intensification via machines. Once slaughter is *consciously* acknowledged to work at the very limits of the human body, it is the shimmering variable vitality within each human physiological form that is being managed, measured, and contained. The result is a Biological System in a fourth sense: one that includes two thousand human workers whose labor on pigs' carcasses remakes their bodies.

THE END OF INDUSTRIAL TIME

This outcome both resonates with and diverges from discussions concerning the state of humanity in industrial capitalism. The idea that human beings are *culturally* industrialized is an old one. Edward P. Thompson (1967) illustrated how rural British conceptions of lived time were brought into alignment with early factory systems. Sigfried Giedion (1948) and Susan Buck-Morss (2000) described how art and aesthetic tastes of the early twentieth century were inseparable from industrial rationalities. Gramsci (1971) analyzed how Henry Ford's Sociological Department sought to construct new kinds of moral subjects alongside making cars, instilling staid domestic mannerisms into workers that would ensure that their diversions did not affect their ability to assemble cars (see Muehlebach and Shoshan 2012). Silvia Federici (2004) redescribed early modern European witch-hunting as a spectacular form of violence against women in ways that were designed to produce docile female subjects who would reproduce workers for capital. Aihwa Ong (1987), in a classic analysis of spirit possession on early Malaysian shop floors, demonstrated just how deeply U.S. dwellers' sense of the world was subtly engineered for them to tolerate the monotony of industrial work. These excavations of Western commonsense affects point to how the engineering of cultural sensibilities was necessary to make people willing and able to sell their time to industrial capitalists, to rent out their labor power for the enrichment of others, no matter how repetitive and boring the work.

Yet this is also more complicated than industrial capital requiring healthy physical bodies for the purposes of working the insemination or disassembly lines. As I noted in chapter 7, by 2010 a surplus of potential workers was available to Dover Foods as the aftermath of the 2008 financial crisis brought people in from the U.S. coasts. Kaushik Sunder Rajan (2006, 2007), Joseph Dumit (2012a), and Melinda Cooper (2008) have done creative conceptual work to develop a notion of "surplus health" that is tethered to increasing the value of the human body as a market in the American biocapitalist present. From extending the life of Americans so that they consume more drugs, to constantly limiting what counts as a healthy body that does not need drugs, these scholars have theorized how the human body has shifted from being an "arm of capital" to "an industry in itself" (Sunder Rajan 2007). Human life, rather than labor alone, is the site of investment.

What I have been charting across this chapter is a kind of surplus health that emerges *through* industrialization and work. The health clinic's series of tests and physicals for new employees are designed, one could say, to measure the vibrant matter that inheres in parts of each worker's irreducibly singular body. In those offices, Dover Foods is studying the state of working-class human embodiment in the United States, measuring how past labor, behavior, and lifestyle manifest within workers' muscle groups. In the absence of the ability of corporations to refine machines, tied to remaining variation in hog muscles, it is the body of the worker that is being industrialized by matching it to an ideal motion or part of the line where it has the least chance of breaking down after breaking in. The health clinic brings states of human and hog muscles into novel forms of entanglement, instantiating emerging forms of industrial engineering at the interspecies conjunction. The speed and scale of the factory farm's slaughterhouse—at the end of industrial time, after two hundred years of mechanization, when architects can no longer easily find ways to profitably refine the labor process—is turning slaughter into more of a "Biological System" than ever before.

What the Biological System of the slaughterhouse underlines is how industrialism is not a finished project, with fixed logics, at the end of an era. It is still evolving to find new terrains and substances for extraction and will continue to do so until we collectively and deliberately construct another social and economic world. The anthropologist Kim Fortun (2012, 2013) has argued that we are not inhabiting a postindustrial world underpinned by novel and emergent forms of digital entrepreneurialism or financial accumulation—or, at least, the present is also a moment of late industrialism marked by worn-out infrastructures and paradigms of thought (see also Besky 2019). As bridges, chemical factories, and nuclear reactors increasingly go awry due to lack of maintenance or a changing planetary climate, we are all at risk of experiencing industrialism in new ways as these systems more intimately harm life and health. That is, the *waning* phase of industrialism may be when we live with its effects most intimately. But the integration of human muscles and tendons as a dimension of capitalist meat and American animality also suggests other modalities of late industrialism. This is a matter not of industrial exhaustion but of industrial technics compounding in systems of raising and killing hogs to the point at which the central object of production has little room left for industrial expansion. This is a kind of late industrial efficiency that is, paradoxically, out of control. How corporations corral value from hog bodies as differential biologies appears to be emerging a template for finding new value within the human body, pushing beyond classic capitalist frames of using humans as labor power—and managing workers as a dimension of industrial swine.

PART V
VISCERA

9.2 **THIRTY-TWO THOUSAND POUNDS OF BONE** This is one batch of front leg bones from which Sakai Minerals is about to extract soup bases and oils. Each batch consists of twenty roughly 1,600-pound "combo boxes" of bones.

9.1 **LOCKER** (overleaf)
One thousand carcasses chill after evisceration in the slaughterhouse as they await further processing.

NINE MAYBE SOME BLOOD, BUT MOSTLY GREASE

GELATIN IS EVERYWHERE. It is an invisible dimension of scores of objects that compose our routine lives. Animal gelatin is hydrolyzed collagen derived from the bones, skin, and tendons of horses, cows, and especially pigs. Most readers are likely familiar with the substance from encountering it as a textural element in candy sweets such as marshmallows, gummies, or Jell-O desserts. The list just goes on from there (see Gelatin Manufacturers Institute of America 2012; Meindertma 2009): photographic prints, makeup and other cosmetics, gel-based medical pills, sandpaper, water proofed fabrics, some wines, simulated mammal tissues for ammunition testing, material for culturing cells in laboratories, paper money. There is a possibility that gelatin congeals on every single page of this book, allowing ink to bind to the sheets, and binding them together. One simple consequence is that it is difficult even to write and read about industrial pigs without touching their bodies. The printing of this book, in its own small way, may have contributed to the reproduction of the industrial pig as a model of animal life. And yet gelatin is but one commodity that comes from these hogs. Hundreds of others emerge from substances within the porcine body.

It was John Travers who first got me thinking about the viscera of slaughter, along with the political consequences of the fact that there is no part of the hog that goes un-slaughtered. John, like the vast majority of people in this area of the Great Plains, owes his livelihood to the rise of the pork industry. But he has never killed a pig. Born in a destitute section of the area, he had become a national- and state-level lobbyist on behalf of rural economic development issues by the time we met in his cramped office in the back of a run-down cell-phone store. The appearance of his ramshackle office was deceptive, for it was little more than a place where he could receive mail. The closet-like office was a sign that his real job was to make visits elsewhere, scratch people's backs, and create new friends. When I trailed him around the state capital for an afternoon, I was surprised to find his gait, accent, and facial expressions shifting with each lawmaker's hand that he shook. John had introduced me to local power brokers and bankers over the few weeks before we met in his office, while helping me enroll me in a Chamber of Commerce program that selected twelve "future community leaders" for a year and taught us about rural economy.

John started his career as a landfill manager in a small municipality, and it often seemed as if he had never left. "I just loooove garbage," he declared as we

9.3 **INTACT FRONT LEG BONES, CIRCA 2010** This close-up is of the top layer of a "combo box," circa 2010. By 2012, Dover Foods would employ new ways to crush the bones and reserve the meat. The company suddenly began sending Sakai Minerals chipped and fragmented bones, causing Sakai to revise its extraction process.

started discussing how his biography is inseparable from factory farms. "Take me out to a junkyard or a landfill. I could spend days going through there. You can see history unfold." He moved to Dixon in 1993 just before he "saw th[e] town grow from 7,500 to 15,500 people." Falling into the position of assistant building inspector for the slaughterhouse, he was also tasked with monitoring the construction of houses, trailers, and motels springing up to serve the expected eight thousand new residents. This gave him a unique perspective on Dover Foods' inner workings and the hidden electromechanical architecture necessary for the relative automation of slaughter. For three years he examined a "seventy-pound stack of plans" to charge for the miles of drains and wires that run across the foundation of what now appears as a gray concrete rectangle. Following this three-year period of construction, John was hired as Dixon's city manager based on his knowledge of rural waste, Dover Foods' infrastructure, and the corporation's internal culture. When his term ended, he became a lobbyist for wind energy companies that wanted public funding to offset the cost of transmission lines; his new job was to convince people that we were sitting amid "the Saudi Arabia of wind."

Amid these changes in his professional life the one constant in our conversations was John's passion for wastewater and solid waste disposal. "I guess I'm just fascinated by whose [the garbage] was, where it came from, where it's headed, and [what] the hell we're gonna do with it all. I could go through your garbage tonight and just be tickled to death. I mean seriously, it shows so much about our society, about people, who they are, what they are," he declared. John was proud of his and the city of Dixon's efforts in the 1990s to "stay on top of the bubble so that we wouldn't be behind with all these eight thousand people coming to town." In two years, Dixon monitored the building of four massive "trailer camps" for workers, retrofitted a homeless shelter, saw a dozen motels spring up overnight, tripled the size of the police force, set up "temporary cities" of recreational vehicles for construction crews, found water for the new population, started "one hell of a recycling program," and ensured that it had all of the access the city needed to solid waste landfills. John's one regret was that "someone forgot about the three million gallons of water coming out of Dover's plant, contaminated out the wazoo with nitrates." The result, after the city was almost fined for disposal of untreated sewage onto open fields, was a new state-of-the-art wastewater treatment plant built largely without subsidies, using local taxpayer dollars. Utility rates skyrocketed in the town shortly after John stepped down as city manager, once Dover Foods "lobbied the City Council pretty hard" to acquire a lower industrial rate on their water usage: "They use well over half the water in this town. It's not right that they get thirty-five cents a gallon and I get fifty cents a gallon. But, you know . . . , people with the deepest pockets win."

Thinking that his knowledge of trash politics could inspire insights into agribusiness, I asked him what kinds of waste came out of the slaughterhouse:

JOHN: Whoooo-wheee! That was something that's coming out of the drains; that's what caused the city of Dixon to have to spend $16 million to $20 million [for a new wastewater facility] because of the high nitrates coming out of the plant. There were some ungodly things in there. We got some samples. . . . The worst thing there was nitrates. High in nitrates. There was some metals in it, some heavies. Of course, there was some sodium. I don't know what else bad little creatures was out there, but the nitrates were the

9.4 **PORK OIL** Buckets of concentrated pork oil sit on pallets ready for shipment to Japan by boat.

killers. That was the biggest issue that we had to deal with. The other thing was just the increase of solid waste itself.

ALEX: Solid waste? You mean not just from the increase in population, but from the plant? I assume there have to be piles of bones going somewhere.

JOHN: Well, no. They was using everything. Jesus, it's fascinating. There's nothing! No Thing! You know what comes out of there? Cardboard. Gloves. Latex. If there's meat coming out of there, it's some old boy's bologna in a trash can. But as far as that hog, there's nothing coming out of the waste streams, of the municipal waste streams. Not a thing. Because they capture all that blood, because they use all that blood for the protein [plasma]. They've got their own little centrifuge. There's nothing really that ever really comes out of that plant that resembles a hog. Or, well . . . unless maybe . . . well, very little.

ALEX: So maybe a little blood in the water?

JOHN: Maybe some blood, but mostly grease.

There's nothing that comes out of that plant that resembles a hog. John's discussion of Dover Foods' waste stream points to a space of full biological absorption in which the corporation controls every fragment of the pig's body, the only exception being minute particles of fat and feces that are invisible to the naked eye. The primary sign that nineteen thousand pigs die in this town each day—that some 5.5 million pounds of biological matter move through this place each day—are merely some washed-away smears of grease that cling to the surfaces of metal knives and slaughterhouse conveyor belts, along with some feces from cleaning out intestines. The only remaining visible traces of the company's daily kill are traces of human labor: cardboard, latex, deli meat. At the same moment, while one cannot perceive anything resembling a hog in public, novel corporate externalities, municipal politics, and particulate risk cohere through the compounded nitrates of some 100,000 pigs leaking each week into the wastewater. Invisible traces, measurable only microscopically as substances that are not materially unique to hogs, nonetheless overwhelm sanitation systems in their scale of concentration. What John was pointing

9.5 **UNUSUAL BACTERIA** A wastewater manager's drawings of strange bacteria that he found in the slaughterhouse's water stream, which led him to send samples to specialists around the country.

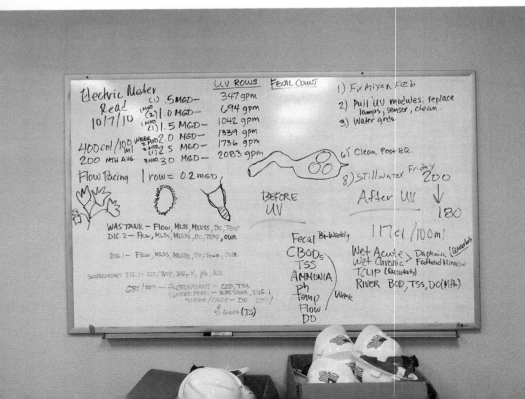

to is a kind of industrial carcass that cannot be fully comprehended in terms of chops, tenderloins, ribs, or other muscles. All of this suggests an animal species in which there is barely any room left for value-free biology; the industrial pig in John's narrative is one in which every bodily substance save for the microscopic has been measured and acquired some worth. It begs the question of what kinds of labor, history, power, and social relations underlie the corporate monopolization of a life-form to its chemical compounds.

Sidney Mintz (1984), in his justly celebrated account of the global circulation of sugar, famously argued that we are unable to understand an agricultural commodity without attention to its production and its consumption. The two reverberate through each other, entangling distant populations together such that even a stalk of sugarcane ripples with ongoing practices. Yet there are 1,100 product codes within Dover Foods' hogs; there are as many as 1,100 different preexisting claims on portions and substances of each pig's

9.6 **TESTING FEEDSTOCKS** These mason jars contain completed designer bio-oils for racecars. A local entrepreneur was building a startup for fat-based high-performance engine inputs. Pictured are two batches derived from pig fat and one from castor oil.

body. What this suggests is that it is impossible to account for the worlds and practices that cohere through, and ripple back to sustain, industrial pigs. There are just too many beings eating and consuming these animals' bodies. What I find remarkable is that, under these terms, the industrial pig—even after its death—is at some level an unknowable entity.

The fat used to be the basis of candles and soap; today, traces of Dover Foods' lard are blended into diesel pumps at commercial gas stations across the country (see chapter 10). The skins generate leather, gelatin, and collagen that can then appear as hair gels and moisturizers. The bones are cooked and processed in so many different stages that the same leg can become a source of soup base, pork oil, glue, and concrete filler. Each gland plays host to future drugs and hormones in the form of estrogen, epinephrine, insulin, trypsin, and somatotropin. Hog blood can become piglet food, sausage, or fibrin for surgical repair. The foam from hogs' (and cows') lungs—pulmonary surfactant—in some other slaughterhouses is used to help premature human babies and those with respiratory distress syndrome breathe (Boodman 2018). A fibrous substance in the hog's bladder is being developed to help humans regenerate tissue (Piore and Lewis 2011). The world's largest pork company, Smithfield Foods, has opened a new biomedical unit for exploring xenotransplantation of hog parts into human beings (Steenhuysen and Hirtzer 2017).

The next chapter is about what it means to use all of the pig and the kinds of human waste that ensue *because* of ardent efforts to try to make every single microgram of carnal terrain within hogs carry unique forms of value and use. Or, if the previous chapter was about the changing qualities of labor within factory farms, this one is about the capitalist inability to limit the quantities of labor that have come to course through porcine forms.

TEN **LIFECYCLE**

On Using All of the Porcine Species

SURPLUS DEATH

In her art project *Pig 05049* (2009), Christien Meindertsma tracks the long, essentially interminable death of a single hog in the Netherlands by recovering all of the commodities that emerged from this one animal's body. As a visual artist, Meindertsma offers her viewers little commentary. She instead takes 1:1 pictures of the 185 items she uncovered during her globe-spanning investigation. The products went far beyond cuts of meat to include bullets, biodiesel, inkjet paper, wine, and holograms. The North Carolina Pork Producers Council estimates that as many as four hundred nonedible products depend on hog substances either for their material composition or as an irreplaceable dimension of their manufacturing process. Over the nearly three-decade history of Dover Foods' plant in Dixon, it has used some 3,600 different SKUs (product codes). In 2010, it was making 1,100 of these commodities from hogs. Many of these codes are just identical cuts of meat shipped to different places and wholesalers. Some others are designer portions of custom meat such as thinly sliced shoulders for Japanese wholesalers, or trotters with collagen and bits of flesh above the hoof for Chinese markets. But many others are substances that few could recognize as being rooted in animals.

Across the photographic entries and the book's foreword, Meindertsma's text repeatedly insists on a simple but suggestive point for thinking through forms of carnal value and even power within the factory farm. Killing hogs at the rate of twenty thousand per day opens up different possibilities for capital, imagination, and labor than exists at the scale of two hundred. Deep evisceration of the animal into 1,100 distinct commodities is premised on massive scales of death. It makes little sense to burn the bones of a single pig to generate a few grams of specialty black bone pigment or to build a biodiesel plant to gain energy and glycerin from the fat of five hundred hogs. Carbon offsets will not be granted for the use of tiny pools of pig feces-*cum*-methane biogas (see Mahony 2011). There is similarly no reason to build a health clinic, as we saw in chapter 8, to capitalize on, and vertically integrate, workers' muscles and tendons if a corporation employs only two hundred people. The gallbladders, lungs, pancreatic tissues, heart valves, brains, blood, and workers' arms are more easily transmogrified into new kinds of valuable stuff when they are concentrated in millions of pounds.

In *Pig 05049*'s insightful foreword, Lucas Verweij contrasts Meindertsma's findings with the claims of an old Sicilian gentleman who chided Verweij with the moral message that his generation is wasteful. In his village, the old man reminisced, people frugally saved all pig substance to be good stewards of the environment and pay homage to every piece of a life expended for fleeting human ends. They tried to eat morally, as it is now called in the United States, all the way from "snout to tail" (see Weiss 2016). *Pig 05049* gently illustrates how this old gentleman's nostalgia is complicated and perhaps even misplaced in light of the extreme evisceration that characterizes the corporate pork industry, though in this case one of the key distinctions is that "the overseeable scale of a Sicilian village has been replaced by an unfathomable world scale" (Meindertsma 2009, n.p.).

On the face of it, none of this is new. One need only think of the hygiene industry that sustained the meatpacking operations of nineteenth-century Cincinnati by making soap from excess hog fat, which at that time made up 50–70 percent of pigs' body weight (Gordon 1981; Wrye 2015). As goes the old Chicago cliché, which dates back to the 1920s, meatpackers have long used "everything but the squeal" (Swift and Van Vlissingen 1927). The Armours and Swifts of late nineteenth-century Chicago built their empire on hog hooves, fur, and blood. Historically, the model of profitability in meatpacking has been to break even on meat by charging low prices that undercut competitors such as local butchers (Cronon 1991) or, today, ethically driven pastured and organic farmers (Weiss 2016). In turn, meatpackers tend to build their profit margins through new uses of the "excess" daily haul of 281,500 pounds of fat or 736,000 pounds of internal organs. The sociologist Jen Wrye (2015) points out in a study of pet food that calling such viscera "byproducts" is misleading. She refers to them as co-products, as the sale of organs and blood are what makes cheap and ubiquitous meat possible (see also Walker 2000). Moreover, this process is unending: as the price of meat fell during the twentieth century—or as distributors such as Wal-Mart have taken larger shares of profits—"protein" corporations have kept trying to find new uses, cuts, and presentations of substances to offset low margins and overproduction (Boyd and Watts 1997). The pig's dead body is in history, with capitalists finding new ways to take it apart.

The National Renderers Association—rendering being the process of cooking portions of an animal body that are inedible for humans and separating the substances to extract purified interchangeable forms of fat, bone meal, plasma, and protein—has branded itself the "Original Recyclers" (National Renderers Association 1996; see also Shukin 2009). The association's claim is that the total use of an animal boils down to efficiency; it argues that rendering is an ingenious and neutral technoscientific way to recycle all of the biological material—from poultry feathers to industrial pig brains—that contemporary American society assists into existence. Without dismissing the utility of rendering, I would nonetheless argue that the idea of total animal usage should be seen as profoundly political. The increasing derivation of products from hogs' bodies arguably necessitates ever-growing corporate consolidation and scales of killing. Moreover, it should matter that it is almost impossible to exist today without being in contact with traces of dead pigs. Our everyday actions are forced to provide value to industrial animality. Using all of the pig, as we shall see, is a means through which the model of the factory farm—along with the kinds of standardized life it cultivates—is sustained indefinitely into the future. This, in turn, affects how we can conceptualize viable pathways for transforming food and agriculture.

In 2008, People for the Ethical Treatment of Animals made a proposition that it felt could undercut factory farms: it announced a $1 million award for whoever could commercially manufacture in vitro meat. The ability to grow tissue in a bioreactor, at scale and cost, in a form that mimics the taste, texture, and shape of an intact muscle seems to be a ways off. But there is no shortage of start-ups trying to speculatively enter into product development (see Dutkiewicz 2019). There do appear to be clear benefits to decoupling meat from the bodies of animals: reduction of the risk of zoonotic disease, ecological damage, greenhouse gases, along with the possibility of minimal death (Dutkiewicz 2019; Wolfe 2012, 96–97).[1] For all of the public discussion and hype that the issue of lab-grown meat has generated, however, the flesh-centric basis of the debate risks accentuating a reductive impression of the factory farming system that this technology is supposed to replace. Conversations amongst the general public seem to assume that blood, fur, or organs are burdensome waste. Such a view implies that these animal parts are disposable when, instead, these so-called by-products have long been the very substances that have enabled the corporate concentration and control of animal life and death.[2] While the large-scale success of in vitro meat at a reasonable price would undoubtedly affect factory farms, as evidenced by meat lobbies' strident efforts to try to create legal restrictions on what substances can be labeled "meat," what this debate parses over is the ambiguous question of whether capitalist agribusiness is ultimately (or, at least, necessarily), at the level of its organization and profitability, geared around feeding animal flesh to human beings. It may be counterintuitive, but factory farms are not easily reducible to meat consumption.

The twentieth-century capitalist slaughter model was premised on an economics of what we might call surplus death. At first glance, surplus death can seem like a nonsensical, throwaway phrase. Death is death; it is the consequential end. Along these lines, one of the key contributions of critical animal studies has been the unpacking of the naturalized cultural processes behind how some animals are made "killable," subject to an unflinching and unreflective termination (e.g., Animal Studies Group 2006; Haraway 2008; Lopez and Gillespie 2015; Raffles 2010). But capitalist pigs, we should remember, are not simply being killed. They are industrially slaughtered and disassembled. If we think beyond that split second moment when the hog's carotid arteries are slit—on which a blinding amount of capital and ethical attention is focused (cf. Grandin 2006; Williams 2004)—we might see an excess that emerges across the long path of a hog being disassembled, which affects how its life is sustained. Capitalist slaughter aims to unlock new value through killing at larger scales by cutting more finely into the substances of the animal's carcass and by keeping body parts out of rendering, where they become cheap fungible fats and proteins. While it is true that meatpacking plants have long used *all* of the pig in some manner—the least valuable substances rendered for kibbles or fertilizer—they have also been searching for unique carnal terrains within the pig on which to put people to work.

Over the course of this book, we have seen how capitalist imperatives for growth take hold of industrial pigs. A sampling includes increasing litter sizes, increasing the number of hogs in a place, more finely regimenting the behavior of workers in the face of the hog's fragility, raising the rate of (literal) hog growth, and speeding up the pace of killing. This only continues into postdeath viscera, which are fundamentally about expanding the realms and worlds mediated by porcine substance.

The protagonist of this book's final chapter is the radically disassembled animal—this post-organismal hog—that cannot be grasped as a unitary being, but instead as a parsed collection of discrete proteins, fats, amino acids, and nitrates. I begin with the vision of one of Dover Foods' architects of monopolized life, tracing his sense of what "finished" vertical integration would look like. I then complicate his sense of finality by rethinking the factory farm through several of its distinct commodity chains such as lungs, feces, fat, logistical meat, front leg bones, and animals that do not match specs. These are fleeting snapshots of various ways that companies make surplus death. Such arts of fashioning livelihoods that thrive in the periphery of a modern Porkopolis illustrate how the factory farm generates, and relies on, alternative capitalisms and interspecies assemblages, toward surprising and uncertain ends.[3] Thus, my closing aim is to offer some open-ended portraits of how people get by in the fissures of this Porkopolis and the new worlds that it summons into existence. My premise is that we cannot understand the ongoing lives of industrial pigs—along with the extreme uniformity of their bodies—without attention to the thousands of pathways through which their dead ancestors' body parts circulate. And each of these portraits is rooted in a simple question of totality, one that has, in a sense, been this book's most basic query from its very first pages: what does it mean to use *all* of the pig? What emerges, across sites, is not so much a finished achievement as a fragile and ongoing process that must continually enlist new kinds of consumers to sustain its growth.

THE LIFECYCLE OF THE POSTDEATH PIG

When I first met Ryan Jenkins, I expected a simple lesson on how Dover Foods raises pigs in an agricultural context in which 50–70 percent of input costs tend to be tied to feed rather than labor. Instead, I heard an ambiguously utopian rendition of what it means to use all of the pig. Ryan gave a narrative on vertical integration that suggested how the nature of the industrial pig can be grasped only long after its death as a collection of parts and chemicals rather than as a single coherent organism. In so doing, he offered a relatively unusual portrait of capitalist agribusiness in which the factory farm's project is to expand the realms of existence that are mediated by, and dependent on, industrial pigs.

"You get numb at these figures," Ryan cautioned while he wrote a long stream of numbers on a whiteboard. He was trying to provide a group of interns drawn from U.S. agricultural colleges with a line of sight into the regional and global significance of Dover's operations. As he passed around various feed components—types of dried corn, wheat, jars of bright white beef fat, baggies of antibiotics, glycerin, dried blood plasma, a black briefcase containing twenty small glass vials of minerals, and ground bakery byproducts (expired kid's breakfast cereal from Pennsylvania that "tastes like Lucky Charms")—Ryan was trying to articulate his awe at the scale of production that the company had achieved after two decades of gradual organizational refinement.

We were sitting in a low-ceilinged corporate-style meeting room just outside the rural hamlet of Franca (population, four hundred). This modular room looked identical to other Dover management offices that dot outposts on the Great Plains and in the Midwest: white walls, a projector for video conferences, folding plastic tables, giant maps of company operations, motivational posters with quaint leadership slogans, continuous quality improvement circle diagrams, and metal chairs. As Ryan spoke to this group of eight interns, wind shrieked outside and pounded through the cheap thin walls and single-pane windows, forcing him to smile and pause his overview of the economic, social, and nutritional factors in animal feed. The noise reminded me of the corporation's bare-bones frugality alongside the long history of fleeting capital investment in these rural parts.

This is a "place in the middle of nowhere," he admitted, "but our world isn't really that large anymore." Franca had become a tiny outpost where "if you can keep up" and watch the movement of commodities from around the world absorbed into pigs and reemerging as incarnate, he said, "you can actually see the world market moving through here." The numbers that he had written on the whiteboard were indeed numbing. Dover Foods' five million animals consume thirty thousand tons of feed per week, with three of their feed mills alone processing eight thousand tons each. That is about 800,000 bushels of grain coming in from across the Midwest every week, filling thirty-two rail cars. It is 260,000 tons per year of soybean meal, a byproduct of cooking oil extraction. This is in addition to the pallets of fifty-pound bags of antibiotics stacked in the feed mills, minerals from a dozen countries, amino acids and vitamin supplements, and gallons of "choice white grease" from a cow slaughterhouse. In a year, as Ryan wrote, Dover would feed its hogs forty million bushels of corn, or a full 10 percent of the Kansas corn crop. Whether it is phosphates sourced out of eastern Siberia or detritus cheaply recovered from a Pittsburgh cereal processing factory, Ryan was trying to make clear that the company was actively suturing distinct global ecologies and supply chains within its pigs' diets. He was attempting to build a vision of a very complex pig whose life must be sustained through global ecologies as a whole rather than from just one place.

Ryan was the commodities buyer for Dover Foods. He was in charge of drawing from "a whole world for possible feedstuffs" to purchase the grain, vitamins, minerals, and antibiotics that will be pelletized and fed to growing hogs. Ryan's job was to survey changes in the volatile prices of grain and petroleum, and in currency exchange rates, to cheaply sustain the company's swine without sacrificing carcass quality. He was something of a capitalist digestion manager who put metabolisms and markets in sync.[4] Thus, Ryan's position gave him a unique perspective on the arc of industrial hogs' life-and-death course, from a growing two-day-old baby piglet to a wide array of disassembled substances marked by barcodes. A tension started emerging in his discussion, however, between feeding the pig to sustain its life (or growing pigs with a high feed-to-weight conversion ratio) and sustaining the profitability of its death (or feeding Dover Foods' pigs the right combination of things to maintain all 1,100 product codes).

"A pig is pretty much what you feed it. . . . If ya eat junk, you're gonna be junk. And that ain't good enough for Japan," Ryan declared, parroting a phrase that his colleagues tended to use to tout the advantages of their premium industrial pork. Dover Foods, unlike some other major corporations, refused to cut corners for quick profitability by using, say, cut-rate dried distillers' grains in place of fresh corn. The company's economic model was premised on exporting as much meat as possible to East Asia, where wholesalers will pay more but demand consistency and quality in terms of fat content, carcass texture, and shelf life. At the same time, the line is a recognizably old expression in pig farming circles, dating back to the quaint slogan that "a pig is twenty bushels of corn on four legs" (see Essig 2015). In this room surrounded by dozens of feed ingredients beyond those bushels of corn, however, Ryan's statement hinted at changing porcine natures. As a solvent for the feed commodity market, one whose omnivorous digestion allows it consume almost anything, including expired breakfast cereal, this hog was both evolving alongside and acting as a key component in the global food system.[5] Yet there are some tensions here. While the industrial hog's very flesh is shifting as new products and detritus emerge on the market, Dover also needs to consistently source similar things over time to maintain a bodily assemblage of chemical components and acids that can lead to 1,100 commodities.

These narratives of interconnection across novel agricultural centers, a global market made visibly incarnate, and the multiple market pressures on the pig's body were a backdrop for Ryan to articulate his true passion: what he dubbed the "Lifecycle" of pork production. "You need a different lens to see this, but our whole area is really one huge playground," he said. He claimed that this zone is now composed of agricultural products where nothing gets out except when it emerges in the pig's body, an agricultural totality funneled through hogs. Minerals from Siberia or South Africa may be imported, but local corn, milo, and beef fat are never exported except in porcine form. The scale of swine has reoriented the crops that farmers decide to grow, dictating the value of the fields and soil where the pig is a dominating presence. Para- doxically, the emergence of this place "in the middle of nowhere" as a player in global agribusiness has made it, in a sense, distinct from the rest of the world. It is a one hundred-mile-radius zone that is re-regionalized via this hog whose body is metabolically designed for circulation to East Asia, and a place where swine diets dictate all value and futures for every locally farmed organism.

Tracing his fingers along the roads and fields of a company map dotted with 1,200 farm sites, Ryan declared that "this is a 'local' operation" that absorbs the entirety of the region's agricultural outputs. Hence, as he was hinting for the benefit of a new generation of agriculture students schooled to acknowledge the importance of local breadbaskets, it is not fully disconnected from local ecologies. But he continued by saying that it is an operation that "has to be understood as local within a huge area." "This area here," he declared as his hands moved across a map that indexed a unique territorialization, encom- passing many counties and states, "is now a total living system." In Ryan's vision, this region has essentially become one massive farm for making pigs.

"The level of integration here is simply incredible," he continued, drawing a circle around the one hundred-mile-radius region. "The natural Lifecycle here is fully integrated." Describing how *disconnected* monocultures in American agriculture create a monocultural imagination, he claimed, "From an agricul- ture perspective . . . people have gotten so in their little world, they are dis- connected from the original Lifecycle that is all integrated." Ryan's statement might appear contradictory, for he seems to cite nostalgia for the 1950s small- scale diverse farm of pigs, corn, tomatoes, and wheat that has been decimated by the very industrial monocropping that led to the factory farm (Berry 1977; Pollan 2006). Yet his point was that only a higher-scale order of industrialization could reunite the natural lifecycle in the twenty-first century. His countervision was the promise of "finished" vertical integration. The proposition latent in the Lifecycle is that we need to shift our vision of the original lifecycle from the single farmer on his property managing pigs and corn to the corporation coordinating the movements of "the [industrial] Lifecycle" across a one hundred-mile-radius region, or even the globe. His workplace philosophy is loaded with tensions, for it suggests that the endpoint of the factory farm is the total monopolization of life and death across all global species that come into contact with or are mediated by the industrial pig.[6]

Put differently, the lens of the Lifecycle depicts a species of animal that never really lives or dies; one that constitutes itself out of the whole of a global material world while, in turn, sustaining the elements that make up its chain of being in the form of payment to farmers, fertilizer for crops, or energy for transport. The industrial Lifecycle is a market vision of porcine vitality in terms of the substances that are predestined to be detached after the hog's death, one where the life of the hog is inseparable from the manner of its death. Throughout this book, we have seen how, from ownership of farms to meticulous slaughter, from feed mills to genetics, from workers' housing to health clinics, Dover Foods tries to control every stage and aspect of pig production. Ryan's market-driven version is perhaps the apotheosis of this agribusiness model, a seamless vision whereby corporations are no longer managing unique life forms but a purified mode of vitality. The Lifecycle is a vision of the industrial pig and the factory farm as a completed, modular project at the end of an era; it offers a sense of the industrial pig as a doubly globalized species. On the one hand, this animal is hooked into so many worldly ecologies, and reshaping the local agro-ecologies where it lives, that it seems to be capable of being reemplaced elsewhere. On the other, this pig's bodily substances are circulating finely into everyday life around the globe.

What Ryan's narrative ignores are the many (not necessarily industrial) practices and values that sustain this contemporary Lifecycle. Following Marianne Lien's (2015, 107) push against "too-smooth account[s] of industrial success" in farming, all of this points to the fragility, unpredictable entanglements, and unintentionality of such a system. So many beings need to do work to maintain the profitability of this model of a factory farm; so many lives and technologies are recruited to handle its biological excess. The routine practices of cats, drivers, internet browsers, transnational shippers, ramen soup chefs, and family farmers are being converted into working on standardized life. Each is consuming the carcass of industrial pigs. I offer snapshots of six of these worlds, but it should be remembered that there are 1,094 more that could be described. What emerges is not a finished and total Lifecycle at the end of an era but tenuous worlds that prop up the industrial pig.

LUNGS AND LIVERS, OR OFFSHORE ANIMALITY

A squat white metal and concrete building sits in a dusty industrial park outside Dixon. It is deliberately unremarkable. There are no brands or signs announcing the building's purpose. A few cars sit in its gravel parking lot. Three metal chemical storage cylinders poke out from the back. When I first spent time in the facility, shortly after it opened in the early 2010s, locals were calling it the "kibble plant." Prior to meeting with its eight employees, I assumed it made small batches of designer pet food. Instead, this building, along with six others that have been built next to the United States' largest slaughterhouses within the past ten years, makes a powdered substance called a palatant. This building is part of an ambitious logistical process to transform how all the world's cats and dogs experience the sensation of taste.

On the building's so-called hot side, boilers, reactors, and centrifuges run on automated cycles for eighteen hours per day. There is a dry storage room with pallets of some twenty different chemicals that are used in the "cooking" process and a sparkling laboratory for sampling the end product. The cold side, a two thousand-square-foot refrigerated concrete warehouse, is stacked to its rafters with blue plastic bins that are the shape and size of oil drums. The bins are covered with warnings that the contents are not for human consumption. "Inedible," in capital letters, is stenciled with black spray paint on their surface. Inside are hog lungs and livers—which formerly would have been used in rendering—that have been splashed with black food coloring to ensure they are not accidentally ground up with muscle for human food.[7] The reddish-white piles of inky black-stained viscera resemble squid. In this cold chamber at any given moment, there are thirty thousand of these hog organs awaiting chemical processing into liquid and powdered palatants.

As a routine step in the process of making commercial pet food, manufacturers have long been cooking fatty flavoring slurries of mixed hydrolyzed animal parts known as "digests." Their purpose has always been an interspecies balancing act. Digests make extruded pellets or moist cans of foodstuffs sensorially appealing to both nonhuman eaters and their human feeders (Nestle 2008). They mask the intense rendered stench that would be disagreeable to most human noses while enticing cats to ingest a host of processed grain meals, vitamins, and muscle proteins that they would not consider edible. These principles remained the same after the 1990s when the industry shifted to palatants. But a palatant differs from a digest in a few crucial ways. As (typically, but not always) a powder, it is more intense and used sparingly to coat kibbles. It is closer to a material substance that is "pure taste" rather than a substance that carries nutritive qualities. This allows animal feed manufacturers more flexibility in their kibble mixes. Second, palatants are more precise and selective than digests in their composition of material sources (livers, lungs, stomachs, etc.) to create a more uniform base for a flavor. Third, they are treated with amino acids to create chemical reactions—such as Maillard reactions, emphasizing meaty sensations—that intensify certain qualities of taste for a given "target species" (Eiler 2015; Nagodawithana et al. 2010). In sum, palatants are made from the coproducts of industrialized hog killing and, since the 1990s, have been added to pet food to compel other species to rapidly consume even more wastes of industrialized hog killing.

"My bosses told me to tell you that they've completed their Bermuda Triangle around the competition," Jeff DeLong informed me as we walked around BFG Essences' new facility in Dixon. What he meant was that this building ensured that BFG Essences had access to three U.S. pork packers while geographically encompassing its two main competitors with organ-cooking stations. Jeff was a stocky and jovial fellow in his mid-thirties who took pride in running buildings—he walked me through each of his framed industrial certifications on the wall—while maintaining a sense of humor about his odd line of work. But when we first met, he was a bit stressed. At that early juncture, a month into opening, there were still a lot of issues to work out. For one, the floors were overrun with cockroaches, and dense hordes of flies covered the back of the building. This had never happened at the other BFG facilities that Jeff had set up. He maintained the building meticulously, at one point even picking up a broom to dust overhead pipes as we strolled around. But some odd combination of the Great Plains ecology and dense viscera vapors made insects "throw themselves at us, at the building."

This facility is officially called BFG Essences North. But when the company bosses flew in for a day from Europe and saw the flat landscape, they informally renamed it BFG Essences Moon. The metaphor of a natural resource extraction expedition to the moon felt fitting, for Jeff kept insisting that he was "just a stooge with a machine." He was a temporary transplant from North

Carolina who had moved to Dixon for a few months to train a few hired locals who would eventually run the factory. Following each "cook," he sampled the substance and sent the raw data to Europe, where flavor scientists told him what to adjust to match the substance to the other organ factories. Jeff and three other company operatives would stay until they were done tinkering with this viscera recipe. Then they would move to a different meatpacking town to set up another one. As the flavor scientists at corporate headquarters changed the recipe, they repeated the process to ensure that the company's four extraction facilities were making a similar substance, despite differences in regions along with the properties of a source of viscera.[8]

The company's logistical practices of trying to source standardized viscera give a striking portrait of how corporate pork production has reshaped the ecologies of select American places over the past twenty years. These parts of the rural United States come to appear as globally unique. There are now eight to ten locations in the country that contain so many hogs that global corporations are offshoring their facilities to "mine" porcine bodies that cannot be found at this carnal concentration elsewhere in the world. It cuttingly pushes against subtle fantasies of American empire and postindustrial temporalities, which always figure other places as the appropriate site for grueling work and environmental degradation (see Tsing 2015). The United States is typically imagined as the clean "intellectual" site that coordinates these processes, not the host that endures their environmental effects. Yet few other countries allow this degree of carnal production density, such that massive formations of animality cohere that can be treated as akin to environmental deposits for extraction.

The palatants made by BFG Essences rely on what we might call bodily monocultures. By having exclusive access to the largest pools of viscera, palatant companies can more easily create consistency across sites. Moreover, confinement becomes manifest in seemingly identical lungs that have all breathed the same ammonia and hydrogen sulfide-ridden air and livers that have all processed the same standardized rations of feed. Standardized life leads to qualitatively new kinds of value. This logistical work of setting up automated extraction centers is part of the work of making pigs into *the* pig, or livers into *the* liver. It is one step in terms of doing and stabilizing materials to manufacture a single taste for the feline species. In turn, cats and pigs are becoming entangled in new ways: global feline sensations are changing alongside the living conditions of industrial pigs—while these cats' increasingly voracious eating practices come to sustain confinement.

The efforts of BFG Essences to secure ample pools of uniform viscera from American factory farms are only part of the company's logistical program for making cat taste. When I spent time with Jeff, most of our conversation centered on the sites where the organ recipe itself is refined. The company's claim to fame is its investment to maintain, as Jeff put it, "a worldwide network of expert tasters." They "employ" (his words) more than five hundred cats—of different breeds and habits—across a series of testing facilities located on different continents. These feline workers are designed to overcome the major hurdle of designing palatants: "The problem is that the cat can't tell us what it likes." Indeed, the flavors being manufactured—largely based on pyrophosphates (Roach 2013)—are not detectable by the human palate (just as cats, for instance, cannot taste sweetness).

These testing sites for experimenting with variations on organ recipes were first initiated in the mid-2000s. If a company such as Hill's Science Diet chooses to source its palatants with BFG Essences, then BFG Essences uses its tests to determine the correct palatant recipe and intensity for the given kibble. But they are also sites of comparison. The company tests its contracted manufacturers' feeds against other brands—for example, Friskies or Meow Mix—that might be aligned with a different palatant company. It does this to see how those competitors' taste recipes are changing over time, or if they are starting to "outperform" (as they call it) one of BFG's brands that were previously dominant. In this manner, the flavor of each company is meant to become more "agentive" and "cat-like" over time in its ability to make felines consume; cat panels are designed to continuously refine and maximize the circulation of rendered pig detritus and organs through another species.

What makes a cat an expert taster is its consistency. Each cat is slightly (or starkly) different—BFG Essences acknowledges that—but what it wants are cats that are predictable in their quirks or preferences. My understanding is that the company cultivates such feline differences within the so-called worldwide network: cats with certain allergies, for instance, are useful for some trials concerning niche-market pet foods. The basic trial—the "Gold Standard," as BFG Essences calls it—is the two-bowl test (see Roach 2013). A cat is given two bowls of kibble, one with BFG's palatant and another with a competitor's palatant, and various parameters are measured. They include which food the cat eats in greatest total quantity, the speed at which it eats, the first bowl it eats from, and the first bowl that it approaches. Another company, Diana Pet Foods, also measures what it calls "emotional palatability," or the signs given off by cats that, based on survey data, U.S.-based pet owners deem significant. As this company puts it, "To make meal time a shared enjoyable moment, pet food manufacturers not only need to satisfy pets' appetite, they also need this satisfaction to be clearly perceptible by the owner" (quoted in Beaton 2015). Palatants are designed to not just act on target species but on the target relationship.

The diverse collection of cats employed for tests in their multisite, so-called worldwide network are what palatant companies such as BFG Essences use to claim that they know what "the" cat as a species prefers. As AFB International (n.d.), one of the three major flavoring companies, puts it in literature about its tests, "Some variations include the number of pet participants, the environment, the feeding length, the 'normal' diet of pet participants, the breed of the pet participant, and even the region where the test is run." Palatants offer a portrait of attempting to use cats' work to operate at the level of a species—to identify a taste that drives all of a species' earthly manifestations to consume—by conducting tests across breeds, geographies, and facilities that simulate everyday lives of cats. As a whole, they are trying to produce an interspecies universal out of the intersection of immense quantities of standardized swine, coupled with cats that are enacted through tests as iconic representatives of the global feline population as a whole.

From the perspective of lungs and livers, the project of using all *of the pig is something that cannot be enacted by the human species alone.* While cats have been sinks for the detritus of animal slaughter over much of the twentieth century, now even their sensate experience functions to create specialized forms of value in the industrial pig. As cats' experience is more finely parsed and made into sites of capital, in turn, discrete porcine physiologies come to accrue new and unique claims.

SHIT, OR THE INDUSTRIAL PIG AS AN UNENDING PROJECT

In 2012, factory farms across the United States generated 369 million tons of untreated waste. That is roughly thirteen times more than was generated by the digestion and excretion of the entire human population of the United States (Food and Water Watch 2015). Dover Foods' pigs annually produce the equivalent feces of fifty million human beings—more than all people in California. As the agrarian philosopher Wendell Berry (2009) frames factory farms' mass-production of shit, "Once plants and animals were raised together on the same farm—which therefore neither produced unmanageable surpluses of manure, to be wasted and to pollute the water supply, nor depended on such quantities of commercial fertilizer. The genius of American farm experts is very well demonstrated here: they can take a solution and divide it neatly into two problems." Plants once played a vital infrastructural role in acting as sinks to collect animal waste. But there is no longer enough agricultural vegetation in the United States to absorb factory farms' feces. Moreover, a study found that antibiotics such as sulfamethoxazole, leached from animal waste, can accumulate in small quantities in cabbage tissues (Beecher 2015). Animal shit is becoming postagricultural—both exceeding and becoming hostile to plants. Moreover, while most Americans have long existed in cities and towns founded on what the anthropologist Nicholas Kawa (2016) calls "a modernist magic trick" of vast subterranean sewer systems to cleverly conceal our own feces right under our apartments and streets, it turns out that the factory farm's efforts to use *all* the pig is only making us more intimate with distant porcine shit.

Almost since the founding of factory hog farms in the 1990s, agricultural colleges tied to the pork industry have been trying to invent schemes that would turn pig waste into a kind of petroleum equivalent, or into "the new black gold" (cf. Jordahl 2011). These capitalist fantasies of farming both pork and feces are usually framed in a language of environmental solutions and stewardship. But I would argue they are better described as an effort to normalize the status quo concentration of porcine waste by entangling it more finely into human life. Many of Dover Foods' breeding barns run on methane-*cum*-biogas, as do the slaughterhouse's rendering boilers. In North Carolina, Google is helping fund digesters around corporate hog farms to capture their carbon offsets and cheap energy (Mahony 2011). In coming years, the rocks in American highways' asphalt probably will have been bound together with bioadhesive from oils in pig feces (ter Beek 2016). *Using all of the pig turns out to be an unending and shifting project, inseparable from the factory farm. What counts as a "part of the pig" for profit mining is constantly expanding.*

FAT, OR THE POLITICS OF USING ALL OF THE PIG

Tied to this, factory farms effectively turn many of our routine activities into sinks for industrialized biology. This is not usually treated as a political matter, but I would argue that this is a mistake. It should be possible to use the internet, drive down a highway, or have something delivered in a truck without being in contact with porcine particles. Everyday human life in the United States is increasingly lived as a subsidy to industrial meat. *Meanwhile, using* all *of the pig is also reshaping how pigs live.*

Pigs' lives are tethered to the current standards of their death. Recall the old saying, invoked by Ryan, that "you are what you eat." The factory farm, as a model, is challenged by such ontologies of consumption because, from the point of view of its post-slaughter disassembly, the modern pig is not a unified living organism. It is many things; the industrial pig is thousands of discrete substances. Today's pigs are born with 1,100 preexisting claims on their bodies, in the form of products that might be as diverse as shoulder, blood plasma, leather, heparin, palatants, collagen, and bone glue.

Take Dover Foods' decision to build a large biodiesel factory using swine fat as its feedstock. In a 2000s context, when petroleum prices were forecast to perpetually rise and there were dwindling market routes through which to move the company's annual harvest of 80,509,000 pounds of hog fat, the venture was economically alluring. The fat in the 2000s version of the Dover Foods hog, however, contained properties such as fatty acids that made certification for high-grade commercial biodiesel cost-prohibitive. These properties were a major stumbling point for blending the product into generic diesel at gas stations. Nutritionists at the company determined that they could incorporate glycerin into hogs' diets to minimize these properties of the fat— and glycerin is a byproduct of biodiesel transesterification—but only if it had no chemical effect on the other 1,099 product codes that were already slotted and reserved within its carcass. For example, the company requires a firm type of fat to thinly slice parts of the shoulder in the style that has already been promised to food wholesalers for the Japanese pork market.

The goal here is to make fat into a doubly alienated commodity: capable of freely circulating on the market and imperceptibly detached from its origins in living porcine substance. Beyond desiring the greater market access that such blending with regular diesel would entail, the company was seeking to ensure that its product would not be associated as rooted in pigs' fat. Although the exact reasoning was not always clear on this score, this was perhaps due to cultural scandals with relation to vegetarians or people who choose to avoid pork for cultural or religious reasons. Diesel at most commercial gas stations now contains small quantities of pig. *Using* all *of the pig is an active project of reshaping the organism to make it more invisibly intertwined with our routine lives—and to have everything from certain human cultural tastes to shipping trucks pulsing through pigs' bodies.* From scholars such as Paula Young Lee

(2008) and Timothy Pachirat (2011), we know that slaughterhouses are designed to be invisible. But that is perhaps the tip of the iceberg, for the hog's very carcass is made to imperceptibly snake through the world. The industrial pig is designed, down to the level of its fatty acids, as a hidden creature.

MEAT, OR GLOBAL INEQUALITY

Nearly all of the major pork corporations use *all* of the pig. But they do not do so in the same way. The industrial pig that I have traced across this book is a supply-chain project whose very biophysical existence is premised on circulating to East Asia.[9] Complex tiers of porcine value emerge from how the pig's substances circulate regionally and across the globe. At its simplest, there is a division between "meat" and "other." Yet even in "meat" there is a hierarchy of value. Piece of Meat (1) is static in value. Dover Foods is always trying to turn it into Meat (2) by moving it to Japan or South Korea rather than the United States, where pork commands a lower price. For example, Dover Foods is constantly trying to sell 22 percent rather than 20 percent of its meat to East Asia for higher returns, increasing the price of the carcass as a whole. The category "Other" can also be split into hierarchical circulations. Other (1) is sold to other companies across the globe for human consumption (say, glands for drugs or heart valves for surgical implantation), while Other (2) stays in internal circuits and is recycled back into the process (say, blood plasma for piglets). Finally, perhaps the most crucial division of value within porcine physiologies is between the "intact" and "essentialized" substances. Rendering pieces of pig—the hooves, for instance—is always treated as a loss in potential value. The goal is to keep pieces of pig intact. Finding a wholesaler that will take 456,000 raw hooves for dog toys—or trotters for French and Chinese culinary preparations—every week is challenging, but the hooves bring in more profit if they can be sold intact than if they have been boiled for fat, bone meal, and fertilizer alongside the brains, floor trimmings, and dead stock. This model relies on tapping into and, in turn, offloading pig parts onto global cuisines and cultures that can consume large supplies of tongues, heads, caul fat, and glands. The pig is itself a logistical model, and Dover Foods functions as a transnational export zone set up in the middle of America.

All of this suggests a simple point, but it is one I would want to underline: using *all* of the industrial pig in profitable ways is premised on global difference—sometimes innocuous cultural differences, to be certain, but also matters of economic inequality. It is perhaps banal but still striking to state that the very material bodies of hogs are infused with human tastes. Over the twentieth century, the amount of fat on a hog's body has been inseparably tied to shifting human desires (see Weiss 2016). Human dietary whims resulted in an industrial animal with barely any body fat, physiologically fused to indoor confinement to the point at which it would be stricken with pneumonia if it left its barn environment in northern climates. But it is also true that those who are willing and able to pay more for flesh will shape the carnal composition of the porcine species. The Dover Foods hog—from the firmness and texture of its fat to its muscles' capacity to retain water over a long boat ride overseas—is fed and shaped for the highest bidder. To sell the remainder that does not meet these specifications relies on gradients of human buyers who are unable (or unwilling) to pay more for food. The industrial pig is not only made through unequal class relations in the workplace; it is a being whose very mode of life and death is premised on human hierarchies. *Using all of the pig—in ways that are obvious yet still jarring—depends on, and generates, global inequality at a biophysical level.*[10]

BONES, OR THE FRONTIERS OF CARNAL TERRAIN

My multiple walks through the production floor of Sakai Minerals, with its current president, Kaoru Noguchi, revealed a curiously cosmopolitan world hidden in the rural United States. The Sakai Minerals workplace reflected both the global particularity of this region in terms of its excess of porcine materials and cultural possibilities in an economic boomtown where children in the elementary school speak twenty-six primary languages.

Our tours began in the steaming-hot boiler rooms where pressure cookers boil thirty-two thousand pounds of bones at a time. From there, the liquid passes through pipes and dryers to make desiccated pork essence and pork oil for ramen flavoring. The company offshored their operations from Japan in search of an abundance of front leg bones. Dover Foods, Noguchi explained to me, is ten times larger than the biggest slaughterhouse that he can access in Japan. The result is that, in Japan, companies must make extracts using the ribs, hips, or back legs. As he put it, "We just take the front arm or leg bone [from Dover]. We Japanese consider these bones better than the other [bones available in the pig]." Images of meaty front leg bones adorned the product's casing, entailing the beginning of a new mode of even deeper forms of disassembly once there was a novel claim on segments of porcine skeletons.

At first glance, akin to its insistence on using only two precisely located bones per pig, Sakai Minerals appears to have refused to accommodate itself in any way to regional labor practices. The workrooms off the production floor were designed in the mold of a stereotypical Japanese office. Its main administrative room is no larger than a U.S. executive's office, some twenty feet by fifteen feet. In this space, twelve people work at computers around a single long desk, with Noguchi wedged so tightly against the wall at the end that everyone needs to stand up as he gets to his seat. Not only is there little division of labor architecturally, but crews across maintenance divisions were forced to share tools and equipment in ways that the company learned was rare in the United States. The working days stretch from 9 AM to 9 PM, ending with a teleconference call to the parent company and its outposts in China and Germany. Every two years a new president comes from Tokyo for a tour of duty—speaking little English and using Dutch multilingual translators to conduct meetings with Dover Foods—with the hope of returning to the parent company at a higher position.

At the same time, Sakai Minerals has created a hybrid form of Mexican and Japanese workplace environment. As I toured the facility on a couple of occasions, it became clear that Spanish is the universal language—including among the five Japanese expatriates who manage the administrative side and the European translators. Julio, the general floor manager, remembers being the first Mexican migrant to enter Dixon's high school when he was fifteen and his father moved in search of meatpacking labor in the 1990s. Upon graduation, he went to work for another East Asian animal extract company before starting at Sakai. Traveling back and forth between the United States and Japan—while living in Japan for months at a time—Julio taught the parent company about the Mexican workforce's expectations (such as not sharing tools), which led to a reorganization of workplace hierarchies that decreased the rate of turnover. He was the longest-serving employee along with Naoki, who ran the laboratory for sampling the product. She moved to the region because she did not believe she would be able to attain a supervisory position in mainland Japan. Every two years, however, she and Julio must relearn certain basic processes of soup base production when a new president comes from Japan and, perhaps more important, because the bones themselves change slowly and continually over time.

After visiting with people at Sakai Minerals over the course of three years, I started to see clearly that their operation was struggling as the bones shifted in form, substance, and quantity. Over dinner one summer evening Naoki explained, "We are losing our bones to China. We're getting less and less ingredient." Dover Foods was finding Chinese wholesalers to take the meat from the intact front legs of the pig at a rate that was driving up the price of the bones, in turn increasing the global claims coursing through this single piece of the pig's body. Even more significant, however, was that the form of the bones was changing each year. Dover found additional ways to extract meat, fat, blood, marrow, and other substances from their surfaces. In 2010, Sakai Minerals received "whole huge bones" with meat and fat clinging to their surface (see figure 9.3). But Dover gradually started running the bones through "special machinery," she said, "and now they come out crushed." She explained that these historical transformations to the front leg bones caused changes to the fat and moisture content of the product: "It takes more work from the centrifuge to separate the little particles out since it's crushed. And it gives us less fat. . . . So it changes all of these little things. The taste and smells are a little different, too." In essence, the quantity of porcine essence in the bones was shrinking as Dover Foods took over more portions of the material, risking the reduction of these shards of front leg bones to pure fungible "bones." Indeed, Naoki was worried that Sakai might not even receive front leg bones anymore, as their skeletal origins were being rendered untraceable through the grinding.

Even the hog's skeleton—perhaps in a parallel to differential use of working bodies in the slaughterhouse—is being subjected to different valuations based on its location (front leg bone versus spine) along with Dover Foods' move to work closer to the level of the chemical makeup of bones themselves. Surplus death is a historical process of gradually carving labor deeper into the inner substances of pigs and making others—such as Sakai Minerals—dependent on particular porcine physiologies. *Using all of the pig means constantly opening up new carnal terrain within the animal on which to develop (and exploit) labor processes, of finding and making discrete new substance for work.*

OFF-ANIMALS, OR SLAUGHTERING THE SPECIES

In these vignettes we can begin to see some ways that, in the past fifteen years, industrialization has turned the industrial pig into a(n) (inter)national project. A whole host of sites, values, consumers, and companies—which extend far beyond the factory farm proper—have been enlisted to prop up and sustain this agribusiness's model of animality. This is even more extreme within the pork industry. At this moment, virtually everyone who works with pig substance in the United States—with the exception of a couple hundred heritage or pasture-based farmers (cf. Weiss 2016)—is now tied in some way to a few corporations' biologies. The porcine species is gradually being monopolized. Yet I was surprised to find that this project of building a national animal—of making both concrete standardized pigs and exportable models of American capitalist animality—depends on older epochs of slaughter. What we are starting to see, I suggest in this final vignette, is a shift in surplus death from trying to use all of the individual pig body to slaughtering all of the species.

After working on the insemination floor of industrial breeding farms, visiting the stockyards of Tuffit Meats was like entering an alternative porcine universe. The holding space in its barn is half the size of a football field, with large pens that give its 1,000 animals room to move. Unlike the scenes of identical forms of pigs in breeding barns—where animals appear as fungible tokens of one another—these hogs were of different shapes, sizes, sexes, colors, breeds, and genetics. The only traces of an ordering impulse were the brightly marked symbols in pink, green, and blue crayon on the animals' backs indexing their origin from different stages. With the creatures drawn from across farm sites, this was the industrial division of porcine "labor" reunited for the first time inside one barn. Tuffit Meats' holding pens included semen and pheromone boars that had grown too large for their cages. Many of the sows looked healthy, but they had been sent to this barn because their reproductive potency had diminished over multiple pregnancies. The tiny piglets must have been the runts that did not make it past the nursery barns, and the midweight animals were the "fall-behinds" in the feeder barns that put on weight too slowly to become industrial "finisher" hogs. In this barn were some of the thirteen different types, sexes, and breeds of pig that jointly help make the standardized Dover meat hog.

Across this book, we have seen that the capitalist horizon of porcine value has been shifting over the past twenty years. To kill and disassemble nineteen thousand pigs in eighteen hours, for instance, has required a new type of animal: a standardized meat pig with a *relatively* regularized distribution of weight, tendons, posture, and fat-to-muscle ratios around which corporations can divide the actions of one thousand workers into the most fixed and minute of knife slices. The speculative promise and eco-social threat of the factory farm—as a vertically integrated complex of genetics, barns, feed mills, and slaughterhouses—is that it can reliably deliver such a creature. But visiting the Tuffit Meats barn underlined to me that there is a big catch: such an effort results in vast amounts of biological excess in the form of nonstandardized and destandardized animals that no longer fit the industrial model. While corporations may find ways to use all of the individual pig, they are not singlehandedly able to contain the vital entirety of the species emerging from the fissures of standardization.

Frank Hill, a man in his fifties who managed the barn, was quiet as I explained my research. We had been trying to meet for three months at this holding barn—one of twelve across Canada, the United States, and Mexico—but he kept calling to cancel because he was in Florida, California, or Pennsylvania "opening up new markets." He nodded from behind his desk, papers strewn about in no apparent order, fiddling with two smartphones. I got the feeling that he was placing me in his imagination of food publics to get a read on how he should speak. "Our end of the deal is totally different," he declared after a pause, distancing Tuffit Meats from the other companies that he referred to as "the corporates." "We're not in the production end of [raising pigs]. We don't process anything [killing pigs]. What we actually do is bring in all assorted type animals of everything—'off-animals.' And we put 'em together, and we sell 'em where we have markets."

Off-animals, as Frank called them, are the closest thing to organic waste that one can find on factory farms. But unlike expendable trash animals such as cockroaches (see Nagy and Johnson 2013), even they are not quite negative value (see Reno 2009). Off-animals are a vast pool of beings that include overgrown boars, infertile sows, small runts from large litters, slow-growing "fall-behinds," animals riddled with abscesses from faulty injections, herniated piglets whose guts were ruptured during castration, hogs with severe bedsores and leg trauma, fatty pigs, and emaciated pigs. Their number is growing as genetic refinement in sows produces larger litters with more internal variation and, alongside that, the specifications of the Dover standardized pig narrow even further as the company attempts to kill upward of more than twenty thousand pigs per day. Whether because they have been used up as breeding "workers" in the mass-production of life, the subjects of regularized industrial violence whose bodies absorb and accumulate aberrant forms of human labor, or newly noticed as abnormal based on shifts in specifications, off-animals are generated by the interspecies work of making standardized life. They are the vital byproducts of the industrial.[11]

I would call Frank an aggregator of surplus death. He is the world's largest buyer and distributor of these off-animals, shipping hogs to fifty locations in North America. He has specialized in the logistics of porcine difference, trying to find value in creatures that a generation ago more than likely would have been euthanized on farms. If the factory farm's vision of standardized life cannot ultimately be perfected—if it will inevitably manifest unwanted, singular, particular porcine bodily forms—Frank found a tense livelihood in directing this explosion of vitality across the United States. It is his work that enables something closer to the use of "all of the pig"—making feasible standardized life itself by finding outlets for its necessary biological waste.

Frank's absorption into the world of off-animals is a story of dispossession, adaptation, and survival based on clinging to the last remaining open flow of porcine life remaining in the United States. A small farmer in Illinois, he was swept up in what he called "inevitable" forces in the 1990s as corporations came to undercut the price of pork and monopolize porcine value. "[We] saw the corporates, the contracts, and the direct-to-the-farm movements," he said, "and [we] said, 'Well, I guess we're gonna have to do something different.'" Acknowledging the violence of his work—one of his grades of off-animals is herniated pigs—he often seemed to speak about himself as a certain kind of byproduct of the factory farm as he and his generational cohort of small farmers maintained a tenuous connection to agriculture through these off-animals. He started by specializing in cull sows, buying from three hundred to four hundred different small farms in Iowa. By the 2000s, even this pool of discarded animals had been depleted: there are now only a couple dozen farms across the United States from which he can buy sows, requiring his company to diversify into multiple kinds of pigs if it wanted to keep operating.

As Frank put it during our interview, "We take all the pigs that [don't] have much value. . . . You got this big, that big, this long, this fat, under-fat, a boar, a busted up—You know . . . . Something." This motley crew of pigs that he shepherds across the United States was too irregular to be put through a single automated disassembly line. In essence, Frank explained, the pigs were "for different ethnic groups and different types of packers. [The butcher's] gotta do handwork on it, so he's gotta buy it cheap enough that he can do the handwork." Frank has eked out a living through his skill in reading the regularity of industrial differences, along with the fact that American farm animals are now so concentrated—the U.S. hog herds numbering in the millions—that he is able to aggregate off-animals into new classes. He is inventing new kinds of pig, restandardizing "off-life" in what seems to be a form of reverse imitation of the factory farm's industrial processes.

"On the sows we got the SBS, the SGS . . . , roughly six grades on the sows," he explained as he made some calculations in his head and listed the odd grades that he used to classify animals: "sGs, suws, U67s, MJ2s. We probably have twenty different sorts then, roughly." By expanding ways to group and aggregate the factory farm's output, Frank has been part of a vast national expansion of slaughter that allows a different kind of surplus death to ensue. He wryly notes that this parsing of the factory farm's waste stream has made it easier to acquire a suckling pig for Chinese New Year or medium-weight hogs for family spit roasts. Unlike the factory farm's surplus death of slaughtering each animal more deeply, Frank has developed a logistical infrastructure for more specialized styles of killing. He has redeemed other "parts" of the pig *species*—other horizontal manifestations of pigness—through modes of standardized aggregation based on giving himself over to the so-called inevitability of having to imitate corporate modes of killing.

As I listened to Frank, it became clear that this space was what made the industrial pig possible as a biological creature in two senses. First, it was where corporations could sell their nonstandard hogs at only a small loss, mitigating the cost of the still-existing natural variation in their animals. Second, Tuffit Meats is a secret sort of place, one that allows Dover Foods and the other "corporates" to maintain the veneer of total control over animal life to their wholesalers, who know and encounter only identical cuts of meat. The particular types of pigs that Frank corrals may no longer officially exist within the factory farm. But in his own way, perhaps, Frank remains the farmer from the 1980s whose labor keeps a particular way of life thriving long after the current era of porcine monopoly became a dominant form. Yet it is a process riddled with tension.

There is an ascendant heritage, pasture, craft, and niche animal movement that has been well described in the scholarship of Heather Paxson (2013) and Brad Weiss (2016). But Frank and his peers have overseen the resurgence of aged animal slaughter facilities that most of us thought disappeared in the 1990s period of corporate consolidation; they have kept afloat the "traditional" industrialism of prior generations through the movement of these off-animals. Some fifty butchers and slaughterhouses now specialize in a single kind of off-animal: "bony sows," "runts," "wet sows," "number one barn sows," and others that, because of variations in their body shapes, cannot be killed together on an automated disassembly line. They include aging small-town slaughterhouses of the East Coast that kill one hundred animals a day; the independent sausage makers that dot the U.S. South; the ethnic butchers on various midwestern towns' Main Streets; and the iconic ramshackle meat shops with bright yellow signs advertising $1.99 chops. The labor process of each has been redesigned through the movement of Frank's off-animals to slaughter one precise restandardized type of pig. The circulation of his off-animals has, in essence, kept afloat swathes of small-scale meat producers by specializing them in one niche of porcine deviation that is generated by factory farms. American animality—the contemporary model of standardized meat—is being sustained in part through animality Americana.

Off-animals provide some much-needed clarity for critically examining the state of American animal life. The past decade has seen a robust debate emerge about the consolidation of U.S. food, riddled with threatened yet failed efforts to enforce antitrust actions against corporate meatpacking. The bestselling books at the center of this debate present such monopolies as a threat to the American food supply through reduced competition in terms of the control and distribution of meat (see Leonard 2014). But I think the larger question here is not whether pork chops will cost $1.99 or $2.99 per pound, or even whether the "family" farm will remain a viable institution. It is, instead, to ask what it means that there is growing valuation over all vital expressions of pigness—the factory farm's model requires not only that it can derive value from every piece of an individual pig, but also that no worldly manifestation of the species is left unslaughtered.

TOWARD A POSITIVE POLITICS OF WASTE

For years, following talks and lectures, someone in the audience has always asked me, What can be done about this? I am often apprehensive about this question, as it fits too neatly into our technocratic present of each "expert" presenting their own clever silver-bullet solution. The demand also entails a sense of exceptionalism that marks the factory farm as especially deviant. The question is always what can be done about *this industrial site*, not what can be done about industrial capitalism in general. Symptomatically, most books like this one end with a bullet list of things that you—some middle-class American—can do right now to make a difference. Do not consume animal products, or buy them from a local farmer. Donate to an animal welfare organization. Lobby for the end of gestation crates. These things are important in their own right—while one should keep in mind my own economic privileges, I do endorse and practice many of these acts—but they are not currently imperiling American agribusiness.

Despite the industrial pig's omnipresence in our everyday lives—that, in a sense, we can all be said to be working on capitalist animality in some way—my point in recounting these vignettes has not been to narrate the factory farm as inescapable. It is not to generate despair. Rather, my point is that, at its most totalizing, this agribusiness model also appears most tenuous. The ingestion of human eaters alone cannot sustain the factory farm and its modes of growth, which seek to intertwine pigs invisibly into distinct worlds in ever more finely grained forms. On the one hand, I do believe that the primary adage of contemporary U.S. food movements—that you can change the world of industrial agriculture by "voting with your fork" (cf. Pollan 2006)—is in serious need of qualification, given that factory farms profit from things more extensive than meat for human consumption, and they are not primarily designed to feed human populations in the United States. On the other, these vignettes force us to consider how capitalist pigs are sustained through multitudes of consumption practices—many modes of ingestion that remain in formation—and always need to find more outlets to generate surplus death. What all of this suggests is the need for a politics of food, along with a food studies, that cannot be reduced to an anthropocentric focus on what humans consume. Our companions and prosthetics, ranging from cats to computers, are also being enlisted into maintaining, subsidizing, and working on industrial meat. The vulnerabilities of this model of "growth" hints at the radical possibilities of a more extensive politics of refusal and care than one that is mindful of human diets alone, and instead makes common cause with all our companions' entanglements. Rather than simply refusing to eat meat, a basic demand should be the right to remain autonomous from the factory farm— not to be forced to subsidize these operations within our mundane actions. There are no magic bullets. While a modest campaign such as the banning of unmarked animal gelatin in consumer products alone might not grievously affect these agribusiness models, it would make clear how much human energy is put in their service.

Rather than allowing the use of *all* of the pig to stand as a neutral good, perhaps what we need is a positive politics of inefficiency. It is true that there is virtually no waste of the hog's body parts in factory farming—outside, of course, of externalized nitrates that are creating a dead zone in the Gulf of Mexico and antibiotic resistance genes that are transforming the nature of microbial life (see Schneider 2015; Landecker 2016; Blanchette 2019). What should be questioned is the profound amount of human energy, creativity, and science that is needed to keep this system afloat. From university resources and careers diverted to mine poop for its methane biogas, to the human knowledge and education that is marshaled to develop a new injectable hormone to decrease the price of pork by a penny per pound, the collec-

tive social resources mobilized to maintain the factory farm's model of standardized life—and industrialism as a whole—is what is truly jarring. From
this perspective, the value of small and local farms is not just their agrarian
worth or support for rural communities. It is that they nurture animals in a
fashion whereby every moment of their lives, and every microgram of their
bodies, is not saturated by economic value. This is the symptom and sign of
our times: it has come to feel radical to advocate merely leaving something
unworked. But I do think this, ultimately, is what we do need to demand—the
right to be "un-efficient" creatures. It is not wasteful or lazy if every dimension
of our everyday life and routine labor does not course with capitalist value. It
means that we are, as both human and non-human beings, more than simply
economic creatures. That is the demand for human and animal life that is
truly incompatible with the logic of late industrial factory farms.

EPILOGUE
The (De-)Industrialization of the World

The grease and chemicals that are poured into it undergo all sorts of strange transformations, which are the cause of its name; it is constantly in motion, as if huge fish were feeding in it, or great leviathans disporting themselves in its depths. Bubbles of carbonic acid gas will rise to the surface and burst, and make rings two or three feet wide. Here and there the grease and filth have caked solid, and the creek looks like a bed of lava; chickens walk about on it, feeding, and many times an unwary stranger has started to stroll across, and vanished temporarily. The packers used to leave the creek that way, till every now and then the surface would catch on fire and burn furiously, and the fire department would have to come and put it out. Once, however, an ingenious stranger came and started to gather this filth in scows, to make lard out of; then the packers took the cue, and got out an injunction to stop him, and afterward gathered it themselves. The banks of "Bubbly Creek" are plastered thick with hairs, and this also the packers gather and clean.—UPTON SINCLAIR, *THE JUNGLE*

IN 2018, I spent time in Chicago's Back of the Yards, the home of the Union Stock Yards until their closure in 1971 signaled the imminent rise of companies such as Dover Foods. I found myself taking frequent walks along the banks of Bubbly Creek, thinking about how we remain tied to the histories that unfolded along this stream. The south fork of the south Chicago River, the creek can still give the visual effect of being permanently subject to a faint drizzle of rain as tiny pockets of methane gas and hydrogen sulfide—at this point smaller than the ones Upton Sinclair described—pop out of its surface. The bubbles are from still-decomposing, century-old hog offal and blood. At a public forum, a member of the U.S. Corps of Engineers described it as a pudding-like material piled eighteen feet deep in parts. It remains uncertain whether Bubbly Creek can be remediated.

Within the packinghouses that concentrated so many dead body parts into the stream that the bubbling river appeared almost animate, many pivotal transformations to industrial society started coming about. That is where historians train their attention: battles for the eight-hour workday and the limiting of labor, the development of (dis)assembly lines and the reduction of laboring people to motions, and the invention of refrigerated transport that eventually allowed the abandonment of Chicago itself in favor of far-flung places such as Dixon. Only a few small packers are left in the city; they now specialize in off-animals. But that river remains a consequential reflection of the state of industrialism today.

This was a truly ruined ecological body, yet also one where industrial architects first appeared as if they might be capable of redeeming themselves by corralling their vast scales of life and death. Dumping entrails and blood annihilated nonmicrobial aquatic life while turning the neighborhood into a sensorium of rot, with profoundly negative consequences for the surrounding immigrant community's quality of life (see Washington 2005). Then the packers, as Sinclair suggests, experimenting with forms of waste recycling and rendering technologies, devised methods to put all the porcine excess to use (see also Shukin 2009). Or, as I would prefer, they discovered new ways to put humans to work on pig biology. That slowdown in the flow of intact offal into Bubbly Creek marked a crucial moment in the gradual transformation of pigs into one of the planet's most labored species and a harbinger for processes of industrial transformation that still plague the planet today. Bubbly Creek may no longer be a biological dumping ground, but the corollary is that there are few spaces that remain in the United States where we are not in contact with pigs. It might be better to say that the world—from the soil to our houses—is now the dumping ground.

This became more than metaphorical when, in 2016, the Working Group on the Anthropocene, a team of geologists tasked with determining whether the planet has entered a new epoch defined by traces of human activity, made an affirmative recommendation to the International Geological Congress (Carrington 2016a).[1] Their parameters for declaring the change are highly specific to the discipline of geology. They are based on whether a signal marking a clear break from the Holocene is detectable across the planet, and whether future geologists will be able to identify this new period in the earth's sedimentary layers. Few of the signals under investigation are surprising. They include radioactive elements from nuclear explosions, immortal plastics in waterways, or fertilizers developed during the Green Revolution leaving their mark in the planet's soils. However, there is an additional—and decidedly odd—signal under investigation, and that is the highly enlarged skeleton of the post–World War II industrial chicken.

Bioarchaeologists believe that industrial chicken skeletons, with their distinctive osteopathologies rooted in rapid rates of growth, may be accumulating across much of the planet amid the surging exportation of both animal carcasses and industrial animal-rearing systems from Euro-American locales (Bennett et al. 2018; Carrington 2016b). Moreover, these intact bones' potential for preservation in the anaerobic conditions of landfills—or in graves following disease-induced mass culls—means that they could one day be a globally distributed "key fossil index taxon of the Anthropocene" (Bennett et al. 2018, 8). The chicken is a relative latecomer to the kinds of industrial processes this book has considered, even if its mode of contract-based vertical integration would later inspire and remake the pork industry (Silbergeld 2016). Starting in the 1940s, chickens were transformed from egg-laying animals, kept in sheds primarily for rural subsistence and whose flesh was rarely served on urban dinner plates, into the planet's most populous species of bird (Bennett et al. 2018; Horowitz 2008; Striffler 2005). The pounds of meat per year that the average American ate absolutely soared, as did the size of the average bird's carcass. In an experiment that measured the effects of breeding selection over time, scientists found that strains of chicken from 2005 grew at a 400 percent higher rate than strains from 1957 raised under identical conditions (Zuidhof et al. 2014). In turn, some commentators suggest, these swollen chicken "bones could become the key fossil evidence for the dawn of the age in which humankind came to dominate the planet" (Carrington 2016b).

My hope, after reading this book, is that you will question whether the mass-fossilization of poultry indicates a unified humanity's anthropocentric "domination" of the planet. Instead, each of those engorged skeletons is a record of conjoined human and avian exploitation (see also Stuesse 2016). Another way to put this book's argument is to say that we are mistaken when we see industrial meat as a sterile matter of detaching hogs from human (and other) lives, or a fully anthropocentric process. This was how I was accustomed to think before I lived in Dixon. But it is too close to American agribusiness's own ideal of clean technoscientific control over animals. Dover Foods and other animal agribusiness corporations have instead created a division of human labor around, and embedded workers as prosthetics within, facets and fissures of biology. One of the stories that the mass deposits of swollen chicken skeletons should tell is one of work: those bones' qualities and quantities are an embodied reflection of the exploitation of certain populations *through* capitalist animal biology. This is a story of intraspecies and interspecies domination, reflecting how labor disproportionately circumscribes the ways in which Americans, as a society, relate to and engage animals such as chickens or hogs.

For an anthropologist, the value of sorting these signals is that they provoke us to invent new lines of sight into, and stories about, what industrial capitalism was really about all along. Each of these signals suggests a different narrative about what the lasting significance of industrialism will entail; each can home attention in on interrelated but distinct ways that militarism, consumerism, (settler) colonialism, and speciesism carve disproportionate marks into swathes of the planet. The image of a chickenized stratigraphic record, and the subterranean earth as a burial site that records the changing human diet, is certainly an uncomfortable one to contemplate. I imagine that this image of billions upon billions of discarded sentient lives circulated in popular media because, like a mirror, it reflects back a certain image of society. It can and should bring forth reflection on society's paradoxically profound investment in and callous indifference to nonhuman animals today: vast social and scientific resources are being expended to enlarge quantities and qualities of avian bodies, and equally powerful processes lead chickens to be killed and consumed without a second thought (see Haraway 2008). Indeed, I suspect that careful examination of the chickenized earth will potentially provoke even more than reflection on the ethics of consuming and discarding animal lives. Not unlike what is occurring in the American pork industry, fewer companies have come to coordinate greater shares of poultry markets since the 1980s (Hendrickson et al. 2014; Leonard 2014, 233). The earth is likely to now contain billions of poultry skeletons whose shape and density will overwhelmingly reflect the changing genetics, growing regimens, labor strategies, and feed rations of specific named corporations such as Tyson Foods and Pilgrim's Pride. The fossil record—at least in the subterranean United States—may one day become legible as something of an inadvertently branded and trademarked reflection of a moment of corporate consolidation of one of the planet's life forms.

But ultimately I do not think that intact chicken wings are an adequate proxy for even the state of industrialism, much less an able image for defining the planet in one swoop. Indeed, billions of intact chicken skeletons sinking underground might actually be more indicative of the *infancy* of how industrial technics have come to coordinate avian life and death. Intact chicken wings might comparatively reflect a scarcity of value and labor relations coursing through poultry. What is more jarring, and I think an equally potent sign of human-animal relations today, is the relative absence of intact hog bones in the earth's crust. These inedible substances in pigs' bodies are accumulating less thickly in the earth precisely because they are the built environment. Missing hog skeletons tell us a different story about what it means to live in a highly industrialized world than does trying to imagine chicken skeletons changing in size at each layer of strata. And you would be challenged to find anything identifiable as hog skeletons accumulating in the subterranean environment precisely because they envelop you in a totalizing yet diluted way: in the bone fertilizers in your potted plants, the concrete in the roadways you drive, the glue that seams together your household objects, and the drugs in your medicine cabinet.

What I find most problematic is that few, I suspect, would even recognize that this is a problem (see Graeber 2018, 270). Many people would likely feel compelled to treat the pigification of the built environment as a rational story of efficiency, as a responsible use of resources, or even as a signal of an odd kind of respect for the life of the animal by letting little of its body go to waste. But this is the same kind of logic that leads writers to see industrialism as signaling the collective human "domination" of the planet. It is an ideological reading of the world that assumes humanity is a unified agent consciously acting in concert. Instead, I prefer to see in all of those invisible hog bones something else: a society that is unable to moderate its exploitation of labor; a region of the world that cannot help but pour more and more social energy into doing the same thing. The United States is a place that cannot help but constantly find new terrains to put people to work, and that fact has conditioned—more so than appetites, consumer choices, or indifference—both the lives of pigs and the collective social knowledge of their nature. One banal yet profound sign of the times is the fact that it is rare even to encounter a living pig today outside a workplace, whether that is a farm or a petting zoo.

Another is the sheer depth at which the porcine body has become subjected to formal positions of labor: at the level of hormones, metabolism, instinct, immune systems, epidermis, calcium phosphate, amino acids, and nitrates. The United States struggles to leave any single pig, or dimension of the species, unlabored.

What the relative absence of hog bones perhaps does tell us, then, is that we are not *when* some think we are. Those missing bones suggest we remain within the world of the Chicago meatpackers of the 1890s and the processes that unfolded from Bubbly Creek. At a time that many insist we should call the United States "postindustrial" because fewer people are employed in manufacturing—and even fewer work on farms or encounter living pigs—this book has taken a different path to articulate how things are becoming ever more unendingly industrialized in some hidden places. In a corporate boardroom or university laboratory somewhere, right now, people are sitting around a table planning how to derive yet another commodity from pigs' bodies, compounding yet another industrial labor process into the biology of this species. As I write this, many of the major American animal agribusiness companies are making plans to replicate their operations abroad to capture the even cheaper labor of Latin America, or the even cheaper grain of Eastern Europe. Even if they are successful in moving out of the United States, none of this should be seen as true deindustrialization. It is an effort to incorporate more spaces and lives into a model of industrial animality.

Some people in the United States, as Heather Paxson (2015) once put it, are living "after industrialism": they imagine their existence as no longer organized around the standardized rhythms of industrial machines and manual workflows yet hope to return to some aspects of the social life that they believe factories generated (see also Muehlebach and Shoshan 2012; Walley 2013). Over the course of many years of research and writing I thought of factory farms as decidedly *untimely*—an odd kind of exception to American norms; an ardent and seemingly outdated industrialization project. I now see them as prescient, ahead of the curve. As triumphant images of resurgent industrialism and returns to manufacturing became some of the vehicles through which a new kind of American political rule was mobilized in the 2016 presidential election, it seems better to say that these agribusinesses are intensely normal. Industrialism haunts both our imaginations and material environments. And while it is certainly true that fewer people, at least in the United States, work in large-scale factories than did fifty years ago, I think it is equally true that very few of us can imagine what a life without industrial objects, categories of personhood, and aesthetics would entail. The industrial processes developed in germinal form by the Chicago meatpackers of the 1890s were supposed to herald a new world. That world was realized. The challenge today is how to get out of it once everything from the built environment to commonplace senses of being a productive person is, in however diffuse a sense, inseparably tied to things like industrial killing. And while we may not be able to detect the noxious concentrated effects of these efforts in a single glance or smell like in the heyday of Bubbly Creek, the out-of-control efficiency that aims to wring yet infinitely more value from animals will be marked—permanently—in the nature and drug resistances of the microbial world, in the planet's greenhouse gas levels, in the heavy metals in American soils, and even in the bodies and behavior of what is later recognized as a standard pig.

In *The Great Derangement*, Amitav Ghosh (2016) suggests that the first step to addressing climate change and other planetary problems that portend far-reaching transformations to habituated forms of life is not to ask, "What can I do to change this?" It is instead to ask what we are already very actively doing to ignore, conceal, and forget that there is a massive problem. How, he asks, do our celebrated and popular forms of writing and public engagement seem almost conspiratorially out of tune with the looming disasters of our age? I have encountered startlingly few people, including within the upper echelons of agribusinesses, who think that factory farms are an unmitigated "good thing." Yet I am struck by the quantity of social knowledge, energy, and resources that are being expended each day to keep them in the world. For the story I have tried to tell across this book is not one of domination and unmitigated agribusiness power but, instead, one of creative desperation to keep this system afloat (see Lien 2015). So many processes, from the blood of mares and the taste of cats, to human kinship relations and musculoskeletal systems, are riveted through hogs to create this system of cheap meat. And many more will have to be added in the future to keep it running. Large-scale agribusiness is totalizing because it is so fragile (and fragile because it is so totalizing); it is a story not just of domination but also of desperation in its effort to cling to shopworn forms of value that no longer seem sustainable.

What I want to suggest in closing is, quite simply, that we need to redeem the idea of *actual* deindustrialization as a positive political project—and inhabit that term in ways that do not lead to, as it currently tends to mean, economic precarity and a lack of livelihood for most working people. Put differently, our collective social escape from industrialism will not come about automatically. Learning what it means to deindustrialize the pig is a good place to start thinking about what actual deindustrialization might entail. Not because this animal has suddenly been subjected to unnatural industrial processes. But because, like many human beings, hogs are the product of hundreds of years of compounded engineering. Learning to relate to hogs outside of industry—that is, outside of work, outside of meat, outside of economic value—might better teach us how to live that way ourselves. For the lives and deaths of the American hog are a reflection of how we humans live together.

NOTES

INTRODUCTION: THE "FACTORY" FARM

1 Pork is technically red meat. Many Americans think of it otherwise because of a campaign by the National Pork Board in the 1990s to brand pork as a low-fat muscle—"the other white meat"—at a moment when industrial chicken was rising in popularity. There are also cows raised in the region.

2 See also records of visitors' reactions to the stockyards in the introduction to Lee 2008; in Giedion 1948; Pacyga 2015. For analysis of slaughterhouse tours, see Shukin 2009.

3 Even Upton Sinclair, in his infamous muckraking novel *The Jungle*, believed that parts of industrial systems of organizing human and natural energy could be redeemed for the project of building a new socialist world. For the ethos of American mass-production, whose roots lie partially in the meatpacking systems that inspired Henry Ford's assembly line, see Hounshell 1984.

4 For further analyses of how industrialism creates unruly environs, see Checker 2005; Kirksey 2015; Murphy 2017.

5 All company, personal, and place-names in this book are pseudonyms, intended to provide a measure of anonymity to individuals in the four pork corporations where I conducted research. I am unable to specify with precision the exact locale where most of my fieldwork took place, as the largest pork corporations in the United States are each centrally located out of a single state. Colorado, Illinois, Iowa, Kansas, Minnesota, Missouri, Nebraska, Oklahoma, Texas, and Utah all contain major corporate pork installations that resemble the operations in this book. I have rounded and changed these numbers slightly, matching them to a series of hog slaughterhouses across the Great Plains and the Midwest such that this could be one of a small handful of places. While this is among the largest single-line slaughterhouses in history, the Chicago Stock Yards, across

many slaughterhouses and species, killed more animals at their peak—as many as ninety million in a year.

6   All of these figures are approximations. The figure on fecal material is based on an estimate of a hog generating eleven pounds of manure per day. The weights of body material are based on the assumption of a 285-pound live weight hog. The percentage of each substance within the hog is derived from a breakdown supplied by Meindertoma (2009).

7   For *worlds* and *worlding*, which she defines as "the practice of creating relations of life in a place and the place itself," see de la Cadena 2015, 291fn4. Worlds, under these terms, are not fixed containers. They are places where things happen and unfold. One primary project of the factory farm, as we shall see across chapters, is to make those new actions and becomings always be the same. It is not unlike how Walter Benjamin (1999, 26) labeled modernity as the time of hell: "pains eternal and always new."

8   "Grueling monotony" is the anthropologist Steve Striffler's (2005) perfect phrase to describe the burdensome repetition of cutting a single piece of an animal with one motion all day. The phrase was inspired by Striffler's experiences working undercover in a Tyson Foods chicken slaughterhouse in Arkansas, when he would come home after work exhausted and unable to fulfill rudimentary household tasks. For a portrait of repetitive assembly work more generally as mental and physical endurance, see Peña 1997.

9   To protect this person's anonymity to the greatest extent possible, I use the pronouns "they" and "them" to prevent local identification by gender.

10 For an explanation of how this access came about, see chapter 4.

11 As time went by and I became friends with some bankers, and met Dover Foods' own land manager, I learned about this fraught history of purchasing territory from absentee owners. In a different context and place, Annie Proulx's novel *That Old Ace in the Hole* (2002) satirically enlivens this process by following the exploits of a man sent from Chicago to Texas to convince farmers to sell land for hogs.

12 Until 2018 in North Carolina, most of these nuisance suits were unsuccessful (see Centner 2004; Chapin et al. 1998; DeLind 1995). The work of Susan Schiffinan and her colleagues (1998) was an inspired scientific effort to "materialize" hog odor, an effort that has also been developed by Steven Wing and his colleagues (2008). Kendall Thu (2010), who sat for two years on the National Agricultural Air Quality Task Force, along with Kelly Donham (1998), has done important work to detail the respiratory and health problems facing workers and neighbors who are exposed to the manure pits of CAFOS.

13 For a deep analysis of absent presences, see Stewart 1996. Reading Elayne Oliphant's (2012) dissertation and forthcoming ethnography on the Catholic church's quiet domination of the Parisian cityscape has taught me how to think about and become more attuned to omnipresent invisibilities.

14 In addition, see García (2010) and Lien (2015) for how models of industrialized animality are being taken up in guinea pig–rearing and salmon farming, respectively.

15   For important anthropological and geographical work on early phases of hog restructuring, see Bonanno and Constance 2006; Thu and Durrenberger 1998.

16   Key texts on the industrialization of chicken production, along with its imitation by other "protein" companies, include Boyd 2001; Boyd and Watts 1997; Silbergeld 2016; Striffler 2005.

17   Agricultural contracting is becoming increasingly common, more generally, as part of an economic movement toward "supply chain capitalism" (see Tsing 2009a; Watts 2004). There are few broad histories of the shifts across the twentieth century from small-scale diverse farms with pigs to intensively raised corporate protein production. Dawn Coppin's (2002) doctoral thesis on the minute steps that led to the transformation of the pig alongside broader industrial restructuring is an important exception. Ronald Rich's (2003) doctoral dissertation on Illinois hog contracting provides a robust political economic portrait of the contracting form as it unfolded in the Upper Midwest. Stull and Broadway (2013) provide a comparative survey of the transformation of rural communities facing large integrated meatpackers, with a focus in Kansas. A number of books explore the cultural history of the pig, see esp. Horwitz 1998; Mizelle 2012. For a broad overview of this literature, see Blanchette 2018.

18   Vitality—whether in biological or cultural forms—is typically employed as a word to name that which exceeds dominating human agency and cessation, or that which resists both biological death and cultural deadening (see Bennett 2010). Industrial rationality, technics, and routinization are often taken as the sign of de-vitalized "death" (Jones 2011; Lemke 2011). I put the factory farm's project in the oxymoronic terms of "vital industrialization" to magnify the contradictions and ambitions at the very heart of the endeavor. For parallel thoughts on the exploitation of vitality, see also Beldo 2017. I should add that Dover Foods is no longer unique in this regard of seeking maximal vertical integration, either within the United States or elsewhere. Many companies have made similar investments in the conversion of waste products into internally recycled inputs.

19   For a sampling of the better pieces of popular journalism on factory farms, see Eiznitz 2007; Genoways 2014; Leonard 2014; Pollan 2002; and, esp., Schlosser 2001.

20   To analyze agribusiness in these terms is to think alongside an ongoing feminist effort to examine how large-scale capitalist institutions (or, better, capitalisms in the multiple) are shaped and generated in and through mundane practice (Appel 2012; Bear et al. 2015; Salzinger 2004; Yanagisako 2002). Some recent ethnographies, in parallel, have tried to take the industrial out of the factory proper, illustrating how people consciously wield and aspire to achieve its values and affects—especially in post-Fordist contexts where industrial work is no longer a norm but, for working-class communities, more often than not a (tensely nostalgic) memory (Muehlebach 2011; Walley 2013).

21   See also Besky (2019), and Patel and Moore (2017), for broader analyses of the value of cheapness in global agribusiness.

22   See Blanchette (2018, 2019) on agricultural exemption laws around air pollution. Unionization is difficult to achieve in workplaces regulated as "agricultural"—

and this is reflected in Dover Foods' wages, which are marked by a sudden drop once one exits the unionized slaughterhouse. In parallel, one should also read parts of this book's analytical method as influenced by a motivation to reject agricultural exceptions, politically and intellectually, by primarily drawing from literatures in labor and industrial studies. Taking reflexive industrialization at its word, I analytically act as if they are "really" factories.

23 We will see that this is not my own abstract point: standardization is an ongoing and never-quite-complete process even within Dover Foods' own adopted industrial manufacturing philosophies (chapters 4 and 8). On ways to think about the idea that no being is an island—that pigs cannot be industrialized without attention to their bio-social relations—see Tsing 2012b. For an earlier attempt to think about farm animal industrialization in these extensive terms, using the case of milk production, see DuPuis 2002.

24 I thank Jake Kosek for pushing me on this point. For a general critique of standardization's constant overreach, see Scott 1998. For the limitations of efforts to achieve "scalability," such that (in our case) making one pig is akin to making one million, see Tsing 2012a, 2009b.

25 I use the word "skirmish" because of its overtones of quiet, mundane, everyday conflict. This is not a space, as we shall see, in which there is—at least during the very specific period of my own research—much in the way of robust labor organizing or social movements. See Stuesse (2016), however, for an instructive text on the conditions of possibility in which those movements might arise in meatpacking.

26 In other words, one part of this book is solidly within the long-standing tradition of ethnographies of the industrial labor process in terms of control, hierarchy, and exploitation: see, e.g., Burawoy 1982; Collins 2003; Nash 1979; Ong 1987; Salzinger 2004. But one of my key assumptions is that how we write and analyze industrialism must shift alongside the object of production.

27 For elaboration of this point, see Cochoy 2005. This also provides some insight into Dover Foods' corporate model. The company controls a very large percentage of American swine with little branding and prefers to sell raw commodity pork to wholesalers and other processing companies. While one is unlikely to find a Dover-brand tenderloin in a grocery store, it is likely that every pork eater in North America or East Asia has consumed a piece of these hogs.

28 For analyses of how capitalist value is becoming increasingly affective, tied to desires and modes of sociality rather than simply encased in material commodities, see Hardt and Negri 2000; Virno 2004.

29 In Gastón Gordillo's (2014) dialectical terms, one might say that these pursuits of totality contain within themselves their own "negativity."

30 On the stakes of these kinds of debates, see, e.g., Graeber 2001; Jay 1986; Tsing 2012a. It is usually invoked when discussing allegedly "big things": global capitalism as a whole (Arrighi and Moore 2001), how capitalism incorporates nonhuman worlds (Moore 2015), or abstractions such as "the U.S. food system" (Neff

2015). For an excellent and creative example to think about the politics and use of totality in places we might not expect to find the word and form of thinking to have much relevance—notably, given this book's topic, in small-scale "local" pork production—see Weiss 2016.

31 Things like the barcode also require new approaches to capitalist animality. There are stellar scholarly ethnographies that take place in growing farms (Rich 2003) and slaughterhouses (Pachirat 2011; Ribas 2016; Striffler 2005) in relative isolation. But a shortcoming of this writing is that it centers its relative attention on one node of living or killing. This book instead attempts to inhabit integration as a political process, as it is integration itself—more so than confinement, disassembly speeds, or corporate finance—that has distinguished capitalist meat since the 1980s.

32 For an analysis of what they critically call "damage narratives," or efforts to ascribe exceptional pain and suffering to particular peoples, communities, and places in a (perhaps naïve) effort to ameliorate these conditions, see Murphy 2017; Tuck 2009.

33 In other words, I am not dismissing the very real struggles, actual and potential, unfolding in other diverse agricultures outside of this place (see esp. Alkon and Agyeman 2011; Lyons 2016; McMichael 2012; Paxson 2013; Penniman 2018; Weiss 2016). My nudge is to allow potentially radical alternatives to be unpacked on their own dynamic terms, amid the specific agribusinesses they confront.

34 For a broader take on this book's method as one of immanent critique, see Mazzarella 2013.

CHAPTER ONE: THE DOVER FILES

1 Corporations such as Dover Foods explain this differently. They claim that many barns were constructed in the 1990s for, say, ten thousand animals but only house five thousand as the company manages territories and disease. Thus, the company claims to rarely need to empty some of its lagoons because they were constructed with larger pits than were necessary for the number of defecating animals that are currently housed in some barns. The company is, however, certainly allowing the vast majority of the pits' contents to evaporate (see Blanchette 2019).

CHAPTER TWO: THE HERD

1 The bulk of this conversation occurred in Spanish but shifted to English as technical workplace terms such as "biosecurity" became the subject of discussion. This was the norm on farms, where the primary spoken languages were Spanish or K'iche', mixed with the English farming phrases taught during training. At the time of my research, a complicated racial division of labor extended across the factory farm's various work sites. For example, the people I encountered in

breeding were of Mexican, Guatemalan, or Cuban descent, while migrants from Burma tended to staff the slaughterhouse's overnight sanitation shift. With a few exceptions, the most senior managers tended to be white and born in the United States, and they spoke English as their primary language.

2   Public health researchers have started to find evidence that hog farmworkers can carry antibiotic-resistant bacteria on their bodies for several days, despite showering protocols (Nadimpalli et al. 2014). Forms of hog-to-human-to-human-to-hog infection are considered rare and are labeled "tertiary exposure" in the pork industry biosecurity literature, as distinguished from the relatively more common forms of hog-to-hog (primary) or direct hog-human-hog (secondary) exposure (Morrow and Roberts 2002). But this biosecurity protocol is not unique to Dover Foods. For example, an Australian biosecurity organization suggests that all hog farm employees sign a declaration that includes, among other stipulations, a pledge that they will not live with other animal farmworkers (Animal Health Australia 2012).

3   There is no formal rule, to my knowledge, dictating that managers across different nodes of porcine life and death cannot socialize. There remain situations at work—such as planning meetings—when some managers must be copresent. Still, this burgeoning consciousness and rule of thumb was further made clear to me when a couple of managers expressed uncertainty about how (or whether) to interact with *my* embodied self as a researcher who spoke with people of different social classes and spent time at multiple firms.

4   This is in addition to more obvious forms of class inequality in terms of wages, such as the fact that workers in the early 2010s were making $9–$10 per hour while senior managers' annual salaries can range from $70,000 to more than $100,000.

5   For an account of an anthropology of suspension in which beings are diluted, intermingled, and held together through the shared medium of the atmosphere, see Choy and Zee 2015. The term "atmospheric attunement" is derived from Kathleen Stewart (2011).

6   Nor is it unprecedented in other, smaller forms of animal agriculture. In her remarkable study of small-scale slaughterhouses in Minnesota, Kara Wentworth (personal communication, email March 2015) describes how farming families would strip off clothes outside their homes and between house and barn after attending community events such as high school basketball games, church, or 4-H competitions, where they would have encountered other agriculturalists. Moreover, scholars such as Catherine McNeur (2014) have shown how, even in cities such as Manhattan, people used to cohabit and share households with pigs. This is, in some ways, a very old story—perhaps even one of an industrial "return" to more typical relationships between pigs and humans.

7   See also Michelle Murphy's (2011) notion of distributed reproduction, whereby biophysical reproduction (in humans, in her writing) is distributed across an economy.

8   For this reason, I characterize the factory farm as ambiguously postanthropocentric—that is, neither fully anthropocentric in its local realiza-

tion on the ground and quite obviously not purely porcine-centric, given that it is a matter of making life and death for human consumption.

9   In other words, this should not be read as a critique of the (academic) posthumanities. Quite the opposite: I see this as a matter of corporations trying to capture some of this contemporary zeitgeist, incorporating it in ways that dull and pacify its radical edges. For an incisive and original approach to theorizing the ways that capital is itself a process of incorporating radical oppositions, see Braun 2015.

10 Emily Yates-Doerr (2015, 309) has expansively called for a multispecies scholarship that rejects the taxonomic urge to preemptively classify things into fixed natural categories, and instead illustrates the ongoing work of enacting species needed to make "an occurrence of coherence situated amid ever-transforming divisions and connections."

11 While farmers and pastoralists have called groups of owned hogs a herd for centuries, when I refer to the Herd I am describing an organizational technology that is specific to industrial animal production.

12 For an insightful philosophical analysis of farm animal massification, and how seeing in mass affects off-farm apparatuses such as animal welfare science, see Buller 2013.

13 In other words, I am interested here in how the subject positions of "workers" and "managers" are processually created at a local level through pigs (cf. Salzinger 2004). One thing to remember is that these categories did not really exist in American animal agribusiness twenty years ago (at least outside of the slaughterhouse). These managers, among the first generation of factory farm managers, have had to create these positions. My focus on the division of labor at this very broad level leads me to emphasize "class" as an analytic in this chapter. But one could just as easily characterize this as a process of racialization through industrial animality. Those who are hired to "work with" the Herd are almost all people of color, while those who are employed to abstractly "work on" the Herd tend to be white. I examine this in more detail in chapters 3 and 6.

14 For a different—arch-anthropocentric—kind of privatization of public biosecurities through the development of transgenic animals that would not shed disease and would require no modification of contemporary human activities, see Lezaun and Porter 2015.

15 For important analyses of biosecurity's *infelicity*, or how "security . . . has itself become a significant source of insecurity," see Caduff 2014, 115; Masco 2014.

16 This is not a pseudonym. The word *pollo* means chicken in Spanish.

17 For a broader history of trucking and its relation to building large-scale rural animal-based agribusiness, see Hamilton (2008).

18 Or, less a blanket statement on the nature of nature, see chapters 4 and 8 for how even these managers, within their manufacturing theory courses, see "full" standardization as impossible.

19   Steve Hinchliffe (2014) and Steve Hinchcliffe and Kim J. Ward (2014) discuss
     building immunities in hogs and managing endemic illnesses, noting how sup-
     posedly disease-free barns would only result in the emergence of new illnesses.

20   While disturbing exposé videos of workers beating animals have been picked
     up by the media to create the impression that employees are alienated from
     and indifferent to pigs, I often found the opposite. Workers would often go
     to incredible lengths to intimately heal the pigs with which they worked (see
     chapter 6).

21   Although, it is important to note, these pod managers do not cross over into the
     death phases.

CHAPTER THREE: SOMOS PUERCOS

1   Twenty-six different languages are spoken by the children at Dixon's elementary
    school. However, farmworkers tend to hail from Latin America, while people
    working in the slaughterhouse might have been born in Burma, Ethiopia, Viet-
    nam, China, Somalia, or Sudan.

2   For an analysis of how the colonial plantation—with its clean lines, monocul-
    tures, and ordering of nature—serves as the original model of contemporary
    industrial agriculture, see Tsing 2012b. For a discussion of how the modern
    slaughterhouse is constituted by a "plantation capitalism" of neocolonial divi-
    sions between white managers and nonwhite workers, see Stuesse 2016.

CHAPTER FOUR: STIMULATION

1   I am implicitly thinking (albeit in interspecies ways) across this chapter with
    some of the arguments in Leslie Salzinger's *Genders in Production* (2004). There
    she argues that gender in Mexico's maquiladoras is a performance brought to
    life on the shop floor, that the gendered roles that female (and male) work-
    ers are forced to inhabit are simulacra—copies without originals (Baudrillard
    1994)—transplanted from the globally circulating image of the "nimble-
    fingered" woman from 1970s Malaysia. On the AI line, both workers and sows
    are brought into being through practices. For the notion of enactment, which
    is a practice that does (or "enacts"; makes real) a given object or thing, see
    Mol 2002. The term is useful for me because it implies that porcine sexual
    natures are not just "in" sows but, rather, co-enacted across species in ongoing
    practices.

2   Each sow, on average, is inseminated 2.5 times over the course of its estrous
    cycle. Thus, the 122 sows being bred that week will lead to about 303 total
    inseminations, or about sixty per day in a five-day workweek. For reasons that
    are made clear in chapter 6, Sow #6 aims for 1,071 piglets weaned per week, with
    an average pre-wean mortality rate of 15 percent (meaning that 1,265 piglets will
    be born per week, and a little over 190 will die). The ideal figure that Berkamp

Meats tries to hit across its six breeding farms is 331,500 piglets weaned, raised, and slaughtered in a year.

3   On critiques of how the animal is often framed as a being that is not open to the ongoingness of the world and that is fundamentally reactive and predetermined, see Agamben 2004; Derrida 2008.

4   I have, despite some reticence, come to think of artificial insemination as a form of "sex work" through the humor and conversations that unfold on the production line. But I am also inspired by Gabriel Rosenberg's (2017) and Jeanette Vaught's (2016) pathbreaking efforts to develop queer readings of American agribusiness, with attention to how human sexualities are inseparable from histories of managing nonhuman sexualities.

5   I am thinking here with Anna Lowenhaupt Tsing (2012b) and Rebecca Cassidy and Molly H. Mullin (2007) in terms of domestication never being a one-way street. Domestication of animals (or plants) ends up transforming the domesticators' social relations, senses of self, and social organization.

6   A key exception here is Thom Van Dooren's (2013) discussions of bird imprinting and attempts to make animal natures flourish in captivity.

7   Frederickson (2014) is careful to note that there were many tensions within the equation of work, instinct, and industrial capitalism. Not only did it present the factory system as animalizing people, but the figure of an instinctual laborer is one who is static and unable to take on forms of capitalistic self-improvement.

8   In this sense, we might note an irony about working on instincts. Classically, especially in the Marxist tradition (such as Braverman 1974), human labor has been framed as that which overcomes merely repetitive, "reproductive" instinctual behavior. It makes new things and changes the world with each action (unlike, say, the figurative bird's nest, which is said to be always similar). But inhabiting pig instincts is about always doing things the same; instinctual labor is an oxymoron in these terms.

9   I thank Timothy Pachirat for pushing me on this point.

10   In their tours of Denmark's family-*cum*-industrial insemination farms, both Tsing (2016) and Inger Anneberg and her colleagues (2013) narrate this odd inbetweenness of intimacy and detachment that suffuses the practice of AI—with the former nicely putting the issue as "this is sex, and this is not sex" (Tsing 2016, 7).

11   My coworkers were initially apprehensive about the idea of a researcher writing about them. After being permitted to shadow managers at Dover Foods, executives at Berkamp Meats decided that it was acceptable to allow me to work in a breeding farm. As Blanca later explained to me, she and a few others were skeptical about the idea of another white person making them feel bad by complaining all day about how they could not possibly do this type of dirty work. I indirectly assuaged much of this by trying to work harder than everyone else. While that would not be a wise strategy for achieving solidarity in a line-based production method, Sow #6 has a fixed number of tasks and sows to

inseminate on any given day, and people frequently expressed happiness that I was there to work. For my part, I asked the company's owners to treat me as an extra hire, which gave Sow #6 an extra available hand. In retrospect, this was fortuitous because it slowed down the pace of work, allowed for extra breaks, and facilitated conversation. Most research in these kinds of facilities, especially on the slaughtering side, has been conducted through undercover ethnography (see, e.g., Fink 1998; Pachirat 2011). This comes with many ethical issues, which those authors often address. But so does the seemingly more innocuous route of gaining access to work through the bosses. Workers, at first glance, are not given much in the way of a choice over whether they will be a part of a study. After explaining my research on the second day of my time in the barns, I also described the terms of my Institutional Review Board forms with everyone. I distributed the forms and said that anyone who was willing to be featured in this book could return the signed form to me at any point during the following two months. At that point we would also discuss what each individual was comfortable with me writing about. I made clear that I would not let the bosses know who had (or had not) submitted forms, and I would not pester anyone for forms. Three people did not return forms, and they are largely unmentioned in this book.

12 "El Chapo" Joaquim Guzman was the head of the Sinaloa Cartel, whose wars with rival cartels and the Mexican military were raging in northern Mexico during the time of my primary research in 2010. The violence was a source of worry and lunchtime speculation for coworkers who had family residing in those regions.

13 For a discussion of how capitalism is itself a process of reducing attention to the pluripotency of nonhuman worlds—that is, a matter of reducing complex behavior to archetypes—see Johnson and Goldstein 2015.

14 There did seem to be some consideration of biosecurity in terms of who was placed into each of the three class sessions, especially among relatively lower-ranked managers in frequent contact with pigs.

15 Continuous quality improvement courses were a testament to the bureaucratic power of the Live Side's ongoing experimental sensibilities over the Plant Side at this moment in Dover Foods' history. Live Side managers had introduced CQI to the national pork industry, and now they were attempting to export CQI into Plant Side planning, along with the various positions that are glossed as "support" functions by the corporation (e.g., human resources, shipping, ground maintenance). This is striking for two reasons. First, even at this one pork corporation competing industrial practices and philosophies animated the central divisions. The slaughterhouse used a machine-driven, centrally coordinated Fordist labor process to kill pigs, while the Live Side employed its own version of post-Fordist ("Toyotist") team-driven statistical analyses to help practice industrial innovation in raising the pigs (see also Boyd and Watts 1997). Second, in spite of the slaughterhouse being one of the original industrial forms

(see Cronon 1991; Hounshell 1984), the Live Side was intellectually directing the factory farm as a whole.

16 For a broader examination of fractal processes within social practice, see Irvine and Gal 2000.

17 When giving presentations, I am often asked how I was granted forms of access to this corporation. Although I have no way to know the behind-the-scenes negotiations that took place, a number of the pod managers felt that it was better to keep me close than distant—that perhaps the strategy of barring all outsiders was not very effective—and in the end they were proud of the system they had built in spite of their many constraints. A number of them advocated for me to be given some kind of research access. I did not plan my research expecting to receive this kind of entry into the corporation, and my own approach was to simply be extremely honest about my intentions, research angles, and ideological approach. For instance, I volunteered to share my prior grant applications with managers. I expected that one of my basic guiding questions—How can we think about the "factory" in the factory farm?—would be the sort of thing that would annoy managers, given the term's negative connotations. But it turned out to be helpful because it made clear that I was writing a scholarly book, which opened some doors. Yet it also closed others when executives questioned whether participating was worth the effort. Fortuitously, and as reflected by these CQI classes, some senior managers and executives were asking themselves similar questions. That said, my "access" to senior management and sites was not even across space and time. It ebbed and flowed, especially with changes to upper-level management, and I was granted much less (official) access to the slaughterhouse and packinghouse managers. I suspect this was so partly because I was seen as aligned more with the Live Side, and, as I show, there were strong divisions between the life and death sides. In addition, my initial stated focus was on the lives of workers and the politics of work, not so much on the conditions of animal life (which I now see as an untenable distinction). This suited the concerns of managers on the Live Side well, given that their practices are more often critiqued from the perspective of animal well-being. I imagine that this played less well on the Plant Side, where abuse of human workers is more thoroughly documented (see chapter 8).

18 This should be read as a heuristic distinction. Many scholars have noted that even the assembly line, that seemingly most effective or "objective" of machines, is not at all capable—or, at least, is not solely capable—of perfectly controlling labor. For just one example, see Peña 1997.

19 I thank Brad Weiss for elaborating and pushing me on this point.

20 Actual change to farrowing rate, litter sizes, and litter quality is a complicated issue in the literature on AI. Scores of factors, including genetics, sperm quality, time of insemination, quantity of inseminations during estrous, diet, environmental conditions such as temperature, boar presence, and injections of oxytocin can affect the output of pigs (see, e.g., Flowers and Esbenshade 1993; Gadd

2003; Vansickle 2002). However, AI "technicians" (as they are called in the literature) have been shown to have great effect on at least the farrowing rate and the litters sizes—with changes, say, to the farrowing rate based on workers' fatigue, time of day, illness, and so forth (see Rix and Ketchem 2011a, 2011b, 2012). Part of this is due to proper heat detection (identifying when a sow enters estrous). But it can even get into questions of sentience and perception, as studies demonstrate that breeding animals proliferate more on farms where hogs are not scared of humans due to a history of mistreatment (Hemsworth 2003).

21 Following Kay Milton (2005), Matei Candea (2010, 252), and Alex Nading (2012, 587), I do not think we need to see Felipe's practice as a matter of anthropomorphism, or the assignment of humanlike qualities to nonhuman animal behavior. That term is perhaps too broad. During his fieldwork in Nicaragua with *brigadistas*, public health practitioners who were trying to eradicate dengue-carrying mosquitos, Nading noted that many would joke that "mosquitos are like single mothers." While the typical impulse might be to call this "anthropomorphism," as if it were a projection of "the human," Nading (rightly, in my mind) thinks of it in terms of egomorphism: for these women, the mosquitos were not "humanlike" but, instead, "like me." Along these lines, I think of Felipe's practice as masculine heteromorphism, of assigning normative gender motivations across species.

22 Merck stopped acquiring blood from South America after this report. They continue to source from Europe, and other pharmaceutical companies maintain ties to South American facilities.

CHAPTER FIVE: LUTALYSE

1 For a discussion of soaring rates of milk replacement, see Mavromichalis 2011a.

2 Induction drugs can be harmful to animals in that they can cause litters of pigs to come out of the birth canal too quickly, potentially causing some to suffocate if a group gets stuck. Most managers claimed that, in an ideal world, they would try to avoid using them with great regularity.

3 The only invocation of animal-based hormonal drugs that I can find in U.S. media are perennial legends, spread by the Christian right, that kids are breaking into farms to steal birth induction drugs such as prostaglandins to conduct auto-abortions. Intriguingly, following some of Sarah Pinto's (2008) work, there is a remarkable class politics to the use of these drugs in India, with poor women forced to take (harsher, fast-acting) injectable forms of oxytocin that, to my knowledge, are typically used in this form only to stimulate contractions in animals in the United States.

4 By "alienation" I am referring here to the Marxist notion of estrangement, whereby the product of the worker's labor is taken from her and becomes hostile (cf. Berardi 2009). For a systematic attempt to think about alienation with respect to farm animals, see Stuart et al. 2012.

1   For an analysis of how clinical trials are about growing "health," such that cap-
    italist medicine makes us take more and more drugs to be healthy, see Dumit
    2012b. I have learned to think and write about pig litters and their incessant
    "growth" largely through Dumit's example in *Drugs for Life*.

2   See Martineau and Badouard (2009). Some observers would argue against this
    statement, claiming that hyperprolific sows are a uniquely European experi-
    ment. It is true that American producers have been slower to adopt the specific
    genetics that are explicitly labeled "hyperprolific." However, there were experi-
    ments underway in barns where I have worked, which were testing the adoption
    of sows that produce far more offspring than they have teats. Current litter size
    averages for some American companies are very similar to what was considered
    a European "hyperprolific" sow in the above report by Martineau and Badouard
    from 2009. In the following pages, I refer to new lines of American sows as hav-
    ing "hyperprolific qualities" to articulate this distinction.

3   Only 7.6 percent of pigs died prior to weaning on small farms. These data on swine
    production statistics come from the USDA's quarterly *Hogs and Pigs Report*.

4   For an early theorization of postmodern feral life—as beings that are rendered
    "wild" *through* industrial engineering—see Tsing 2016.

5   See Mavromichalis 2011b; Wu et al. 2016. Mavromichalis (2011b) estimates that
    hyperprolific sows have resulted in up to 10 percent of pigs in European farms
    being runted. A runt is typically defined as being born with a birthweight of
    under 2.2 pounds.

6   Put differently, the coolers do not recruit essentialized "female" sentiments for
    work in farrowing. There is nothing inherently "female" or "male" about cooler
    versus thumping modes of euthanasia. They instead invoke ideological forms of
    femininity as a trope for organizing production (see Salzinger 2004, 15).

7   There are no "gangs" in this section of the Great Plains. Since Dover Foods'
    packing plant opened in the early 1990s, newspapers feature perennial gang
    sightings. These are nothing more than nativist hallucinations. The graffiti that
    might show up on a building once or twice per year can usually be attributed to
    a group of high school kids (as I was told by the police chief of Dixon, who was
    still adamant that these young pranksters constitute a "gang").

8   By "industrial universalization" I am referring to the flipside of deskilling and
    interchangeability, which, since at least the invention of the assembly line, has
    been framed as incorporating more of the national body politic into formerly
    delimited spaces of work (and, as a consequence, cheapening labor). Henry
    Ford, for example, argued in *My Life and Work* (1923) that his assembly line was
    "democratic" because its strict division of labor could incorporate even maimed
    paraplegic war veterans (cf. Buck-Morss 2000).

9   Recall that *profound knowledge* is a CQI term for people who have deeply in-
    grained familiarity with one task, a euphemism for "manual laborer," such as the
    person who only power-washes rooms all day.

10   On care as a practice that is not abstract, but rather responsive to ongoing situations and occurrences, see Puig de la Bellacasa 2012; Van Dooren 2014.

11   Making a sow overproduce is not *just* a matter of genetics. As we have seen in the previous chapter, it is also about insemination technique, feeding, and properly "stimulating" the herd of animals. Francisco usually maintained this as a good thing—at least in the current moment when the Runt was not (yet) universal every day. Ideally, for example, one might get an "extra" piglet, and then people could choose which is the weakest and requires euthanasia. The trouble is when the entire litter—or, at least, a majority of animals—become runts and the ability to selectively euthanize weak ones becomes an impossibility.

12   For a keyword approach to the shifting resonances of the term "life-form" as it has developed with respect to a generalizing theory of biology in the life sciences over the past two centuries, see Helmreich and Roosth 2011.

13   On the cultural politics, practices, and ideologies of engagement and detachment, especially as they inform human-animal relations, see the pathbreaking writing of Matei Candea (2010, 2013, 2015).

14   For wide-ranging discussions of prosthetic politics, see Grosz 2005, chap. 9; Scarry 1985.

15   I take this notion of the condition of being subaltern from Fortun 2013. For the long American history of refusing farmworkers—in her case, African slaves in South Carolina—any degree of knowledge or agency, see Carney 2001.

CHAPTER EIGHT: BIOLOGICAL SYSTEM

1   Moreover, these kinds of "post-offer employment testing" facilities are by no means unique to Dover Foods or the meatpacking industry. They appear to be ascendant in large companies in an era of high health-care costs.

2   For a broader look at the politics of labor disposability in American farmwork, see Guthman 2019.

3   Work in the unionized packing plant—albeit one where the union's strength is severely curtailed by right-to-work legislation, which means that all workers in a contract do not need to pay union dues—is a relatively well-paying job for this area. Employees in 2010 began at almost $13 per hour, with consistent overtime and full benefits after the sixty-day probation period. This was a solid salary in a place where a decent home could be had for $60,000; virtually every worker I met was content with her or his salary and cited it as the reason for working in the plant. This is the product of unionization. People who wash trucks just outside the slaughterhouse—perhaps the hardest job on the factory farm since they are always bent over—make only $9 because they are not "in" the plant and part of the contract. But these salaries also have to be put in historical context. The average slaughterhouse worker made the contemporary equivalent of $35 per hour in 1980, prior to the "IBP revolution" and the cancellation of the national union contract (see Schlosser 2001). Older managers today look back

with nostalgia at that pre-1980s era of growing up in meatpacking towns as part of an upwardly mobile working class. One remembered driving a Mercedes-Benz at twenty-two as a symbol of how hard work was well rewarded. Unfortunately, many of them blame the migrant workforce rather than supply-side agricultural policy that favors cheap food for this economic shift in the industry. Still, the occasional manager clandestinely told me about his hopes for a new wave of union power that might rise all tides and create new forms of solidarity across the packing plant.

4 Catherine Fennell (2011) has written on the topic of shared forms of "sensory publics" as modes of memory and collective politics with respect to the experience of good heat in low-income housing in Chicago.

5 A human resources manager estimated that before the 2008 recession, turnover was verging on 100 percent per year but had now decreased to "44–52 percent across all company operations." The slaughterhouse is likely still on the higher end of that estimate relative to the farms and feed mills. Turnover is complicated in meatpacking. The six-day workweek and limited vacation time mean that people will often quit to take a vacation, or rest their bodies, before returning to work. Regional slaughterhouses will also compete for employees, and people do tend to cycle over companies across the Great Plains, especially when one company is offering some kind of incentive. Dover Foods' packing plant generally rehires approved employees as long as they have not quit three times previously.

6 A full history of the slaughterhouse is outside this book's scope. Horowitz (1997, 2006, 2008; Halpern and Horowitz 1999) has long documented changing labor relations in slaughter across the twentieth century. Anthropologists have been among the most careful documenters of present-day slaughterhouses. Stull and Broadway 2013 and Stull et al. 1995 offer detailed empirical portraits of the ways that slaughterhouses transform rural communities, alongside the plight of human laborers in these systems. Deborah Fink (1998) helps us understand how the slaughterhouse (and the working class) has been written out of dominant narratives of American rurality. Striffler's (2005) undercover work in an Arkansas chicken plant provides a brilliant examination of the violence of "manual" labor. Timothy Pachirat's (2011) detailed undercover ethnography of the slaughterhouse as a space of death is, in my opinion, the single most important text for understanding the processes of industrial killing. For the politics of labor, race, and migration in southern U.S. slaughterhouses, see Ribas 2016. For other excellent recent studies, see Angela Stuesse's (2016) activist ethnography of organizing chicken packinghouse workers, along with Faranak Miraftab's (2016) detailed examination of changing small towns and globalization in the wake of corporate moves to locate slaughterhouses in rural areas.

7 For additional notes on this point see Horowitz and Miller 1999, cited in Stull and Broadway 2013, 99.

8 Note that this is not just a matter of quantity and accumulated weight over the eight- to ten-hour shift. One could simply add more people if that was the case.

Instead, if the conveyer is moving too quickly, the worker cannot read and scan the label for sorting. Alternatively, moving any faster could result in people being acutely hurt beyond repetitive motion injuries by boxes smashing into their hands.

9 This should be read as the archetypal male body. Some women do work on the kill floor, but for the most part women work on the cut floor. It is very rare to hear of a woman working in shipping and box movements.

CHAPTER TEN: LIFECYCLE

1 For skepticism on this issue, however, see Agapakis 2012.

2 Rendering managers, despite working in the muck of euthanized piglet corpses and blood, were accorded a certain prestige by others in the company because, as one put it, "They're the bottom line." For an attempt to quantify the value of "byproducts," see Marti et al. 2011.

3 I learned to think in this manner from Susan Squier's *Poultry Science, Chicken Culture* (2010), which addresses how "industrial" and other agricultures are interlocked (see also Gibson-Graham 2008).

4 On metabolisms and eating practices, including, notably, the nonhuman metabolisms that affect human metabolisms and how we are transformed by the food of our food, see Landecker 2013, and Landecker forthcoming.

5 In an incisive article on pet food diets, Molly Mullin (2007) argues that we risk placing excess influence on breeding to establish the identity and domesticated nature of the animal. What makes an animal "industrial" or "domestic"—here, in the sense of being connected to circuits and networks of broader industrial agricultures to sustain its being—is also legible through its diet and paths of sustenance.

6 The term "Lifecycle" also derives from Ryan's position as a commodities buyer. "Lifecycle feeding" is an expression and technology in the national pork industry that appeared in the 1960s. It refers to using specialized diets at each precise stage or age in a growing pig's life to maximize its growth rates, or "feed conversion ratios." For the origin of this term, see Finlay 2004.

7 Hog lungs, or "lights" (as they were once called in the English-speaking culinary world), have been banned for sale for human consumption by the U.S. Department of Agriculture due to the difficulty of removing bacteria from their inner surfaces. Of course, they are still consumed elsewhere for food—think, for example, of Scotland's haggis, a traditional preparation that is illegal in the United States.

8 One can imagine a whole array of factors that could make industrial pig lungs and livers starkly distinct across sites: breeds and genetic stock, the typical kill age of a given corporation's hogs, different feeds, perhaps building and fan construction styles that circulate air and chemical vapors from pooled feces differently, or even how a given corporation's feed ration affects the chemicals that are wafting up.

9   For supply chain capitalism, along with Japan as a fundamental originator and coordinator of such processes, see Tsing 2015.

10 For a very rich elaboration of this point based on research into the ways that New Zealand unloads its cheap, fatty, and unhealthy "flaps" of lamb to poor island nations, see Gewertz and Errington 2010.

11 They are akin, perhaps, to what Anna Tsing (2016) has been developing as a form of "feral biology," or creatures that are the uncontrolled, unmoored offshoots of anthropogenic engineering.

EPILOGUE: (DE-)INDUSTRIALIZATION

1   See Blanchette (2018) for a very different analysis of the Working Group on the Anthropocene's discoveries.

REFERENCES

AFB International. n.d. *Principles of Pet Food Palatability*. White paper. https://afbinternational.com/downloads/principles-of-pet-food-palatability/.

Agamben, Giorgio. 2004. *The Open: Man and Animal*. Palo Alto, CA: Stanford University Press.

Agapakis, Christina. 2012. "Steak of the Art: The Fatal Flaws of In Vitro Meat." *The Crux, Discover Magazine* blog, April 24. http://blogs.discovermagazine.com/crux/2012/04/24/steak-of-the-art-the-fatal-flaws-of-in-vitro-meat/.

Alkon, Alison Hope, and Julian Agyeman. 2011. *Cultivating Food Justice: Race, Class, and Sustainability*. Cambridge, MA: MIT Press.

Allen, John, and Stephanie Lavau. 2015. "'Just-in-Time' Disease: Biosecurity, Poultry and Power." *Journal of Cultural Economy* 8, no. 3: 342–60.

Andrews, Thomas. 2008. *Killing for Coal*. Cambridge, MA: Harvard University Press.

Animal Health Australia. 2012. "Employee Biosecurity Declaration Template." Accessed August 9, 2015. http://www.farmbiosecurity.com.au/wp-content/uploads/2012/11/Employee-Biosecurity-Declaration-Template.pdf.

Animal Studies Group. 2006. *Killing Animals*. Champaign: University of Illinois Press.

Anneberg, Inger, Mette Vaarst, and Nils Bubandt. 2013. "Pigs and Profits: Hybrids of Animals, Technologies, and Humans in Danish Industrialized Farming." *Social Anthropology* 21, no. 4: 542–49.

Appel, Hannah. 2012. "Offshore Work: Oil, Modularity, and the How of Capitalism in Equatorial Guinea." *American Ethnologist* 39, no. 4: 692–709.

Arrighi, Giovanni, and Jason W. Moore. 2001. "Capitalist Development in World Historical Perspective." In *Phases of Capitalist Development: Booms, Crises, and Globalizations*, edited by Robert Albritton, Makoto Itoh, Richard Westra, and Alan Zuege, 56–75. London: Palgrave.

Ashwood, Loka, Danielle Diamond, and Kendall Thu. 2014. "Where's the Farmer? Limiting Liability in Midwestern Industrial Hog Production." *Rural Sociology* 79, no. 1: 2–27.

Avant, Sandra. 2014. "Myelin Matters to Piglet Movement, Reflexes, and Coordination." *Agricultural Research*. February 2014.

Bateson, Gregory. 1972. *Steps to an Ecology of Mind*. Chicago: University of Chicago Press.

Baudrillard, Jean. 1994. *Simulacra and Simulation*. Ann Arbor: University of Michigan Press.

Bear, Laura, Karen Ho, Anna Lowenhaupt Tsing, and Sylvia Yanagisako. 2015. "Gens: A Feminist Manifesto for the Study of Capitalism." Theorizing the Contemporary, *Fieldsights*. March 30. https://culanth.org/fieldsights/gens-a-feminist-manifesto -for-the-study-of-capitalism.

Beaton, Lindsay. 2015. "Palatability Technologies in the Petfood Industry." Petfoodindustry.com, September 1. http://www.petfoodindustry.com/articles/5349 -palatability-technologies-in-the-pet-food-industry.

Beecher, Cookson. 2015. "Managing Black Gold: Animal Manure and Antibiotic Resistance." Food Safety News, November 9. http://www.foodsafetynews.com /2015/11/managing-black-gold-animal-manure-and-antibiotic-resistance/#.V6 -XkFfbkhY.

Beldo, Les. 2017. "Metabolic Labor: Broiler Chickens and the Exploitation of Vitality." *Environmental Humanities* 9, no. 1: 108–28.

Bell, Daniel. 1947. "The Study of Man: Adjusting Men to Machines." *Commentary Magazine*, January.

Benjamin, Walter. 1999. *The Arcades Project*. Cambridge, MA: Harvard University Press.

Bennett, Carys, Richard Thomas, Mark Williams, Jan Zalasiewicz, Matt Edgeworth, Holly Miller, Ben Coles, Alison Foster, Emily Burton, and Upenyu Marume. 2018. "The Broiler Chicken as a Signal of a Human Reconfigured Biosphere." *Royal Society Open Science* 5, no. 12: 1–11.

Bennett, Jane. 2010. *Vibrant Matter: A Political Ecology of Things*. Durham, NC: Duke University Press.

Benson, Peter. 2011. *Tobacco Capitalism: Growers, Migrant Workers, and the Changing Face of a Global Industry*. Princeton, NJ: Princeton University Press.

Berardi, Franco. 2009. *The Soul at Work: From Alienation to Autonomy*. Cambridge, MA: Semiotext(e).

Berg, Lora. 2009. "Fetal Imprinting May Affect Pigs' Lifetime Performances." *National Hog Farmer*, January 15. https://www.nationalhogfarmer.com/genetics -reproduction/0109-fetal-imprinting-effects.

Berger, John. 1979. *Pig Earth*, vol. 1. London: Vintage.

Berman, Marshal. 1983. *All That Is Solid Melts into Air: The Experience of Modernity*. New York: Verso.

Berry, Wendell. 1977. *The Unsettling of America*. San Francisco: Sierra Club Books.

Berry, Wendell. 2009. *Bringing It to the Table: On Farming and Food*. Berkeley, CA: Counterpoint.

Bershadker, Matthew. 2015. "USDA's Meat Animal Research Center: An American Horror Story." *Huffington Post*, January 23. http://www.huffingtonpost.com/matt -bershadker/usdas-meat-animal-researc_b_6532210.html.

Besky, Sarah. 2019. "Exhaustion and Endurance in Sick Landscapes: Cheap Tea and the Work of Monoculture in the Dooars, India" In *How Nature Works: Rethinking Labor on a Troubled Planet*, edited by Sarah Besky and Alex Blanchette, 23–40. Albuquerque: SAR Press/University of New Mexico Press.

Besky, Sarah, and Alex Blanchette, eds. 2019. *How Nature Works: Rethinking Labor on a Troubled Planet*. Albuquerque: SAR Press/University of New Mexico Press.

Bird, Isabella L. 1856. *The Englishwoman in America*. London: John Murray.

Blanchette, Alex. 2018. "Industrial Meat Production." *Annual Review of Anthropology* 47: 185–99.

Blanchette, Alex. 2019. "Living Waste and the Labor of Toxic Health on American Factory Farms." *Medical Anthropology Quarterly* 33, no. 1: 80–100.

Bonanno, Alessandro, and Douglas H. Constance. 2006. "Corporations and the State in the Global Era: The Case of Seaboard Farms and Texas." *Rural Sociology* 71, no. 1: 59–84.

Boodman, Eric. 2018. "How an Inconspicuous Slaughterhouse Keeps the World's Premature Babies Alive." *STAT*, March 12. https://www.statnews.com/2018/03/12 /cow-surfactant-premature-babies/.

Boyd, William. 2001. "Making Meat: Science, Technology, and American Poultry Production." *Technology and Culture* 42, no. 4: 631–64.

Boyd, William, and Michael Watts. 1997. "The Chicken Industry and Postwar American Capitalism." In *Globalising Food: Agrarian Questions and Global Restructuring*, edited by David Goodman and Michael Watts, 192–225. New York: Routledge.

Brassley, Paul. 2007. "Cutting across Nature? The History of Artificial Insemination in Pigs in the United Kingdom." *Studies in the History and Philosophy of Biological and Biomedical Sciences* 38, no. 2: 442–61.

Braun, Bruce. 2015. "New Materialism and Neoliberal Natures." *Antipode* 47, no. 1: 1–14.

Braverman, Harry. 1974. *Labor and Monopoly Capital*. New York: New York University Press.

Broadway, Michael. 1995. "From City to Countryside: Recent Changes in the Structure and Location of the Meat- and Fish-Processing Industries." In *Any Way You Cut It: Meat Processing and Small-Town America*, edited by Donald D. Stull, Michael J. Broadway, and David Griffith, 17–41. Lawrence: University Press of Kansas.

Brown, Wendy. 2010. *Walled States, Waning Sovereignty*. London: Zone.

Buck-Morss, Susan. 1989. *The Dialectics of Seeing: Walter Benjamin and the Arcades Project*. Cambridge, MA: MIT Press.

REFERENCES

Buck-Morss, Susan. 1992. "Aesthetics and Anaesthetics: Walter Benjamin's Artwork Essay Reconsidered." *October* 62: 3–41.

Buck-Morss, Susan. 1995. "The City as Dreamworld and Catastrophe." *October* 73: 3–26.

Buck-Morss, Susan. 2000. *Dreamworld and Catastrophe: The Passing of Mass Utopia in East and West*. Cambridge, MA: MIT Press.

Buller, Henry. 2013. "Individuation, the Mass, and Farm Animals." *Theory, Culture, and Society* 30, no. 7–8: 155–75.

Burawoy, Michael. 1979. "The Anthropology of Industrial Work." *Annual Review of Anthropology* 8: 231–66.

Burawoy, Michael. 1982. *Manufacturing Consent*. Chicago: University of Chicago Press.

Butet-Roach, Laurence. 2015. "Meet the Artists Who Play with the Rules of Documentary Photography." *Time Magazine*, September 1. Lightbox Blog. Accessed September 12, 2019. http://time.com/4003022/meet-the-artists-who-play-with -the-rules-of-documentary-photography/.

Caduff, Carlo. 2014. "On the Verge of Death: Visions of Biological Vulnerability." *Annual Review of Anthropology* 43: 105–21.

Candea, Matei. 2010. "'I Fell in Love with Carlos the Meerkat': Engagement and Detachment in Human-Animal Relations." *American Ethnologist* 37, no. 2: 241–58.

Candea, Matei. 2013. "Suspending Belief: Epoché in Animal Behavior Science." *American Anthropologist* 115, no. 3: 423–36.

Candea, Matei, ed. 2015. *Detachment: Essays on the Limits of Relational Thinking*. Manchester, UK: Manchester University Press.

Carney, Judith. 2001. *Black Rice: The African Origins of Rice Cultivation in the Americas*. Cambridge, MA: Harvard University Press.

Carrington, Damian. 2016a. "The Anthropocene Epoch: Scientists Declare Dawn of Human-Influenced Age." *The Guardian*, August 29. https://www.theguardian .com/environment/2016/aug/29/declare-anthropocene-epoch-experts-urge -geological-congress-human-impact-earth.

Carrington, Damian. 2016b. "How the Domestic Chicken Rose to Define the Anthropocene." *The Guardian*, August 31. https://www.theguardian.com/environment /2016/aug/31/domestic-chicken-anthropocene-humanity-influenced-epoch.

Cassidy, Rebecca, and Molly H. Mullin, eds. 2007. *Where the Wild Things Are Now: Domestication Reconsidered*. London: Berg.

Centner, Terrence. 2004. *Empty Pastures: Confined Animals and the Transformation of the Rural Landscape*. Champaign: University of Illinois Press.

Chakrabarty, Dipesh. 2009. "The Climate of History: Four Theses." *Critical Inquiry* 35, no. 2: 197–222.

Chapin, Amy, Charlotte Boulind, and Amanda Moore. 1998. *Controlling Odor and Gaseous Emission Problems from Industrial Swine Facilities: A Handbook for All Interested Parties*. Yale Environmental Protection Clinic Handbook. Poteau, OK: Kerr Center for Sustainable Agriculture.

Checker, Melissa. 2005. *Polluted Promises: Environmental Racism and the Search for Justice in a Southern Town*. New York: New York University Press.

Chen, Mel Y. 2012. *Animacies: Biopolitics, Racial Mattering, and Queer Affect.* Durham, NC: Duke University Press.

Cho, Jenny G., and Scott A. Dee. 2006. "Porcine Reproductive and Respiratory Syndrome Virus." *Theriogenology* 66, no. 3: 655–62.

Choy, Timothy, and Jerry Zee. 2015. "Condition—Suspension." *Cultural Anthropology* 30, no. 2: 210–23.

Cochoy, Franck. 2005. "A Brief History of 'Customers,' or the Gradual Standardization of Markets and Organizations." *Sociologie du Travail* 47, supp. 1 (December): e36–e56.

Collier, Stephen J., Andrew Lakoff, and Paul Rabinow. 2004. "Biosecurity: Towards an Anthropology of the Contemporary." *Anthropology Today* 20, no. 5: 3–7.

Collins, Jane. 2003. *Threads: Gender, Labor, and Power in the Global Apparel Industry.* Chicago: University of Chicago Press.

Cooper, Melinda. 2008. *Life as Surplus Biotechnology and Capitalism in the Neoliberal Era.* Seattle: University of Washington Press.

Coppin, Dawn Michelle. 2002. "Capitalist Pigs: Large-Scale Swine Facilities and the Mutual Construction of Nature and Society." PhD diss., University of Illinois, Urbana-Champaign.

Cowen, Deborah. 2014. *The Deadly Life of Logistics.* Minneapolis: University of Minnesota Press.

Crawford, Mathew. 2009. *Shop Class as Soulcraft: An Inquiry into the Value of Work.* New York: Penguin.

Cronon, William. 1991. *Nature's Metropolis: Chicago and the Great West.* New York: W. W. Norton.

Curliss, Andrew. 2014. "From Eastern N[orth] C[arolina] to Tokyo: A New Breed of 'Silky' Pork." *Charlotte Observer,* December 13.

Davis, Mike. 2007. *The Monster at Our Door: The Global Threat of Avian Flu.* New York: Holt.

Dee, Scott, John Deen, Kurt Rossow, Carrie Wiese, Satoshi Otake, Han Soo Joo, and Carlos Pijoan. 2002. "Mechanical Transmission of Porcine Reproductive and Respiratory Syndrome Virus through a Coordinated Sequence of Events during Cold Weather." *Canadian Journal of Veterinary Research* 66: 232–39.

De Genova, Nicholas. 2005. *Working the Boundaries: Race, Space, and "Illegality" in Mexican Chicago.* Durham, NC: Duke University Press.

de la Cadena, Marisol. 2015. *Earth Beings: Ecologies of Practice across Andean Worlds.* Durham, NC: Duke University Press.

DeLeon, Jason. 2015. *The Land of Open Graves: Living and Dying on the Migrant Trail.* Berkeley: University of California Press.

DeLind, Laura B. 1995. "The State, Hog Hotels, and the 'Right to Farm': A Curious Relationship." *Agriculture and Human Values* 12, no. 3: 34–44.

Deming, William Edwards. 2000. *The New Economics for Industry, Government, Education.* Cambridge, MA: MIT Press.

Derrida, Jacques. 2008. *The Animal That Therefore I Am.* New York: Fordham University Press.

Desperet, Vinciane. 2016. *What Would Animals Say If We Asked the Right Questions?* Minneapolis: University of Minnesota Press.

Donham, Kelly. 1998. "The Impact of Industrial Swine Production on Human Health." In *Pigs, Profits, and Rural Communities*, edited by Kendall M. Thu and E. Paul Durrenberger, 73–83. Albany: State University of New York Press.

Dudley, Katherine Marie. 2004. *Debt and Dispossession.* Chicago: University of Chicago Press.

Dumit, Joseph. 2012a. "The Biomarx Experiment." In *Lively Capital: Biotechnologies, Ethics, and Governance in Global Markets*, edited by Kaushik Sunder Rajan, 45–92. Durham, NC: Duke University Press.

Dumit, Joseph. 2012b. *Drugs for Life: How Pharmaceutical Companies Define Our Health.* Durham, NC: Duke University Press.

Dunn, Elizabeth. 2003. "Trojan Pig: Paradoxes of Food Safety Regulation." *Environment and Planning A* 35, no. 8: 1493–511.

Dunn, Elizabeth. 2004. *Privatizing Poland: Baby Food, Big Business, and the Remaking of Labor.* Ithaca: Cornell University Press.

DuPuis, Melanie. 2002. *Nature's Perfect Food.* New York: New York University Press.

Dutkiewicz, Jan. 2018. "Capitalist Pigs: The Making of the Corporate Meat Animal." PhD diss., The New School for Social Research.

Dutkiewicz, Jan. 2019. "Socialize Lab Meat." *Jacobin*, August 11. https://jacobinmag .com/2019/08/lab-meat-socialism-green-new-deal.

Eckblad, Marshall. 2011. "Big Litters Put Farms in Hog Heaven." *Wall Street Journal*, July 19.

Egan, Timothy. 2006. *The Worst Hard Time: The Untold Story of Those Who Survived the Great American Dust Bowl.* New York: Houghton Mifflin Harcourt.

Eiler, Brooke. 2015. "Digest versus Palatant: What's the Difference?" *Palatants+*, December 2. http://palatantsplus.com/blog/digestvspalatant.

Eisenstadt, Marpie. 2014. "Deadly Pig Virus Puzzles Scientists with Rapid Spread." Syracuse.com, May 12.

Eiznitz, Gail. 2007. *Slaughterhouse: The Shocking Story of Greed, Neglect, and Inhumane Treatment inside the U.S. Meat Industry.* Amherst, NY: Prometheus.

Ericksson, John R. 2004. *The Modern Cowboy*, 2nd ed. Denton: University of North Texas Press.

Essig, Mark. 2015. *Lesser Beasts: A Snout-to-Tail History of the Humble Pig.* Boston: Hachette.

Fanon, Frantz. 1963. *The Wretched of the Earth.* New York: Grove.

Fearnley, Lyle. 2015. "Wild Goose Chase: The Displacement of Influenza Research in the Fields of Poyang Lake, China." *Cultural Anthropology* 30, no. 1: 12–35.

Federici, Silvia. 1975. *Wages against Housework.* London: Power of Women Collective.

Federici, Silvia. 2004. *Caliban and the Witch: Women, the Body, and Primitive Accumulation.* New York: Autonomedia.

Federici, Silvia. 2018. *Re-Enchanting the World: Feminism and the Politics of the Commons*. New York: PM Press.

Fennell, Catherine. 2011. "'Project Heat' and Sensory Politics in Redeveloping Chicago Public Housing." *Ethnography* 12, no. 1: 40–64.

Fink, Deborah. 1998. *Cutting into the Meatpacking Line: Workers and Change in the Rural Midwest*. Chapel Hill: University of North Carolina Press.

Finkelstein, Maura. 2019. *The Archive of Loss: Lively Ruination in Mill Land Mumbai*. Durham, NC: Duke University Press.

Finlay, Mark R. 2004. "Hogs, Antibiotics, and the Industrial Environments of Postwar Agriculture." In *Industrializing Organisms: Introducing Evolutionary History*, edited by Susan R. Schrepfer and Philip Scranton, 237–60. New York: Routledge.

Fitzgerald, Deborah. 2004. *Every Farm a Factory: The Industrial Ideal in American Agriculture*. New Haven, CT: Yale University Press.

Flowers, W. L. 1998. "Insemination Programs for Swine to Increase Fertility." *Journal of Animal Science* 76: 39–46.

Flowers, W. L., and H. D. Alhusen. 1992. "Reproductive Performance and Estimates of Labor Requirements Associated with Combinations of Artificial Insemination and Natural Service in Swine." *Journal of Animal of Science* 70: 615–21.

Flowers, W. L., and K. L. Esbenshade. 1993. "Optimizing Management of Natural and Artificial Matings in Swine." *Journal of Reproduction and Fertility Supplement* 48: 217–28.

Food and Water Watch. 2015. *Factory Farm Nation: 2015 Edition*. May 27. http://www.foodandwaterwatch.org/sites/default/files/factory-farm-nation-report-may-2015.pdf.

Ford, Henry. 1923. *My Life and Work*. Scotts Valley, CA: Createspace.

Fortun, Kim. 2012. "Ethnography in Late Industrialism." *Cultural Anthropology* 27, no. 3: 446–64.

Fortun, Kim. 2013. "From Latour to Late Industrialism." *HAU: Journal of Ethnographic Theory* 4, no. 1: 309–29.

Foucault, Michel. 1978. *The History of Sexuality, Volume 1: An Introduction*. London: Vintage.

Foucault, Michel. 2003. *Society Must Be Defended: Lectures at the Collège de France, 1975–1976*. New York: Palgrave Macmillan.

Foxcroft, G. R., W.T. Dixon, S. Novak, C. T. Putman, S. C. Town, and M. D. A. Vinksy. 2006. "The Biological Basis for Prenatal Programming of Postnatal Performance in Pigs." *Journal of Animal Science* 84, supp. (April): e105–12.

Foxcroft, George, and Susanna C. Town. 2004. "Prenatal Programming of Postnatal Performance—The Unseen Cause of Variance." *Advances in Pork Production* 15: 269–79.

Franklin, Sarah. 2007. *Dolly Mixtures: The Remaking of Genealogy*. Durham, NC: Duke University Press.

Franklin, Sarah, and Helena Ragoné. 1998. *Reproducing Reproduction: Kinship, Power, and Technological Innovation*. Philadelphia: University of Pennsylvania Press.

Fraser, David. 2008. *Understanding Animal Welfare*. London: Wiley.

Frederickson, Kathleen. 2014. *The Ploy of Instinct*. New York: Fordham University Press.

Freidberg, Susanne. 2009. *Fresh: A Perishable History*. Cambridge, MA: Belknap Press.

Gabor, Andrea. 1992. *The Man Who Discovered Quality*. New York: Penguin.

Gadd, John. 2003. "A Checklist on 'Weak Heats.'" *National Hog Farmer*, July 15, 30.

Gadd, John. 2015. "Opinion: Big Litters and Pre-Weaning Mortality." *Pig Progress*, August 31. https://www.pigprogress.net/Sows/Articles/2015/8/OPINION-Big -litters-and-pre-weaning-mortality-2678324W/.

García, María Elena. 2010. "Super Guinea Pigs?" *Anthropology Now* 2, no. 2: 22–32.

Gelatin Manufacturers Institute of America. 2012. *Gelatin Handbook*. http://www .gelatin-gmia.com/images/GMIA_Gelatin_Manual_2012.pdf.

Genoways, Ted. 2014. *The Chain: Farm, Factory, and the Fate of Our Food*. New York: HarperCollins.

Gewertz, Deborah, and Frederick Errington. 2010. *Cheap Meat: Flap Food Nations in the South Pacific*. Berkeley: University of California Press.

Ghosh, Amitav. 2016. *The Great Derangement: Climate Change and the Unthinkable*. Chicago: University of Chicago Press.

Gibson-Graham, J. K. 2008. "Diverse Economies: Performative Practices for 'Other Worlds.'" *Progress in Human Geography* 32, no. 5: 613–32.

Giedion, Sigfried. 1948. *Mechanization Takes Command: A Contribution to Anonymous History*. London: Oxford University Press.

Glick, Megan H. 2013. "Animal Instincts: Race, Criminality, and the Reversal of the 'Human.'" *American Quarterly* 65, no. 3: 639–59.

Goodman, David, Bernardo Sorj, and John Wilkinson. 1987. *From Farming to Biotechnology: A Theory of Agro-industrial Development*. New York: Blackwell.

Goodman, David, and Michael Watts, eds. 1997. *Globalising Food: Agrarian Questions and Global Restructuring*. New York: Routledge.

Gordillo, Gastón. 2014. *Rubble: The Afterlife of Destruction*. Durham, NC: Duke University Press.

Gordon, Stephen Canning. 1981. "The City as 'Porkopolis': Some Factors in the Rise of the Meat Packing Industry in Cincinnati, 1825–1861." Master's thesis, Miami University, Oxford, OH.

Graeber, David. 2001. *Toward an Anthropological Theory of Value: The False Coin of Our Own Dreams*. New York: Palgrave.

Graeber, David. 2018. *Bullshit Jobs: A Theory*. New York: Simon and Schuster.

Gramsci, Antonio. 1971. "Americanism and Fordism." In *Selections from the Prison Notebooks*, translated and edited by Quintin Hoare and Geoffrey Nowell Smith, 277–318. New York: International Publishers.

Grandin, Greg. 2009. *Fordlandia: The Rise and Fall of Henry Ford's Forgotten Jungle City*. New York: Metropolitan.

Grandin, Temple. 2006. *Animals in Translation: Using the Mysteries of Autism to Decode Animal Behavior*. New York: Scribner.

Gray, Gregory, Troy McCarthy, Ana Capuano, Sharon Setterquist, Christopher Olsen, Michael Alavanja, and Charles Lynch. 2007. "Swine Workers and Swine Influenza Virus Infections." *Emerging Infectious Diseases* 13, no. 1: 1871–78.

Greene, Ann. 2004. "War Horses: Equine Technology in the American Civil War." In *Industrializing Organisms: Introducing Evolutionary History*, edited by Susan R. Schrepfer and Philip Scranton, 143–66. New York: Routledge.

Grosz, Elizabeth. 2005. *Time Travels: Feminism, Nature, and Power*. Durham, NC: Duke University Press.

Guthman, Julie. 2004. *Agrarian Dreams: The Paradox of Organic Farming in California*. Berkeley: University of California Press.

Guthman, Julie. 2011. *Weighing In*. Berkeley: University of California Press.

Guthman, Julie. 2019. *Wilted: Pathogens, Chemicals, and the Fragile Future of the Strawberry Industry*. Berkeley: University of California Press.

Halpern, Rick, and Roger Horowitz. 1999. *Meatpackers: An Oral History of Black Packinghouse Workers and Their Struggle for Racial and Economic Equality*. New York: Monthly Review Press.

Halverson, Marlene. 2000. "The Price We Pay for Corporate Hogs." Institute for Agriculture and Trade Policy. http://www.iatp.org/documents/the-price-we-pay-for-corporate-hogs.

Hamilton, Shane. 2008. *Trucking Country: The Road to America's Wal-Mart Economy*. Princeton, NJ: Princeton University Press.

Haraway, Donna. 2008. *When Species Meet*. Minneapolis: University of Minnesota Press.

Haraway, Donna. 2015. "Anthropocene, Capitalocene, Plantationocene, Chtulucene: Making Kin." *Environmental Humanities* 6: 159–65.

Hardt, Michael, and Antonio Negri. 2000. *Empire*. Cambridge, MA: Harvard University Press.

Harris, Hank. 2004. "PRRS from 30,000 Feet." *Swine Health Report* (fall 2004): 6–8.

Harrison, Ruth. 1964. *Animal Machines*. London: Centre for Agriculture and Bioscience International.

Hayden, Cori. 2012. "Rethinking Reductionism, or The Transformative Work of Making the Same." *Anthropological Forum* 22, no. 3: 271–83.

Hecht, Gabrielle. 2012. "Nuclear Nomads: A Look at the Subcontracted Heroes." *Bulletin of the Atomic Scientists*, January 9.

Helmreich, Stefan. 2008. "Species of Biocapital." *Science as Culture* 17, no. 4: 463–78.

Helmreich, Stefan, and Sophia Roosth. 2011. "Life Forms: A Keyword Entry." *Representations* 112, no. 1: 27–53.

Hemsworth, Paul H. 2003. "Human-Animal Interactions in Livestock Production." *Applied Animal Behavior Science* 81: 185–98.

Hendrickson, Mary, and William Heffernan. 2007. "Concentration of Agricultural Markets." Department of Rural Sociology, University of Missouri, Columbia. http://www.foodcircles.missouri.edu/07contable.pdf.

Hendrickson, Mary, Harvey James, and William Heffernan. 2014. "Vertical Integration and Concentration in U.S. Agriculture." In *Encyclopedia of Food and Agricultural Ethics*, edited by Paul Thompson and David Kaplan, 1791–99.

Hetherington, Kregg. 2013. "Beans before the Law: Knowledge Practices, Responsibility, and the Paraguayan Soy Boom." *Cultural Anthropology* 28, no. 1: 65–85.

Hinchcliffe, Steve. 2014. "More than One World, More than One Health: Reconfiguring Interspecies Health." *Social Science and Medicine* 129: 28–35.

Hinchcliffe, Steve, and Kim J. Ward. 2014. "Geographies of Folded Life: How Immunity Reframes Biosecurity." *Geoforum* 53: 136–44.

Hoelle, Jeffrey. 2015. *Rainforest Cowboys: The Rise of Ranching and Cattle Culture in Western Amazonia.* Austin: University of Texas Press.

Holmes, Seth. 2013. *Fresh Fruit, Broken Bodies: Migrant Farmworkers in the United States.* Berkeley: University of California Press.

Horowitz, Roger. 1997. *Negro and White, Unite and Fight! A Social History of Industrial Unionism in Meatpacking, 1930–90.* Champaign: University of Illinois Press.

Horowitz, Roger. 2006. *Putting Meat on the American Table: Taste, Technology, Transformation.* Baltimore: Johns Hopkins University Press.

Horowitz, Roger. 2008. "'That Was a Dirty Job!' Technology and Workplace Hazards in Meatpacking over the Long Twentieth Century." *Labor* 5, no. 2: 13–25.

Horowitz, Roger, and Mark J. Miller. 1999. *Immigrants in the Delmarva Poultry Processing Industry: The Changing Face of Georgetown, Delaware, and Environs.* JSRI Occasional Paper No. 37, The Julian Samora Research Institute. East Lansing: Michigan State University.

Horwitz, Richard P. 1998. *Hog Ties: Pigs, Manure, and Mortality in American Culture.* New York: St. Martin's.

Hounshell, David. 1984. *From the American System to Mass Production, 1800–1932: The Development of Manufacturing Technology in the United States.* Baltimore: Johns Hopkins University Press.

Hrdy, Sarah. 2000. *Mother Nature: Maternal Instincts and How They Shape the Human Species.* Cambridge, MA: Harvard University Press.

Human Rights Watch. 2005. "Blood, Sweat, and Fear: Workers' Rights in U.S. Meat and Poultry Plants." Report. http://www.hrw.org/reports/2005/01/24/blood-sweat-and-fear.

Imhoff, Daniel, ed. 2010. *The CAFO Reader: The Tragedy of Industrial Animal Factories.* San Rafael, CA: Earth Aware.

Irvine, Judith T., and Susan Gal. 2000. "Language Ideology and Linguistic Differentiation." *Regimes of Language: Ideologies, Polities, and Identities*, edited by Paul V. Kroskrity, 35–83. Albuquerque: SAR Press.

Ishikawa, Kaoru. 1985. *What Is Total Quality Control? The Japanese Way.* Englewood Cliffs, NJ: Prentice-Hall.

Jain, Sarah S. Lochlann. 2006. *Injury: The Politics of Product Design and Safety Law in the United States.* Princeton, NJ: Princeton University Press.

Jay, Martin. 1986. *Marxism and Totality: The Adventures of a Concept from Lukacs to Habermas.* Berkeley: University of California Press.

Johnsen, Carolyn. 2003. *Raising a Stink: The Struggle over Factory Hog Farms in Nebraska.* Omaha: Bison.

Johnson, Colin. 2007. "Heat Detection Critical to Success." *National Hog Farmer*, October 15. https://www.nationalhogfarmer.com/genetics-reproduction/estrus /farming_heat_detection_critical.

Johnson, Colin, James Kliebenstein, John Mabry, and Eric Neumann. 2005. "The Impact of PRRS on the Pig Cost of Production." *Animal Industry Report*: AS 651, ASL R2045. Ames: Iowa State University. https://lib.dr.iastate.edu/ans_air/vol651 /iss1/71/.

Johnson, Elizabeth, and Jesse Goldstein. 2015. "Biomimetic Futures: Life, Death, and the Enclosure of a More-Than-Human Intellect." *Annals of the Association of American Geographers* 105, no. 2: 387–96.

Johnson, Nathanael. 2006. "Swine of the Times: The Making of the Modern Pig." *Harper's Magazine*, May, 47–56.

Jones, Donna. 2011. *The Racial Discourses of Life Philosophy: Négritude, Vitalism, and Modernity*. New York: Columbia University Press.

Jordahl, Rick. 2011. "Manure: The New Black Gold." Pork Network, January 17. http:// www.porknetwork.com/pork-magazine/features/manure-the-new-black-gold -113891669.html.

Kawa, Nicholas. 2016. "Shit." Theorizing the Contemporary, *Fieldsights*. April 6. https://culanth.org/fieldsights/shit.

Kirby, David. 2010. *Animal Factory: The Looming Threat of Industrial Pig, Dairy, and Poultry Farms to Humans and the Environment*. New York: St. Martin's.

Kirchhelle, Claas. 2018. "Pharming Animals: A Global History of Antibiotics in Food Production (1935–2017)." *Palgrave Communications* 4: 1–13.

Kirksey, Eben. 2014. *The Multispecies Salon*. Durham, NC: Duke University Press.

Kirksey, Eben. 2015. *Emergent Ecologies*. Durham, NC: Duke University Press.

Kohn, Eduardo. 2013. *How Forests Think: Toward an Anthropology beyond the Human*. Berkeley: University of California Press.

Kosek, Jake. 2010. "Ecologies of Empire: On the New Uses of the Honeybee." *Cultural Anthropology* 25, no. 4: 650–78.

Labban, Mazen. 2014. "Deterritorializing Extraction: Bioaccumulation and the Planetary Mine." *Annals of the Association of American Geographers* 104, no. 3: 560–76.

LaFlamme, Marcel. 2018. "Remaking the Pilot: Unmanned Aviation and the Transformation of Work in Postagrarian North Dakota." PhD diss., Rice University.

Lakoff, Andrew. 2008. "The Generic Biothreat, or, How We Became Unprepared." *Cultural Anthropology* 23, no. 3: 399–428.

Lakoff, Andrew, and Stephen J. Collier, eds. 2008. *Biosecurity Interventions: Global Health and Security in Question*. New York: Columbia University Press.

Lampland, Martha. 2009. "Classifying Laborers: Instinct, Property, and the Psychology of Productivity in Hungary." In *Standards and Their Stories*, edited by Martha Lampland and Susan Leigh Starr, 123–48. Ithaca, NY: Cornell University Press.

Lampland, Martha, and Susan Leigh Starr, eds. 2009. *Standards and Their Stories*. Ithaca, NY: Cornell University Press.

Landecker, Hannah. 2013. "Post-industrial Metabolism: Fat Knowledge." *Public Culture*. 25, no. 3: 495–522.

Landecker, Hannah. 2016. "Antibiotic Resistance and the Biology of History." *Body and Society* 22, no. 4: 19–52.

Landecker, Hannah. Forthcoming. "The Food of Our Food: Medicated Feed and the Industrialization of Metabolism." In *Eating Besides Ourselves*, edited by Heather Paxson. Durham, NC: Duke University Press.

Latour, Bruno. 2000. *We Have Never Been Modern*. Cambridge, MA: Harvard University Press.

LeDuff, Charlie. 2000. "At a Slaughterhouse, Some Things Never Die." *New York Times*, June 16.

Lee, Paula Young. 2008. *Meat, Modernity, and the Rise of the Slaughterhouse*. Lebanon, NH: University of New Hampshire Press.

Lemke, Thomas. 2011. *Biopolitics: An Advanced Introduction*. New York: New York University Press.

Leonard, Christopher. 2014. *The Meat Racket*. New York: Simon and Schuster.

Lezaun, Javier, and Natalie Porter. 2015. "Containment and Competition: Transgenic Animals in the One Health Agenda." *Social Science and Medicine* 129 (March): 96–105.

Lien, Marianne. 2015. *Becoming Salmon*. Berkeley: University of California Press.

Lopez, Patricia, and Katie Gillespie. 2015. *Economies of Death: Economics Logics of Killable Life and Grievable Death*. London: Routledge.

Lowe, Celia. 2010. "Viral Clouds: Becoming H5N1 in Indonesia." *Cultural Anthropology* 25, no. 4: 625–49.

Lyons, Kristina. 2016. "Decomposition as Life Politics: Soils, Selva, and Small Farmers under the Gun." *Cultural Anthropology* 31, no. 1: 56–81.

MacKenzie, Donald. 1984. "Marx and the Machine." *Technology and Culture* 25, no. 3: 473–502.

Mahony, Melissa. 2011. "Google Takes Stink out of Pig Waste." *Smart Planet*. http://www.smartplanet.com/blog/intelligent-energy/google-takes-stink-out-of-pig-waste/8660.

Marti, Daniel L., Rachel J. Johnson, and Kenneth H. Mathews Jr. 2011. "Where's the (Not) Meat: Byproducts from Beef and Pork Production." Report no. LDP-M-209–01. Economic Research Service, November. Washington, DC: U.S. Department of Agriculture.

Martineau, Guy-Pierre and Brigitte Badouard. 2009. "Managing Highly Prolific Sows." *The Pig Site*, July 8. https://thepigsite.com/articles/managing-highly-prolific-sows.

Marx, Karl. 1992. *Capital: A Critique of Political Economy*, vol. 1. London: Penguin Classics.

Marx, Leo. 1964. *The Machine in the Garden: Technology and the Pastoral Ideal in America*. Oxford: Oxford University Press.

Masco, Joseph. 2014. *The Theater of Operations*. Durham, NC: Duke University Press.

Masco, Joseph. 2015. "The Age of Fallout." *History of the Present* 5, no. 2: 137–68.

Massumi, Brian. 2014. *What Animals Teach Us about Politics.* Durham, NC: Duke University Press.

Mavromichalis, Ioannis. 2011a. "Resurgence of Milk Replacers." Pig Progress, June 22. http://www.pigprogress.net/Breeding/Sow-Feeding/2011/6/Resurgence-of-milk -replacers-PP007492W.

Mavromichalis, Ioannis. 2011b. "Helping Underweight Pigs Thrive With Special Feed." *WATTAgNet*, October 13. https://www.wattagnet.com/articles/10645 -helping-underweight-piglets-thrive-with-special-feed.

Mazzarella, William. 2013. *Censorium: Cinema and the Open Edge of Mass Publicity.* Durham, NC: Duke University Press.

McBride, William D., and Nigel Key. 2013. *U.S. Hog Production from 1992 to 2009: Technology, Restructuring, and Productivity Growth,* ERR-158. Washington, DC: U.S. Department of Agriculture Economic Research Service.

McGlone, John, and Wilson G. Pond. 2003. *Pig Production: Biological Principles and Applications.* Boston: Cengage Learning.

McMichael, Phillip. 2012. "The Land Grab and Corporate Food Regime Restructuring." *Journal of Peasant Studies* 39, no. 3–4: 681–701.

McNeur, Catherine. 2014. *Taming Manhattan: Environmental Battles in the Antebellum City.* Cambridge, MA: Harvard University Press.

Meindertsma, Christien. 2009. *Pig 05049.* Rotterdam: Flocks.

Melgares, Pat. 2016. "Kansas State University Offers New Hope for Saving Runt Pigs." *K-State News,* February 2. https://www.kstate.edu/media/newsreleases/feb16 /runts2216.html.

Meyer, Stephen. 1981. *The Five Dollar Day: Labor Management and Social Control in the Ford Motor Company, 1908–1921.* Albany: State University of New York Press.

Miller, Dale. 2007. "Before You Target 30 P/S/Y Read This." *National Hog Farmer,* February 15. https://www.nationalhogfarmer.com/mag/farming_target_psy_read.

Miller, Dale. 2011a. "The Race to 30 Pigs/Mated/Female/Year." *National Hog Farmer,* August 16. https://www.nationalhogfarmer.com/genetics-reproduction/race-30 -pigs-mated-0815.

Miller, Dale. 2011b. "Flirting with 30 Pigs/Mated/Female/Year Goal." *National Hog Farmer,* September 19. https://www.nationalhogfarmer.com/genetics -reproduction/30pigs-mated-female-year-0919.

Milton, Kay. 2005. "Anthropomorphism or Egomorphism? The Perception of Non-Human Persons by Human Ones." *Animals in Person: Cultural Perspectives on Human-Animal Intimacy,* edited by John Knight, 255–71. Oxford: Berg.

Mintz, Sidney. 1984. *Sweetness and Power.* New York: Penguin.

Miraftab, Faranak. 2016. *Global Heartland: Displaced Labor, Transnational Lives, and Local Placemaking.* Indianapolis: Indiana University Press.

Mizelle, Brett. 2012. *Pig.* Edinburgh: Reaktion.

Mol, Annemarie. 2002. *The Body Multiple: Ontology in Medical Practice.* Durham, NC: Duke University Press.

Moore, Donald S., Jake Kosek, and Anand Pandian. 2003. *Race, Nature, and the Politics of Difference*. Durham, NC: Duke University Press.

Moore, Jason. 2015. *Capitalism in the Web of Life*. New York: Verso.

Morrow, W. E. Morgan, and John Roberts. 2002. "Biosecurity Guidelines for Pork Producers." North Carolina State University Animal Science Facts, ANS 02–818s. http://www.ncsu.edu/project/swine_extension/publications/factsheets/818s.htm.

Morton, Timothy. 2013. *Hyperobjects*. Minneapolis: University of Minnesota Press.

Moss, Michael. 2015a. "Animal Welfare at Risk in Experiments for Meat Industry." *New York Times*, January 19.

Moss, Michael. 2015b. "Stricter Oversight Ordered for Animal Research at Nebraska Center." *New York Times*, March 9.

Muehlebach, Andrea. 2011. "On Affective Labor in Post-Fordist Italy." *Cultural Anthropology* 26, no. 1: 59–82.

Muehlebach, Andrea, and Nitzan Shoshan. 2012. "Post-Fordist Affect: Introduction." *Anthropological Quarterly* 85, no. 2: 317–43.

Mullin, Molly H. 2007. "Feeding the Animals." In *Where the Wild Things Are Now: Domestication Reconsidered*, edited by Rebecca Cassidy and Molly H. Mullin, 277–304. London: Berg.

Murphy, Michelle. 2011. "Distributed Reproduction." In *Corpus: An Interdisciplinary Reader on Bodies and Knowledge*, edited by Monica J. Casper and Paisley Currah, 21–38. New York: Palgrave Macmillan.

Murphy, Michelle. 2017. "Alterlife and Decolonial Chemical Relations." *Cultural Anthropology* 32, no. 4: 494–503.

Myers, Natasha. 2016. "Photosynthesis." Theorizing the Contemporary, *Fieldsights*, January 21. https://culanth.org/fieldsights/photosynthesis.

Nadimpalli, Maya, Jessica Rinsky, Steve Wing, Devon Hall, Jill Stewart, Jesper Lasen, Keeve Nachman, Dave Love, Elizabeth Pierce, Nora Pisanic, Jean Strelitz, Laurel Harduar-Morano, and Christopher Heaney. 2014. "Persistence of Livestock-Associated Antibiotic-Resistant Staphylococcus Aureus among Industrial Hog Operation Workers in North Carolina over Fourteen Days." *Occupational and Environmental Medicine*, no. 72: 90–99.

Nading, Alex. 2012. "Dengue Mosquitos Are Single Mothers: Biopolitics Meets Ecological Aesthetics in Nicaraguan Community Health Work." *Cultural Anthropology* 27, no. 4: 572–96.

Nading, Alex. 2014. *Mosquito Trails*. Berkeley: University of California Press.

Nagodawithana, Tilak W., Lynn Nelles, and Nayan B. Trivedi. 2010. "Protein Hydrolysates as Hypoallergenic, Flavors and Palatants for Companion Animals." In *Protein Hydrolysates in Biotechnology*, edited by Vijai K. Pasupuleti and Arnold L. Dumain, 191–207. New York: Springer.

Nagy, Kelsi, and Phillip David Johnson III. 2013. *Trash Animals*. Minneapolis: University of Minnesota Press.

Nash, June C. 1979. *We Eat the Mines and the Mines Eat Us: Dependency and Exploitation in Bolivian Tin Mines*. New York: Columbia University Press.

National Renderers Association. 1996. *The Original Recyclers*. Alexandria, VA: National Renderers Association.

Neff, Roni. 2015. *Introduction to the U.S. Food System: Public Health, Environment, and Equity*. San Francisco: Jossey-Bass.

Nestle, Marion. 2008. *Pet Food Politics: The Chihuahua in the Coal Mine*. Berkeley: University of California Press.

Noble, David. 1984. *Forces of Production: A Social History of Industrial Automation*. Oxford: Oxford University Press.

Nye, David. 1996. *American Technological Sublime*. Cambridge, MA: MIT Press.

Occupational Safety and Health Administration. 1993. *Ergonomics Program Management Guidelines for Meatpacking Plants*. OSHA 3 123. https://www.osha.gov/Publications/OSHA3123/3123.html.

Oliphant, Elayne. 2012. "Signs of an Unmarked Faith." PhD diss., University of Chicago.

Ong, Aihwa. 1987. *Spirits of Resistance and Capitalist Discipline: Factory Women in Malaysia*. Albany: State University of New York Press.

Orland, Barbara. 2004. "Turbo-Cows: Producing a Competitive Animal in the Nineteenth and Early Twentieth Centuries." In *Industrializing Organisms: Introducing Evolutionary History*, edited by Susan R. Schrepfer and Philip Scranton, 167–90. New York: Routledge.

Oxfam America. 2016. *No Relief: Denial of Bathroom Breaks in the Poultry Industry*. *Oxfam Report*, May 9. https://www.oxfamamerica.org/explore/research-publications/no-relief/.

Paarlberg, Robert. 2010. *Food Politics: What Everyone Needs to Know*. Oxford: Oxford University Press.

Paarlberg, Robert. 2016. "Reply to Jedidah Purdy, Forum: The New Nature." *Boston Review*, January 11.

Pachirat, Timothy. 2011. *Every Twelve Seconds: Industrialized Slaughter and the Politics of Sight*. New Haven, CT: Yale University Press.

Pacyga, Dominic. 2015. *Slaughterhouse: Chicago's Union Stock Yard and the World It Made*. Chicago: University of Chicago Press.

Page, Brian. 1997. "Restructuring Pork Production, Remaking Rural Iowa." In *Globalising Food: Agrarian Questions and Global Restructuring*, edited by David Goodman and Michael Watts, 133–57. New York: Routledge.

Pandian, Anand. 2008. "Pastoral Power in the Postcolony: On the Biopolitics of the Criminal Animal in South India." *Cultural Anthropology* 23, no. 1: 85–117.

Pandian, Anand. 2009. *Crooked Stalks: Cultivating Virtue in South India*. Durham, NC: Duke University Press.

Paxson, Heather. 2008. "Post-Pasteurian Cultures: The Microbiopolitics of Raw-Milk Cheese in the United States." *Cultural Anthropology* 23, no. 1: 15–47.

Paxson, Heather. 2013. *The Life of Cheese: Crafting Food and Value in America*. Berkeley: University of California Press.

Paxson, Heather. 2015. "Commentary." Paper presented at the 2015 Conference of the Society for the Anthropology of North America, New York City, April 17.

REFERENCES

REFERENCES

Peña, Devon Gerardo. 1997. *The Terror of the Machine: Technology, Work, Gender, and Ecology on the U.S.-Mexico Border*. Austin: University of Texas Press.

Penniman, Leah. 2018. *Farming While Black: Soul Fire Farm's Practical Guide to Liberation on the Land*. White River Junction, VT: Chelsea Green.

Perrow, Charles. 1984. *Normal Accidents*. Princeton, NJ: Princeton University Press.

Pinto, Sarah. 2008. *Where There Is No Midwife: Birth and Loss in Rural India*. London: Berghahn.

Piore, Adam, and Scott Lewis. 2011. "How Pig Guts Became the Next Bright Hope for Regenerating Human Limbs." *Discover*, July-August.

Pollan, Michael. 2002. "Power Steer." *New York Times Magazine*, March 31.

Pollan, Michael. 2006. *The Omnivore's Dilemma: A Natural History of Four Meals*. New York: Penguin.

Porter, Natalie. 2013. "Bird Flu Biopower: Strategies for Multispecies Coexistence in Nam." *American Ethnologist* 40, no. 1: 132–48.

Proulx, Annie. 2002. *That Old Ace in the Hole*. New York: Scribner.

Puig de la Bellacasa, Maria. 2012. "Nothing Comes without Its World: Thinking with Care." *Sociological Review* 60, no. 2: 197–216.

Rachleff, Peter J. 1993. *Hard-Pressed in the Heartland: The Hormel Strike and the Future of the Labor Movement*. Boston: South End Press.

Raffles, Hugh. 2010. *Insectopedia*. New York: Vintage.

Reno, Joshua. 2009. "Your Trash Is Someone's Treasure: The Politics of Value at a Michigan Landfill." *Journal of Material Culture* 14, no. 1: 29–46.

Ribas, Vanesa. 2016. *On the Line: Slaughterhouse Lives and the Making of the New South*. Berkeley: University of California Press.

Rich, Ronald. 2003. "Pigs for the Investors: Commoditization, Differentiation and Personalism in Illinois Contract Hog Production." PhD diss., University of Southern Illinois, Carbondale.

Rich, Ronald. 2008. "Fecal Free: Biology and Authority in Industrialized Midwestern Pork Production." *Agriculture and Human Values* 25, no. 1: 79–93.

Ritvo, Harriet. 1987. *The Animal Estate*. Cambridge, MA: Harvard University Press.

Rix, Mark, and Ron Ketchem. 2010. "Checklist to Reduce Heat Stress on Sows and Gilts." *National Hog Farmer*, June 7. https://www.nationalhogfarmer.com/weekly-preview/0607-checklist-reduce-heat-stress-sows.

Rix, Mark, and Ron Ketchem. 2011a. "Heat Detection, AI Skills Impact Farrowing Rate." *National Hog Farmer*, January 10. https://www.nationalhogfarmer.com/genetics-reproduction/swine-heat-detection-ai-skills-impact-farrowing-rate-0110.

Rix, Mark, and Ron Ketchem. 2011b. "Track AI Technician Performance for Clues to Improve Farrowing Rate." *National Hog Farmer*, November 7. https://www.nationalhogfarmer.com/genetics-reproduction/artifical-insemination-technicians-and-farrowing-rates-0207.

Rix, Mark, and Ron Ketchem. 2012. "How AI Technicians Affect Farrowing Rate, Total Born." *National Hog Farmer*, March 12. https://www.nationalhogfarmer.com/health/how-ai-technicians-affect-farrowing-rate-total-born.

Roach, Mary. 2013. *Gulp: Adventures on the Alimentary Canal*. New York: W. W. Norton.

Roediger, David, and Elizabeth Esch. 2014. *The Production of Difference: Race and the Management of Labor in U.S. History*. Oxford: Oxford University Press.

Rose, Nikolas S. 2007. *The Politics of Life Itself: Biomedicine, Power, and Subjectivity in the Twenty-First Century*. Princeton, NJ: Princeton University Press.

Rosenberg, Gabriel. 2015. *The 4-H Harvest*. Philadelphia: University of Pennsylvania Press.

Rosenberg, Gabriel. 2017. "How Meat Changed Sex: The Law of Interspecies Intimacy after Industrial Reproduction." *GLQ* 23, no. 4: 473–507.

Rubin, Gayle. 1975. "The Traffic in Women: Notes on the 'Political Economy' of Sex." In *Toward an Anthropology of Women*, edited by Rayna R. Reiter, 157–210. New York: Monthly Review.

Russell, Edmund. 2004. "Introduction: The Garden in the Machine." In *Industrializing Organisms: Introducing Evolutionary History*, edited by Susan R. Schrepfer and Philip Scranton, 1–16. New York: Routledge.

Salzinger, Leslie. 2004. *Genders in Production: Making Workers in Mexico's Global Factories*. Berkeley: University of California Press.

Sayre, Nathan. 2002. *Ranching, Endangered Species, and Urbanization in the Southwest: Species of Capital*. Phoenix: University of Arizona Press.

Scarry, Elaine. 1985. *The Body in Pain*. Oxford: Oxford University Press.

Schiffinan, Susan S., Elizabeth A. Sanely-Miller, Mark S. Suggs, and Brevick G. Graham. 1998. "Mood Changes Experienced by Persons Living near Commercial Swine Operations." In *Pigs, Profits, and Rural Communities*, edited by Kendall M. Thu and E. Paul Durrenberger, 84–102. Albany: State University of New York Press.

Schlosser, Eric. 2001. *Fast Food Nation: The Dark Side of the All-American Meal*. New York: Perennial.

Schneider, Mindi. 2015. "Wasting the Rural: Meat, Manure, and the Politics of Agro-industrialization in China." *Geoforum* 78, no. 1: 89–97.

Scott, James C. 1998. *Seeing like a State*. New Haven, CT: Yale University Press.

Shannon, Laurie. 2013. *The Accommodated Animal: Cosmopolity in Shakespearean Locales*. Chicago: University of Chicago Press.

Shapiro, Nicholas. 2015. "Attuning to the Chemosphere." *Cultural Anthropology* 30, no. 3: 368–93.

Sharp, Lesley. 2013. *The Transplant Imaginary: Mechanical Hearts, Animal Parts, and Moral Thinking in Highly Experimental Science*. Berkeley: University of California Press.

Shewhart, Walter. 1986. *Statistical Method from the Viewpoint of Quality Control*. New York: Dover.

Shukin, Nicole. 2009. *Animal Capital: Rendering Life in Biopolitical Times*. Minneapolis: University of Minnesota Press.

Silbergeld, Ellen. 2016. *Chickenizing Farms and Food: How Industrial Meat Production Endangers Workers, Animals, and Consumers*. Baltimore, MD: Johns Hopkins University Press.

Sinclair, Upton. 1906. *The Jungle.* London: Penguin Classics.

Singer, Peter. 1978. *Animal Liberation.* New York: PS Books.

Smart, Alan, and Josephine Smart. 2011. "(Im)mobilizing Technology: Slow Science, Food Safety, and Borders." *Identities* 18, no. 6: 529–50.

Smith, Alison, Kenneth Stalder, Timo Serenius, Tom Baas, and John Mabry. 2007. "Effect of Piglet Birth Weight on Weights at Weaning and 42 Days Post Weaning." *Journal of Swine Health and Production* 15, no. 4: 213–18.

"Sow and Pig Care to the Max." 2011. *National Hog Farmer,* August 16. https://www.nationalhogfarmer.com/genetics-reproduction/sow-pig-care-handling-0815.

Spellman, Frank, and Nancy Whiting. 2007. *Environmental Management of Concentrated Animal Feeding Operations.* Boca Raton, FL: CRC Press.

Squier, Susan. 2010. *Poultry Science, Chicken Culture: A Partial Alphabet.* Camden, NJ: Rutgers University Press.

Steenhuysen, Julie and Michael Hirtzer. 2017. "Smithfield Makes Move on Market for Pig-Human Transplants." *Reuters,* April 12. https://finance.yahoo.com/news/smithfield-makes-move-market-pig-human-transplants-040437809--finance.html.

Stewart, Kathleen. 1996. *A Space on the Side of the Road.* Princeton, NJ: Princeton University Press.

Stewart, Kathleen. 2011. "Atmospheric Attunements." *Environment and Planning D* 29, no. 3: 445–53.

Stratman, Frederick W., and H. L. Self. 1961. "Comparison of Natural Mating with Artificial Insemination and Influence of Semen Volume and Sperm Numbers on Conception, Embryo Survival and Litter Size in Sows." *Journal of Animal Science* 20: 708–11.

Striffler, Steve. 2005. *Chicken: The Dangerous Transformation of America's Favorite Food.* New Haven, CT: Yale University Press.

Strom, Stephanie. 2014. "Virus Plagues the Pork Industry, and Environmentalists." *New York Times,* July 4. http://www.nytimes.com/2014/07/05/business/PEDv-plagues-the-pork-industry-and-environmentalists.html.

Stuart, Diane, Rebecca Schewe, and Ryan Gunderson. 2012. "Extending Social Theory to Farm Animals: Addressing Alienation in the Dairy Sector." *Sociologia Ruralis* 53, no. 2: 201–22.

Stuesse, Angela. 2016. *Scratching Out a Living: Latinos, Race, and Work in the Deep South.* Berkeley: University of California Press.

Stull, Donald D., and Michael J. Broadway. 2013. *Slaughterhouse Blues: The Meat and Poultry Industry in North America,* 2nd ed. Belmont, CA: Thomson/Wadsworth.

Stull, Donald D., Michael J. Broadway, and David Griffith, eds. 1995. *Any Way You Cut It: Meat Processing and Small-Town America.* Lawrence: University Press of Kansas.

Sunder Rajan, Kaushik. 2006. *Biocapital: The Constitution of Postgenomic Life.* Durham, NC: Duke University Press.

Sunder Rajan, Kaushik. 2007. "Experimental Values: Indian Clinical Trials and Surplus Health." *New Left Review* 45 (May–June): 67–88.

Sunder Rajan, Kaushik. 2012. "Introduction: The Capitalization of Life and the Liveliness of Capital." In *Lively Capital: Biotechnologies, Ethics, and Governance in Global Markets*, edited by Kaushik Sunder Rajan, 1–41. Durham, NC: Duke University Press.

Swift, Louis Franklin, and Arthur Van Vlissingen. 1927. *Yankee of the Yards: The Biography of Gustavus Franklin Swift*. Chicago: A. W. Shaw Company.

Taylor, Frederick Winslow. 1911. *The Principles of Scientific Management*. New York: Dover.

Taylor, Sunaura. 2017. *Beasts of Burden: Animal and Disability Liberation*. New York: The New Press.

ter Beek, Vincent. 2016. "Pig Manure May Be Used as Road Pavement." *Pig Progress*, July 20. http://www.pigprogress.net/Finishers/Articles/2016/7/Pig-manure-may-be-used-as-road-pavement-2839954W.

Terkel, Studs. 1974. *Working: People Talk about What They Do All Day and How They Feel about What They Do*. New York: Random House.

Thaler, Bob. 2013. "The Impact of PEDv Continues to Grow." *iGrow*, December 26. http://igrow.org/livestock/pork/the-impact-of-pedv-continues-to-grow/.

Thompson, Edward P. 1967. "Time, Work-Discipline, and Industrial Capitalism." *Past and Present*, 38: 56–97.

Thu, Kendall. 2010. "CAFOs Are in Everyone's Backyard: Industrial Agriculture, Democracy, and the Future." In *The CAFO Reader: The Tragedy of Industrial Animal Factories*, edited by Daniel Imhoff, 210–20. San Rafael, CA: Earth Aware.

Thu, Kendall M., and E. Paul Durrenberger, eds. 1998. *Pigs, Profits, and Rural Communities*. Albany: State University of New York Press.

Timmermans, Stefan, and Steven Epstein. 2010. "A World of Standards but Not a Standardized World." *Annual Review of Sociology*, 36: 69–89.

Town, S. C., C. T. Putnam, N, J. Turchinsky, W. T. Dixon, and G. R. Foxcroft. 2004. "Number of Conceptuses in Utero Affects Porcine Fetal Muscle Development." *Reproduction* 128, no. 4: 443–53.

Tsing, Anna Lowenhaupt. 2009a. "Supply Chains and the Human Condition." *Rethinking Marxism: A Journal of Economics, Culture & Society* 21, no. 2: 148–76.

Tsing, Anna Lowenhaupt. 2009b. "Beyond Economic and Ecological Standardisation." *Australian Journal of Anthropology* 20, no. 3: 347–68.

Tsing, Anna Lowenhaupt. 2012a. "On Nonscalability: The Living World Is Not Amenable to Precision-Nested Scales." *Common Knowledge* 18, no. 3: 505–24.

Tsing, Anna Lowenhaupt. 2012b. "Unruly Edges: Mushrooms as Companion Species." *Environmental Humanities* 1, 1: 141–54.

Tsing, Anna Lowenhaupt. 2013. "Sorting Out Commodities: How Capitalist Value Is Made through Gifts." *HAU: Journal of Ethnographic Theory* 3, no. 1: 21–43.

Tsing, Anna Lowenhaupt. 2015. *The Mushroom at the End of the World*. Princeton, NJ: Princeton University Press.

Tsing, Anna Lowenhaupt. 2016. "Earth Stalked by Man." *Cambridge Anthropology* 34, no. 1: 2–16.

Tsutsui, William M. 2001. *Manufacturing Ideology: Scientific Management in Twentieth-Century Japan*. Princeton, NJ: Princeton University Press.

Tuck, Eve. 2009. "Suspending Damage: A Letter to Communities." *Harvard Educational Review* 75: 409–27.

Uexkull, Jakob. 2010. *A Foray into the Worlds of Animals and Humans*. Minneapolis: University of Minnesota Press.

United Nations Food and Agriculture Organization. 2010. "Good Practices for Biosecurity in the Pig Sector." Animal Production and Health Paper no. 169. Rome: FAO.

U.S. Department of Agriculture. 2015. "ARS: U.S. Meat Animal Research Center Review–Interim Report." Agricultural Research Service, September 28.

Vallet, Jeffrey, and Bradley A. Freking. 2006. "Unraveling the Litter Size Riddle." *National Hog Farmer*, June 15. https://www.nationalhogfarmer.com/mag/farming_unraveling_litter_size.

Vallet, Jeffrey, H. G. Klemcke, and R. K. Christenson. 2002. "Interrelationships among Conceptus Size, Uterine Protein Secretion, Fetal Erythropoiesis, and Uterine Capacity." *Journal of Animal Science* 80: 729–37.

Vallet, Jeffrey, Anthony McNeel, Jeremy Miles, and Bradley Freking. 2014. "Placental Accommodations for Transport and Metabolism during Intra-Uterine Crowding in Pigs." *Journal of Animal Science and Biotechnology* 5: 55.

Vander Wal, Gretchen. 2000. "Unique Methods Enhance Sow Productivity." *National Hog Farmer*, September 15, 14.

Van Dooren, Thom. 2013. *Flight Ways: Life and Loss at the Edge of Extinction*. New York: Columbia University Press.

Van Dooren, Thom. 2014. "Care." *Environmental Humanities* 5, no. 1: 291–94.

Vansickle, Joe. 2002. "Ten Ways to Get More Pigs." *National Hog Farmer*, July 15, 32.

Vansickle, Joe. 2009. "Making the 30 P/S/Y Dream Come True." *National Hog Farmer*. January 15. https://www.nationalhogfarmer.com/genetics-reproduction/0109-producers-nearing-thershold.

Vaught, Jeanette. 2016. "Animal Sex Work." *Platypus: The CASTAC Blog*. Posted June 15.

Vialles, Noélie. 1994. *Animal to Edible*. Cambridge: Cambridge University Press.

Virno, Paolo. 2004. *A Grammar of the Multitude*. Cambridge, MA: Semiotext(e).

Vogel, Steven. 1988. "Marx and Alienation from Nature." *Social Theory and Practice* 14, no. 3: 367–87.

Vora, Kalindi. 2015. *Life Support: Biocapital and the New History of Outsourced Labor*. Minneapolis: University of Minnesota Press.

Wade, Louise Carroll. 2003. *Chicago's Pride: The Stockyards, Packingtown, and Environs in the Nineteenth Century*. Urbana: University of Illinois Press.

Walker, Paul. 2000. "Food Residuals: Waste Product, Byproduct or Coproduct." In *Food Waste to Animal Feed*, edited by Michael L. Westendorf, 17–30. Ames: Iowa State University Press.

Wallace, Rob. 2016. *Big Farms Makes Big Flu: Dispatches on Infectious Disease, Agribusiness, and the Nature of Science*. New York: Monthly Review Press.

Walley, Christine. 2013. *Exit Zero.* Chicago: University of Chicago Press.

Wang, Junjun, L. Chen, D. Li, X. Wang, P. Li, L. J. Dangott, W. Hu, G. Wu. 2008. "Intrauterine Growth Restriction Affects the Proteomes of the Small Intestine, Liver, and Skeletal Muscle in Newborn Pigs." *Journal of Nutrition* 138, no. 1: 60–66.

Washington, Sylvia Hood. 2005. *Packing Them In: An Archaeology of Environmental Racism in Chicago, 1865–1954.* Washington, DC: Lexington Books.

Watts, Michael. 2004. "Are Hogs like Chickens? Enclosure and Mechanization in Two 'White Meat' Filières." In *Geographies of Commodity Chains*, edited by Alex Hughes and Suzanne Reimer, 39–62. London: Routledge.

Weeks, Kathi. 2011. *The Problem with Work: Marxism, Feminism, and Post-work Imaginaries.* Durham, NC: Duke University Press.

Weheliye, Alexander. 2014. *Habeus Viscus: Racializing Assemblages, Biopolitics, and Black Feminist Theories of the Human.* Durham, NC: Duke University Press.

Weis, Toni. 2013. *The Ecological Hoofprint.* London: Zed.

Weiss, Brad. 2016. *Real Pigs.* Durham, NC: Duke University Press.

White, Richard. 1996. *The Organic Machine: The Remaking of the Columbia River.* New York: Hill and Wang.

Wilderson, Frank, III. 2003. "Gramsci's Black Marx: Whither the Slave in Civil Society?" *Social Identities* 9, no. 2: 225–40.

Williams, Anna. 2004. "Disciplining Animals: Sentience, Production, and Critique." *International Journal of Sociology and Social Policy* 24, no. 9: 45–57.

Wolfe, Cary. 2008. *What Is Posthumanism?* Minneapolis: University of Minnesota Press.

Wolfe, Cary. 2012. *Before the Law: Humans and Other Animals in a Biopolitical Frame.* Chicago: University of Chicago Press.

Worster, Donald. 1979. *Dust Bowl: The Southern Plains in the 1930s.* New York: Oxford University Press.

Wortley, Emmeline Stuart. 1851. *Travels in the United States, Etc.: During 1849 and 1850.* New York: Harper and Brothers.

Wozniacka, Gosia. 2019. "Less Than 1 Percent of US Farmworkers Belong to a Union. Here's Why." *Civil Eats*, May 7. https://civileats.com/2019/05/07/less-than-1-percent-of-us-farmworkers-belong-to-a-union-heres-why/.

Wrye, Jen. 2015. "Deep Inside Dogs Know What They Want: Animality, Affect, and Killability in Commercial Pet Foods." In *Economies of Death: Economic Logics of Killable Life and Grievable Death*, edited by Patricia J. Lopez and Kathryn A. Gillespie, 95–114. London: Routledge.

Wu, G., F. W. Bazer, J. M. Wallace, and T. E. Spencer. 2006. "Intrauterine Growth Retardation: Implications for the Animal Sciences." *Journal of Animal Science* 84, no. 9: 2316–37.

Yanagisako, Sylvia Junko. 2002. *Producing Culture and Capital: Family Firms in Italy.* Princeton, NJ: Princeton University Press.

Yates-Doerr, Emily. 2015. "Does Meat Come from Animals? A Multispecies Approach to Classification and Belonging in Highland Guatemala." *American Ethnologist* 42, no. 2: 309–23.

REFERENCES

Zuidhof, M. J., B. L. Schneider, V. L. Carney, D. R. Korver, and F. E. Robinson. 2014. "Growth, Efficiency, and Yield of Commercial Broilers from 1957, 1978, and 2005." *Poultry Science* 93, no. 12: 2970–82.

Zurek, Ledek, and Anuradha Ghosh. 2014. "Insects Represent a Link between Food Animal Farms and the Urban Environment or Antibiotic Resistance Traits." *Applied and Environmental Microbiology* 80, no. 12: 3562–67.

INDEX

Page numbers followed by f indicate illustrations.

life-forms versus life force, 160
livers, 220, 222, 262n8
Live Side: and author's access, 257n17; and
    Biological System concept, 193; and
    biosecurity, 48; and CQI classes, 104, 194;
    definition of, 104; and the health clinic,
    179; intellectual dominance of, 197; man-
    ager injuries, 185; pig standardization,
    181; versus Plant Side, 104, 194, 256n15;
    push system slaughter, 179
lungs, 220, 222, 262nn7–8
Lutalyse, 126, 130–31

machines, 106–7, 115–16, 257n18
MacKenzie, Donald, 107
managers: artificial insemination, 89,
    92–93; biological system concept, 193–98;
    and biosecurity, 28, 47–48, 56, 65–66, 74;
    breaking-in stories, 186; Drew Collins,
    21–25; farm tours, 66; and the Herd,
    53–54; human resources, 80–81; and
    industrial animality, 59; and industrial
    pigs, 28, 106; instincts and planning,
    94–95; John (Trenton Produce), 146,
    148; Julio (Sakai Minerals), 229; mi-
    grants, 16; on pig pheromones, 92; and
    pig vitality, 52; and PMMME slogan,
    105; public dress of, 7–8; and public
    image, 8; quality control disagreements,
    194–95; rendering department, 262n2;
    shipping, 197; slaughterhouse, 181, 189,
    193–94, 197, 260n3; specialization of,
    22; standardizing labor, 93; and the
    stockperson, 145; uses of the Herd,
    52–56; on vertical integration, 24–25.
    See also Francisco; manufacturing
    theory classes; pod managers
manufacturing theory classes, 103–6,
    194–95, 256n14. See also Continuous
    Quality Improvement
manure lagoons, 35, 38–40, 56, 250n1
Marx, Karl, 107
Marxism, 115, 258n4

masculine identities and cattle ranching, 80
masculine pride, 183–85
McGlone, John, 92
McNeur, Catherine, 252n6
meat, lab-grown, 213
meat categories, 227
meat industry concentration, 242
meatpacking, 178–79, 212–13. See also
    slaughterhouses
meat prices, 227
Meindertsma, Christien, 211–12
Merck, 114, 258n22
migrant workers: in Dixon, 7; at Dover
    Foods, 16; expertise of, 163; homeless
    shelters, 168, 169f, 186; leaving factory
    farms, 163; Sergio Chavez, 182–85, 190.
    See also Sow #6 workers
Milton, Kay, 258n21
Mintz, Sidney, 209
Moss, Michael, 137
Mullin, Molly, 255n5, 262n5

Nading, Alex, 258n21
Naoki (Sakai Minerals employee), 229–30
National Renders Association, 213
natural mating, 85, 97f, 101, 103
nature, meanings of, 37
nature-history reversals, 37
nitrates, 48, 206, 208, 215, 236, 244
Noguchi, Kaoru, 228
nonhuman work, 132, 134
North Carolina, 14, 56, 61, 211, 225

Occupational Safety and Health
    Administration (OSHA), 185–86
offal, 194, 240
off-animals, 232–35, 240
Oliphant, Elayne, 248n13
Ong, Aihwa, 198
Oxfam chicken plant investigation, 178

Pachirat, Timothy, 19, 169, 227, 261n6
palatants, 220–24

258n21; Fernando, 96; Gonzalo, 151; Janine, 91–92; Maria, 77, 89, 102, 111–12, 116, 131, 151, 163; Miguel, 77, 89, 112–13, 151–52; Raul, 77, 79, 98, 122, 124–25, 151, 163; resistance of, 116; Robin, 150–51, 153–57, 161, 163; Rocio, 81, 83, 151, 157–58; Ruben, 151

sows: breeding for docility, 138; confinement of, 95; C-sections, 150–53; and fear of humans, 135; and hormonal drugs, 134–36; hyperprolific, 139–40, 259n2; ID cards, 120, 121f; induction drugs, 258nn2–3; mundanity of, 83; nesting instincts, 125–26, 132

speciation, 46

standardization: in CQI programs, 105; of death, 144; human work and pig physiology, 134, 190; impossibility of, 62; and off-animals, 232–34; of pet food, 222. *See also* pig standardization

stereotypies, 132, 134

stockperson figure, 145–50, 156, 161

stockyards, 165f

Striffler, Steve, 187, 248n8, 261n6

Super-Pollo (Agrosuper), 57

surplus death, 214–15, 230–32, 234, 236

Taylor, Frederick Winslow, 94

Taylorism, 94

Thompson, Edward P., 198

thumping, 144, 147–48

Tierschutzbund Zurich, 114

totalities, 25, 251n30

Travers, John: and the author, 204; and Dover Foods, 204–5; as lobbyist, 204, 206; political career of, 205–6; on slaughterhouse waste, 206–8; waste management career, 204–6

Trenton Produce, 3, 146–47

Tsing, Anna Lowenhaupt, 255n5, 255n10, 263n11

Tuffit Meats, 231–34

unions, 191–92, 249n22, 260n3

the United States: agrarian political economy, 83; animal density, 222; food debates, 235; industrialism in, 244–45; industrialization of, 244; labor expansion ideologies, 243–44; as postindustrial, 4, 244

U.S. Meat Animal Research Center, 137–38, 141

Utah, 14–15

Vaught, Jeannette, 255n4

vertical integration: barcoding, 23–25; and biological system concept, 196–97; causing social reorganization, 48; conditions enabling, 57; and consumers, 21; and division of labor, 19; extent of, 21; gaps, 24; ideal of, 26; of industrial pigs, 15–17, 215; intensification of, 179; of intimacy, 161–62; Lifecycle model, 218–19; manager views on, 24–25; mentality metaphor, 24; and pig standardization, 17; trucking, 58–59; value of, 23; of worker attachment to pigs, 161–62

viscera. *See* livers; lungs

vitality, 16, 19, 138–39, 249n18

vital materialism, 195–96, 199

waste: antibiotics in, 225; feces, 224–25; management history, 239–40; manure lagoons, 35, 38–40, 56, 250n1; nitrates, 48, 206, 208, 215, 236, 244

Weeks, Kathi, 115

Weiss, Brad, 234

Wentworth, Kara, 252n6

worker attachment to pigs: factory farms exploiting, 157–58, 160–61; factory versus family farms, 147–48; saving piglets, 153–57; sustaining engineered genetics, 161; vertical integration of, 161–62

workers: animal shaping of, 88; and biosecurity, 48, 56, 65–66, 70, 74, 252n3;